WITHDRAWN

Multimedia Technology and Applications

David Hillman

Delmar Publishers

an International Thomson Publishing company I(T)P®

Albany • Bonn • Boston • Cincinnati • Detroit • London • Madrid
Melbourne • Mexico City • New York • Pacific Grove • Paris • San Francisco
Singapore • Tokyo • Toronto • Washington

Cover design: Mick Brady

Delmar Staff
Publisher: Alar Elken
Production Manager: Larry Main

Editorial Assistant: John Fisher
Art and Design Coordinator: Nicole Reamer

COPYRIGHT © 1998
By Delmar Publishers
a division of International Thomson Publishing Inc.

The ITP logo is a trademark under license.

Printed in the United States of America

For more information, contact:
Delmar Publishers
3 Columbia Circle, Box 15015
Albany, New York 12212-5015

International Thomson Editores
Campos Eliseos 385, Piso 7
Col Polanco
11560 Mexico D F Mexico

International Thomson Publishing Europe
Berkshire House 168-173
High Holborn
London, WC1V7AA
England

International Thomson Publishing Gmbh
Königswinterer Strasse 418
53227 Bonn
Germany

Thomas Nelson Australia
102 Dodds Street
South Melbourne, 3205
Victoria, Australia

International Thomson Publishing Asia
221 Henderson Road
#05-10 Henderson Building
Singapore 0315

Nelson Canada
1120 Birchmount Road
Scarborough, Ontario
Canada M1K5G4

International Thomson Publishing – Japan
Hirakawacho Kyowa Building, 3F
2-2-1 Hirakawacho
Chiyoda-ku, 102 Tokyo
Japan

6 7 8 9 10 XXX 02 01 00

Library of Congress Cataloging-in-Publication Data
Hillman, David, 1956-
    Multimedia technology and applications / David Hillman.
       p.   cm.
    ISBN: 0-8273-8498-X
1. Multimedia systems.   I. Title.
QA76.575.H57 1998
006.7–dc21
                           97-33011
                       CIP

Contents

Chapter Two   Products and Evaluation

Chapter Three   Hardware, Operating Systems, and Software

Chapter Four   Text

Chapter Five   Graphics

Chapter Six   Digital Audio

Chapter Seven   Digital Video
and Animation

Chapter Eight   Product Design

Chapter Nine   Authoring Tools

Chapter Ten   Multimedia
and the Internet

Chapter Eleven   The Multimedia
Development Team

Chapter Twelve   The Multimedia Development Process

Preface

The multimedia industry is changing everyday. New technologies and products are announced nearly every week at trade shows or exhibitions. How can you learn about a technology that is constantly changing? One way to learn is by accessing information in a format that reflects the timeliness of the information. First principles, practice, and up-to-the-moment information will be critical to your success in the multimedia field. For example, you will need to understand what digital video is and how to use it. You will learn about digital audio by looking at examples of digital audio files and then become proficient by capturing and using digital audio with the latest hardware and software tools on the market.

The key to learning multimedia is to be exposed to the principles, examples, and latest information so that you can apply your knowledge. This book is an integral part of a three part delivery system that includes:

1. This book, *Multimedia Technology and Applications*

2. An accompanying CD-ROM

3. A World Wide Web site

Each of these components is complimentary and supports each other in delivering instruction.

The Textbook

The textbook component is designed to provide a brief and concise overview of multimedia technology and focuses on technologies and processes that will have a life span of approximately five to seven years—a lifetime in the computer industry. In order to keep the book current, specific references to hardware, operating systems, and software products have been avoided wherever possible. The book should be regarded as a resource that lays a foundation in what multimedia is and what makes it work. This book offers you the opportunity to look at multimedia in three ways:

1. The nuts and bolts of multimedia technology. What is the basic hardware and software needed to develop and run multimedia technology and applications?

2. The creative process behind multimedia. How do you combine technology and content to create multimedia?

3. Management's view of multimedia. What are the steps involved in building a multimedia product?

The book is divided into twelve chapters and is complimented by material on the accompanying CD-ROM and World Wide Web site, also presented in chapter format. To get the maximum benefit from this book, it should be used in conjunction with the CD-ROM and Web site.

The CD-ROM

While the book provides a foundation of first principles, the accompanying CD-ROM provides you with materials to experience multimedia hardware, operating systems, software, and data. It contains examples of files that demonstrate different fonts, text layout, various graphics formats, audio formats, and video examples. In addition to demonstration versions of commercial multimedia development tools, the CD-ROM also contains a Windows software package called *Springboard,* a fully functional authoring tool for developing multimedia products.

The CD-ROM is organized into twelve chapters that match the layout of this book and the accompanying World Wide Web site. The chapters, written in hypertext markup language (HTML), can be viewed by any commercial World Wide Web viewer or by a Microsoft Windows-compatible Web viewer software application provided on the CD-ROM.

The World Wide Web Site

The World Wide Web site provides you with up-to-the-moment information on hardware, software, multimedia products, and tools that you need to know about. It contains references and links to the latest multimedia technologies, tools, products, and vendors that are useful for both novice and experienced multimedia developers. The Web site is updated on a regular basis to keep the information current and useful. Like the book and CD-ROM, the Web site is also divided into twelve corresponding chapters that make finding the latest information convenient and easy.

How to Use the Book, CD-ROM, and Web Site

Multimedia Technology and Applications is a multimedia-based information delivery system. The book is your starting point. Read each chapter thoroughly and try the review questions at the end of each chapter. Throughout the book you will see:

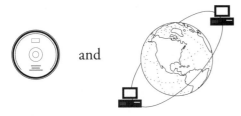 and

These symbols and the accompanying text indicate that you will find related information, software, data, and demonstrations on the accompanying CD-ROM or at the Web site:

www.mmta.delmar.com

Each chapter of the book corresponds to a similarly titled chapter on the CD-ROM and the Web site. The chapters on the CD-ROM describe software, data, and tools that you will find on the CD-ROM. You will be able to use these things to develop a deeper and more practical understanding of multimedia technology and product development. The Web site provides you with current information on technologies and products as well as links to vendors and other resources that you will find useful as you develop your multimedia skills.

After completing your study of the book, CD-ROM, and Web site, use them as a reference to sharpen or add new skills. For example, visit the Web site to learn about a new multimedia authoring tool. Then use the CD-ROM to look at examples of similar authoring tools. Finally, you can go back to the book to refresh your memory on the different types of authoring tools and how they work. This approach means that you will be constantly learning and staying on top of the technology to develop and use multimedia products.

For Students of Multimedia

The key to staying on top of a technology like multimedia is to never stop learning about it. This can be accomplished by reading the latest technical magazines and books, enrolling in classes, and getting hands-on experience by building your own applications. Each person learns differently. Some people require a more formal education while others can adapt knowledge they already have to develop multimedia development skills. It is up to each individual to find the approach that works best for him or her.

The book offers a technical foundation of the facts and concepts behind multimedia technology and products. The CD-ROM offers the opportunity to move from theory to practicality. Finally, the Web site enables you to stay on top of things you will need to apply your knowledge and developing skills.

For Teachers of Multimedia

The book, CD-ROM, and World Wide Web site are intended as a three-prong approach to teaching multimedia technology to those students starting out in this field:

1. Use the book as an outline to teach critical multimedia principles and processes—the foundations of multimedia technology.

2. Use the CD-ROM to provide examples and demonstrations for your students by getting hands-on experience with various multimedia data and products.

3. Use the Web site to enable your students to grow beyond the course by knowing where to find information about changing technologies.

The book intentionally avoids naming trademarked products because each classroom is different. The CD-ROM includes demonstration software products and sample content to be used for student projects. The World Wide Web site will offer late-breaking information about the multimedia industry to facilitate class discussions about the rapidly changing technology they are learning about.

Acknowledgments

Many people are responsible for this book either directly or spiritually. I would like to thank my wife, Leslie, and our daughter, Aubrey, for their patience in this project and especially for the lost weekends. I would like to thank Alan Thormeyer and Bernie Neff for their encouragement and support. I would like to thank Russell Schneck of Delmar for suggesting the idea in the first place. Joan McNamara, my editor, has helped me to become a better writer and I am very grateful for that. I would like to also thank my students at Montgomery College and The Johns Hopkins University who inspired me to create something that others will benefit from.

I would like to recognize and thank the following reviewers of this textbook:

- Jeffery R. Brown, Montana State University
- Richard Browne, Los Angeles Trade-Technical College
- Cynthia Clabough, State University of New York–Oswego
- Sylvia Gist, Chicago State University
- Dr. Gail Jamieson, Phoenix College
- Pat Lehman, Community College of Denver
- Ivan Nunez, Minneapolis College of Art and Design

CHAPTER ONE

Introduction

Multimedia is more than a high technology buzzword—it is a powerful way to educate, entertain, and inform. It has taken the computer from communicating information as text to telling stories using pictures, sound, and video. Multimedia has taken computer users from intimidating mainframe terminals to high-technology desktop systems that offer fun, adventure, and interactive learning. Multimedia technology is one of the main reasons computers are becoming as common in the home as they are in the workplace.

Multimedia products are based on a technology that combines text, pictures, sound, full-motion video, and interactivity into interesting, informative, and often entertaining productions. Multimedia products are used by everyone—from children to adults—to meet a wide range of needs, such as:

- Finding facts and information in encyclopedias on CD-ROM
- Learning new concepts and skills in mathematics, science, art, and languages from home-based and school-based computers
- Entertainment from computer games
- Marketing and technical presentations for business
- Communicating with individuals and corporations all over the world via the Internet

OBJECTIVES

After completing this chapter, you should know:

- How multimedia technology has evolved over the past few decades.
- The definition of multimedia.
- What has impacted the marketing of multimedia technology and applications.
- How copyright impacts the development and distribution of multimedia.

1

Look for information covering issues for multimedia products and development.

Check out the Web site for multimedia market news and organizations.

As the above shows, multimedia technology and applications reach into nearly every aspect of our lives.

Multimedia technology and applications is not a single subject or idea. It is many technologies and ideas with a history that is as old as communication and as new as the latest microprocessor. For example, the lessons learned in art class over many generations influence the use of color and layout in modern multimedia products. Furthermore, as new and more powerful microprocessors and operating systems are developed, there is a corresponding improvement in the quality and power of multimedia content such as audio and/or video.

Brief History of Multimedia

Since the late 1970s, desktop computers used in the home and office have evolved into sophisticated systems that help us get our jobs done, deliver information, and provide entertainment. Figure 1-1 presents a timeline of some of the key technologies that have contributed to the evolution of multimedia computers. Do not worry if some of these terms, especially the ones pertaining to hardware, seem unfamiliar to you right now, because they will be discussed in detail later in this book. The main point is multimedia technology did not happen overnight.

Multimedia technology has changed the way we look at computers. The first computers were seen as single-purpose machines that solved incredibly complex mathematical problems. During the 1960s, mainframe computers were used to manage large corporate databases and financial systems. The 1970s saw computer terminals throughout an organization being used for publishing and information management. The 1980s brought the desktop computer so everyone could have a computer at his or her desk for word processing, spreadsheets, and even games. Bringing the computer to the individual in the office, the home, and the

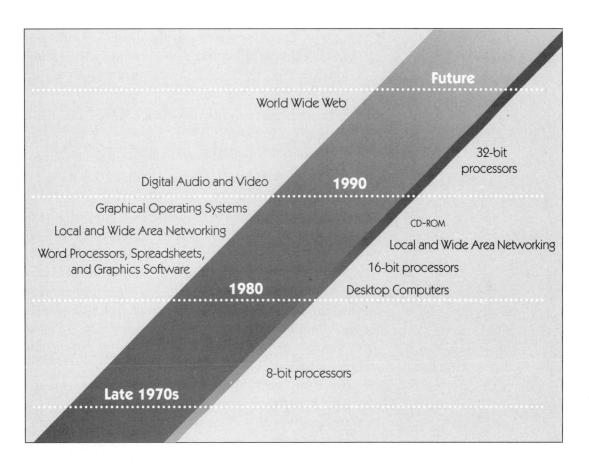

Figure 1-1 Timeline of technology behind the creation of multimedia computers

classroom meant looking at the computer as more than just a fancy typewriter or automated bookkeeper.

In the mid 1980s and into the 1990s, computer developers started looking at how computers could be used as never before. At the same time, advances in technology brought about:

- Faster desktop computers
- Increased working memory capacity in computers
- Higher data storage capacity in disk drives and CD-ROMs
- Digital audio and video

- Graphic operating systems that worked by pointing and clicking at objects on the screen instead of having to remember cryptic command sequences such as "dir *.exe" to find a program
- Local and wide area networks that connected users to the world
- Thousands of applications ranging from word processors to a myriad of multimedia products that have changed the workplace, classroom, and the home

Computer developers started looking to multimedia—the delivery of information using text, pictures, audio, and video—as a way to utilize computers in a uniquely personal way. Multimedia computers could be used to increase efficiency and productivity on the job, provide information at our fingertips in the home, and help students learn more effectively both in and out of the classroom. These personal gains meant that people would see computers as practical and useful tools in their everyday lives.

Since the late 1980s, multimedia technology and applications have found many places in our lives:

- At home where a wide variety of games and reference products such as encyclopedias and cookbooks are put to use
- At the office where marketing presentations and training are essential to learning how to get a new job done
- At school where interactive software programs assist students in learning mathematics, science, and new languages
- In shopping malls where interactive computer terminals, called kiosks, help us to design greeting cards or to find out where specific stores are located

As you can see, the impact of multimedia technology on our daily lives is often more than we realize. The bottom line is that if there is a need to inform, teach, or entertain multimedia technology can play a key role.

Now that a foundation has been laid on the origins of multimedia, let us look at what multimedia is and some of the things that influence its use and development.

What Is Multimedia?

By now you should know that **multimedia** is the use of text, pictures, audio, and/or video to deliver information. Multimedia is technology, content, applications, and people. It encompasses many concepts and ideas that are important to understand. Specific terminology you will encounter throughout this book pertaining to multimedia include:

- **Information**—Facts, ideas, beliefs, and stories that when communicated, provide value to the receiver. In the context of multimedia, information comes in many forms including text, pictures, audio, and video. This term is included because multimedia falls into the greater realm of computer-based information systems technology.

- **Domain**—A domain in the multimedia world is a relatively narrow or focused area of information or knowledge such as astronomy or famous authors, but it can also be a broader area of organized information such as an encyclopedia.

- **Interactivity**—A stimulus-response behavior in which a computer program presents options that the user can select from that lead to further options. Multimedia software applications are designed to logically organize information, making it easily accessible to users. For example, a CD-ROM-based multimedia encyclopedia offers the user a list of letters from A to Z to narrow the search for a specific subject. When the user clicks on a letter, he or she is presented with a list of subjects in alphabetic order within the selected letter to further narrow the search. The user then selects the specific subject and is presented with information.

On the CD-ROM, you will find history, technology, and business perspectives that provide the foundation for multimedia technologies.

Look for current information on key multimedia markets and technologies.

Interactivity, in this case, is used to enable the user to rapidly locate and view information.

- **Application**—A computer program that serves a specific purpose or use such as a word processing or spreadsheet program. Multimedia products include games, educational programs, and corporate briefings to name a few. Multimedia products may also be referred to as products.

- **Content**—Specific information for a multimedia product in the form of text, pictures, audio, and video. Content may start out on paper or videotape but is then captured to digital format for editing and incorporation into a multimedia product. Multimedia products typically contain a set of multimedia content that is specific and unique to that application.

- **Developers**—Managers, designers, programmers, graphic artists, and other skilled individuals who participate in the development of multimedia products. Sometimes referred to as producers.

- **Users (also known as End Users)**—Those individuals or groups who use and/or apply multimedia products for work or play.

- **Authoring Tools**—Software programs for developing and delivering multimedia products. Tools include programs for text and graphic editing, audio and video capture and editing, and multimedia authoring.

- **Product**—A completed multimedia product that is distributed for use by end users. Products are often sold to consumers via commercial outlets.

This list of terminology is enough to get you started in learning about multimedia technology and applications. The glossary in the back of this book provides an extensive list of terms that are defined for your convenience.

On the CD-ROM you will find strategies for learning how to use and develop multimedia technology.

The Multimedia Market

Multimedia technology and applications is a rapidly growing market. The sale of CD-ROM drives, which are used to deliver multimedia products, can be viewed as a barometer for the proliferation of multimedia technology. Personal computers sold in the early 1990s did not include CD-ROM drives except as an expensive add-on. However, by 1995, CD-ROM drives were a common feature for new computers; as the availability of CD-ROM drives in home and business computers increased, there was a corresponding increase in the development and sales of multimedia products.

Another factor in the increasing multimedia market as shown in Figure 1-2 is the relationship between a state-of-the-art computer and its cost versus performance. State-of-

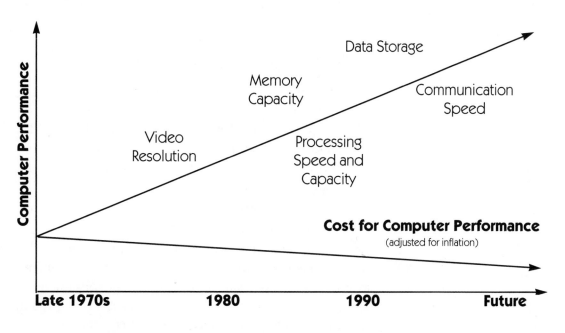

Figure 1-2 Computer performance versus cost. Although the cost of a computer has remained relatively constant, the performance has increased dramatically.

On the Web site look for the latest products and technologies for multimedia.

the-art means that the computer offers the best technology available for processing, storage, video, communications, and other capabilities to support the latest software applications. Although computer performance and capabilities have increased, the cost of a new computer with state-of-the-art capability has remained relatively constant. Even when you factor in inflation, computational power has improved dramatically since the early 1980s. For example, in 1987 a 100 megabyte hard disk cost $300 dollars, in 1996, a 1.2 gigabyte drive cost $300—a twelve-fold increase in storage for the same dollar amount. This has resulted in:

- More powerful computers for the same dollar amount
- More people buying computers
- More products being developed for computers
- Increased expectations for the kinds of things computers can do, especially in the area of multimedia products

Delivering Multimedia Content

The value of multimedia is that interesting applications and products can be created. Sometimes these applications involve large amounts of words, pictures, sound, and video that depend on two things:

1. Enough storage space for content on the computer to support an application
2. Creation of software programs that organize and present the content

As CD-ROM drives became more commonplace, so did the means to deliver multimedia products. Multimedia content, as you will find out later in this book, can consume great amounts of storage space. The basic unit of information in a computer is a byte. A **byte** is eight bits—ones or zeroes that are used to store information. Typical sizes for content data will vary, but the following will give you an idea of how much storage is required for:

- Text—One page of text can require 500 to 1,000 bytes.
- Pictures—A single full-screen picture can require 300,000 to 1,000,000 bytes.
- Audio—One minute of music can require 2,500,000 bytes.
- Video—One minute of video can require 10,000,000 bytes.

CD-ROMs can hold over 650,000,000 bytes of data as compared to a 3.5 inch diskette, which can only hold 1,400,000 bytes. Having so much storage space on a CD-ROM means that you can deliver impressive amounts of content for a wide variety of applications.

The number of software programs on the market that enable developers to create and deliver multimedia products has increased dramatically since 1990. In fact, the number of commercial software programs to author, that is, assemble multimedia content into interactive applications, totaled nearly 200 by the end of 1996. In addition to authoring programs, there are dozens of software programs and tools available for creating and editing text, graphics, audio, and video content. All of these authoring, creation, and editing programs have meant that developers have a wide variety of options from which to choose.

Multimedia products are also riding the wave of the Internet. As computers on networks or via modems communicate faster with each other, so will their ability to distribute multimedia content and applications. The first modems communicated data at a rate of 1200 bits per second or about 150 bytes per second under ideal conditions. It would take 6 to 7 seconds to transmit a single page of text and sending a minute of video could take 18.5 hours. As modem speeds have increased and local and wide area network connections have become more commonplace, transmission of text has become trivial and live video via the network is becoming a reality for many users.

Content and Copyright

Many multimedia products are content intensive. They depend on large amounts of text, pictures, audio, and video that are organized and presented for the benefit of the user. Content can be original to the product or acquired from other sources. Depending on the source, the ownership and rights to use the content can be an issue. Furthermore, once an application has been created, the developer may want to protect it from others taking the content for their own purposes. For example, the developer of a multimedia encyclopedia would not allow others to copy the material into a new application without fair compensation to the original developer.

This section is intended as an overview. Copyright law is a complex area based on national and international laws that are best handled by lawyers, especially when the questions become vague or potentially confusing to interested parties. It is essential, though, that multimedia developers become aware of the basic tenets of copyright law and the associated rules for acquiring content from other parties or protecting their own creations. It is also important to note that laws change from time to time due to legislative or judicial actions and you must constantly be aware of these changes and how they will affect you.

Copyright Law in the United States

Copyright is determined by laws in the various countries around the world as well as by international agreements. These laws and agreements often vary and can be quite difficult for the layman to understand. For the purposes of this discussion we will provide the basis of United States law for copyright and related issues. Remember that you should always check with appropriate experts, such as a copyright and/or intellectual property rights counsel, for specific instances of United States law and international law that may apply.

Copyright in the United States is based on federal law originally found in the Constitution, specifically Article 1, Section 8, Clause 8, which provides Congress with the power "to promote science and the useful arts, by securing for limited times to authors . . . the exclusive right to their . . . writings." A number of federal laws have been enacted to protect authoring and expression. Different mediums of expression include:

- Literary works
- Pictorial, graphic, and sculptural works
- Motion pictures and other audiovisual works
- Musical works
- Dramatic works
- Pantomimes and choreographic works
- Sound recordings

Even though much of the copyright law was enacted prior to the proliferation of computers and multimedia technologies, it is generally accepted that multimedia content and applications are affected by this body of law.

Public Domain

There is a great deal of content available to developers that is not protected by copyright. This content is in the public domain and includes:

- Any work of the Federal Government
- Works in which the copyright has expired—typically copyrights secured more than 75 years ago that have not been renewed

The advantage of public domain content is it is free and technically requires no notification to the owner or creator. However, you should be careful that content is truly in the public domain. This is especially true for works that have been excerpted in more current works under new copyright.

Establishment of Copyright

Generally speaking, most works are copyright protected even if they do not include a notice of copyright. Copyright begins the moment the work is created in fixed form. For multimedia, this would be the moment that a CD-ROM is created with a completed application. Adhering to the copyright is the responsibility of the user who must determine who owns the copyright and to request permission for its use.

Copyright owners have exclusive rights to their own material. This means they can:

- Display the copyrighted work publicly
- Prepare derivative works based on the copyrighted work
- Distribute copies of the copyrighted work
- Reproduce the copyrighted work
- Perform the copyrighted work publicly

Of course, the owner can also authorize others to do these same things with his or her permission. Bear in mind that if you use copyrighted material without obtaining permission you are potentially depriving the owner of their exclusive rights to the material.

Copyright is usually assigned to the person or agency that commissions the work unless prior arrangements are made. This means that multimedia developers working for a company do not own the rights to the application—it is owned by the company.

If you wish to use copyrighted material, you must get the owner's permission. In nearly all cases, you will need to get it in writing with a clear understanding of the limits granted by the owner. In some cases, you will be expected to pay for certain rights and privileges depending on the terms made with the owner of the material. In most cases when you obtain permission to use copyrighted work you must inform the owner of:

- Its intended use
- The market in which it will be used
- The price of the product

- Quantity of the product that will be produced
- United States and international rights for the product

Fair Use

One common misconception about copyright is that it does not apply to teachers, educators, and students. The bottom line is you cannot disregard copyright law just because you are in an educational environment. However, there are guidelines according to federal law that allow for **fair use** of copyrighted material. Fair use means limited use for purposes of criticism, comment, news reporting, teaching, scholarship, and research. However, there are some considerations for fair use, including:

- The amount and use of the copyrighted work must be clearly identified.
- The copyrighted material is used for nonprofit uses only.
- The copyrighted material must be cited; that is, the owner must be acknowledged.
- The market value of the copyrighted work; that is, if significant use of the work will result in financial loss to the owner, some compensation may be necessary.

These criteria are guidelines and should be treated as such. Generally speaking, limited classroom use is acceptable, but when in doubt check with appropriate legal authorities for specific guidance.

Multimedia Copyright Issues

Multimedia is a technology of the 1990s. Copyright law is over 200 years in the making and is constantly being scrutinized for clarification. It is nearly impossible for lawmakers to accurately predict new technologies and how they will impact our lives. Multimedia technology enables scanning, digitizing, and transporting of large amounts of content that was never envisioned by the early lawmakers of our country. The basic rules, however, are the following:

Check the Web site for current issues related to copyright and multimedia.

- Be aware of copyright law and guidelines. If you do not know or are not sure, ask someone who does.
- Just because you can copy it, scan it, or get it using some clever electronic method does not necessarily mean you have the right to use it freely.
- If you obtain content from some other source, make sure you have the rights to use it. The rights should be in writing with specific conditions clearly stated.
- Always acknowledge copyrighted material in the application and in the credits of the application.
- If you create material, provide notice of copyright. A copyright notice on the title page of a book or the first screen of a multimedia product is adequate.
- Look for material in the public domain—it is cheap and there is a great amount of it.

Resources for Multimedia Developers

Regardless of how you learn or what your current situation is, there are a number of resources that can help you. These resources will provide you with information about current products, multimedia authoring tools, state-of-the-art technology, and the best practices for developing and using multimedia products. These resources include:

- Mentors
- Books
- Magazines and periodicals
- Vendors and trade shows
- Internet-World Wide Web and Newsgroups
- Formal Education
- Experience
- Being critical of the multimedia products that you come into contact with every day

The key to utilizing these resources is understanding their unique benefits and how to take advantage of them to continue your education in multimedia.

Mentors

In many companies, educational institutions, and computer support groups you will find people who are willing to help you learn about multimedia technology. Most are often eager to share techniques and strategies they have developed. Look for a mentor who is both experienced in developing multimedia products and willing to share that knowledge. You may want to consider the following strategies for working with a mentor, including:

- Working for them to develop some part of a project they are working on
- Having them advise you on a project you are working on
- Using them for the really hard questions and concepts to help you through the rough spots in your learning

Books

As always, books are one of the best resources for self-help learning. There are a number of books on the market for multimedia product development. You should also consider books in related fields such as desktop publishing, graphics design, and the Internet. These books often provide knowledge that will round out your multimedia skills.

Magazines and Periodicals

Magazines and periodicals offer a number of opportunities to improve and add to your multimedia skill base. They offer a range of resources including:

- Surveys of the latest technologies
- Product, including application and tool, reviews including announcements of new products and comparisons of similar products

- How-to articles

Magazines and periodicals range in coverage from multimedia-specific to the broader-based computer industry. You should also consider periodicals for professional groups such as educators and management as a resource for multimedia technology information. These resources often provide useful information tailored for specific groups of users and developers. You may also want to consider subscriptions to magazines and periodicals to make sure that you stay informed on the latest product and technology information.

Vendors and Trade Shows

Multimedia tool vendors often provide demonstration versions of their software to build product interest. Check with various vendors to see if they have demonstration versions of their products that you can try. In this way you may be able to develop familiarity with tools and products that you might use in a future project or in a job you wish to secure.

Trade shows are a valuable resource for looking at the latest products and technologies. Unfortunately, you have to be able to get to the locations where these are held such as Boston, New York, Atlanta, and San Francisco. Check magazines and Internet resources to find out about shows in your area. If you do see a show, do not be shy about approaching vendors for product demonstrations and information about job opportunities.

Internet

The Internet, specifically the World Wide Web and Newsgroups, is an excellent resource for information that is both comprehensive and current. The primary advantage of the Internet is that information is usually very current. Remember to be careful of rumor mills and product-centered Web sites:

- Make sure that the source for the Web page is credible. Remember that anyone can post a Web page.

Find out who is posting the information and try to determine how reliable their information is.

- Product-centered Web sites are useful for learning about new product releases, software updates, and tips and tricks to better use the product. However, remember that the product vendor's primary goal is to sell his or her product. The buyer must beware—even on the Internet.

When looking at information on the Web, ask yourself if the information is factual or if it is filled with marketing innuendo. If someone is stating an opinion on a product or a technology ask yourself if he or she is a competent and reliable information source. Web and News resources include:

- Corporate Web sites with products and related information.

- Education institutions including faculty and students as developers and as fellow students.

- Newsgroups for multimedia, computer applications, and special interest areas such as education and business.

- World Wide Web Search Engines can be very useful to locate vendors, products, and data samples such as clip art. Simply entering a word such as "multimedia" can reveal thousands of resources for you on the Internet. More specific terms and expressions such as "authoring", "digital video", and/or "clip art" can help you to refine your search.

The Internet via file transfer protocol can be used to download alpha, beta, and even finished software products and tools as well as content matter including text, graphics, audio, and video files.

Education

A formal education is often an effective way to initially develop knowledge and skills and a means to refine current knowledge and skills. Education also provides the basis for developing critical technical skills by allowing you to learn from experts. There are a range of education resources including:

- Vendor seminars from product and tool companies
- One- to multi-day seminars at commercial training centers and at colleges
- Semester-long college courses

Formal education typically takes one of two modes:

1. Degree-seeking—the student will receive formal certification and documentation that they have completed a prescribed course of study. Degree programs can be long term, lasting for months in certification programs to years for academic degrees such as Masters or Doctorate degrees.

2. Job-focused—the student is taking a single course to obtain specific knowledge and/or skills for a particular job-based requirement.

Degree-seeking programs are usually administered and conducted by accredited colleges and universities while job-focused courses are often provided by commercial training vendors.

The value of a formal education in multimedia technology is very high. Formal education can often mean the difference between obtaining a job developing multimedia products and not. However, many companies will look for formal education combined with some level of experience such as an internship, in making hiring decisions. Fortunately, multimedia allows you to develop your own applications so that you can creatively demonstrate your product knowledge, skills, and expertise to potential employers.

Experience

Experience in developing multimedia products cannot be substituted. Unfortunately, sometimes the old chicken and egg problem arises in which you cannot get hired because you lack experience—but you cannot get experience because no one will hire you. Try breaking this vicious cycle by:

- Finding others to mentor and help you develop your skills. Some mentors may be looking for new developers who are willing to work and learn.

- Adapting your current skills, such as word processing or using a video camera, to multimedia skills. For example, graphic artists may want to start using multimedia authoring tools to develop applications based on their own digital art.

- Trying new tools and techniques. As new technologies and tools come on the market, buy them yourself (unfortunately, this can be prohibitively expensive) and start developing your own applications.

- Taking on a project for free to demonstrate your ability and skills. Make sure that you get credit and/or compensation if the final product is sold to others.

- Continuing to learn by reading books and magazines, looking at new technologies, and asking questions.

Check the Web site for upcoming trade shows, magazines, new books, and other events in the multimedia developer community.

Critical Attitude

As you come into contact with various multimedia products you should maintain a critical eye on the quality, operation, and usefulness of these products. You should always be looking for new ideas for your projects or become aware of poor techniques that you should avoid.

SUMMARY

Multimedia technology and applications have changed the way we use computers. As the price of computer hardware has fallen and more people have purchased computers, the number of multimedia products has increased dramatically. Multimedia is found in the workplace, in the home, and in the classrooms. The technology to deliver multimedia has made it possible to deliver large volumes of text, pictures, audio, and video that provide information, training, and entertainment at a moment's notice. As multimedia has proliferated, the use of content for applications has been closely scrutinized by copyright laws that protect both the developer and the user.

This chapter is an introduction to the rest of the book where we will discuss the multimedia products, hardware, software, data, design, tools, and the process or developing multimedia. In the next chapter you will find out about the types of multimedia products and how you evaluate them-both as a user and a developer.

REVIEW QUESTIONS

1. What kind of experience do you have with computers and desktop applications such as word processing and spreadsheets?

2. Given the history of computer technology and how it has impacted multimedia products and products, what trends do you see in the next few years?

3. Describe your experience with multimedia products in the workplace and at home. What applications have you found to be the most useful or entertaining?

4. Why is copyright law so problematic for multimedia technology and applications?

5. What is the responsibility of anyone who uses copyrighted material in his or her own work?

6. What guidelines for fair use apply to students in a multimedia authoring class?

7. What resources have you used in learning about multimedia technology and product development?

CHAPTER TWO

Products and Evaluation

Multimedia products come in many shapes and forms. They are used to market new products, provide research information for a high school student, or simultaneously entertain and educate a young child. In order to develop multimedia products, you need to understand what kinds of products are out there. This chapter describes the various types of multimedia products and provides you with the foundation you need to start developing them.

There are two perspectives to consider when developing multimedia products: the developer's and the end user's. The developer's perspective is based on applying the technology to create a product that is useful, beneficial, and profitable. The end user's perspective is based on his or her need for the product and his or her ability to evaluate its usefulness, benefit, and cost. This chapter focuses on these issues by describing the different types of multimedia products and how they are evaluated.

Types of Products

Multimedia products are as varied as the ideas that spawn them. In most situations, the type of product is defined by who is using it. For example, consider how many ways you can use a CD-ROM-based encyclopedia. A young child might browse the encyclopedia for pleasure, looking at the pictures and video clips, while a high school student uses it for classroom research. In reality, there are almost as many uses for multimedia as there are different kinds of people. However,

OBJECTIVES

After completing this chapter, you should know:

- The different types of multimedia products.
- What is involved in evaluating multimedia products.
- What users need to consider in evaluating multimedia products.
- What developers need to consider in evaluating the development of multimedia products.

Try different examples of multimedia products.

Access the Web site for current multimedia product reviews.

given the large number of products for home, office, and classroom, uses can be grouped as:

- Briefing
- Reference
- Database
- Education and Training
- Kiosk
- Entertainment and Games

Bear in mind that some of these products may overlap each other. For instance, a child plays a computer game in which he is presented arithmetic problems to solve. The child's perspective is that of a game; however, a teacher or parent might view the product as educational.

Briefing

Briefing products are small, straightforward, linear products used to present information quickly and concisely. **Linear** means that the product presents information in sequential order, one page at a time. Briefing products are characterized by:

- Relatively short development cycles typically ranging from a few hours to a couple of days.
- A limited number of presentations after which the product is disposed of or modified for future uses.
- A predominant use of text to present information with a limited use of graphics, audio, and video. This is most often due to lack of time to generate extensive graphics, audio, and video content rather than an explicit desire not to use it.

Examples of briefing products include:

- Corporate presentations such as management or operational summaries
- Sales presentations
- Educational lectures

Briefings usually have few, if any, navigational controls such as buttons to jump to other parts of a product. Moving from page to page is accomplished by clicking the mouse or pressing a button, with limited control available for moving back a page. Briefing products may also use the following control mechanisms to manage or enhance a presentation:

- Zooming control that enlarges and shrinks text and graphics
- Panning control to access specific parts of the display
- Thumbnail pages or bookmarks to review, select, and move to pages within the presentation
- Drawing and graphic editing tools as electronic drawing boards, often referred to as whiteboards, to add content on-the-fly during the presentation

Briefing products are usually delivered to an audience consisting of more than one person. It is essential that the briefing, both format and content, be appropriate for the audience. Furthermore, the content of the briefing should be familiar to the person delivering it. In some situations, the briefing content is used as a guide or an outline for the person conducting the presentation and its success will depend on how effective a speaker the person is.

Briefing products, as shown in Figure 2-1, can be developed by nearly anyone with relatively limited computer skills. Many of the tools to develop briefing products build on existing word processing skills. The advantage is that the expert on the subject, usually the person presenting the briefing, can create and edit content as needed. The disadvantage is that unskilled creation and editing can lead to poorly designed slides (in terms of overall content organization and/or individual page layout). A good briefing presentation depends on:

- A thorough understanding of the subject. A progressive outline can be used to organize concepts at a top level then fleshed out to provide supporting concepts.
- Seamless integration of content. Text, pictures, audio, and video should be effective and fit into the overall context of the briefing. Superfluous content for the sake of humor must be used carefully to avoid dis-

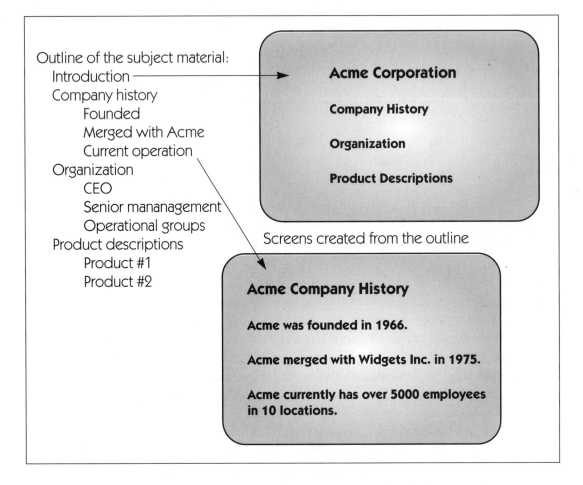

Figure 2-1 Developing a briefing application

tracting the audience from the purpose of the briefing—unless of course the point is to be humorous.

- Consistent page layout, including selecting readable fonts, contrasting background and foreground colors, and managing clutter. Too much clutter, as in too many words or too many pictures or even too many colors can make individual pages difficult for the audience to take in.

- One final point on briefing products is on use. Briefing presenters should be prepared to speak extemporaneously about the content of the briefing rather than directly from the text on the slide. There is nothing more boring than having someone read slides aloud to an audience.

Reference

Reference products are the most common form of commercial multimedia products. There is an extremely broad range of reference products including encyclopedias, dictionaries, cookbooks, and historical and scientific surveys. Unlike briefing products, reference products are long-lived and typically deployed on CD-ROM or a similar high-density media. Reference products are developed and used by a wide range of users from children to adults and from casual to very technical users.

There are two basic classes of reference products: generalized content and detailed content. Generalized reference systems, including encyclopedias and dictionaries, provide broad treatments of content at a limited depth. Detailed content-based reference systems focus on a specific area and provide extensive information. For example, as shown in Figure 2-2, an encyclopedia might contain thousands of entries within each entry, such as astronomy, covered at a very superficial level of detail. Compare this with a reference product on astronomy where comprehensive information is provided on a topic such as "Tour the Galaxy," an astronomy reference product.

Reference products tend to be very structured and easy to navigate. Since they are intended for a variety of users, navigation controls should be clearly identified. Help functions should always be provided to explain how to access and use the information. Most reference products include:

- A layered selection function that allows the information to be organized logically making it easier for the user to quickly find a topic of interest.

- Bookmarking that keeps track of hits during the current and previous uses of the product. Bookmarks quickly return the user to previous information hits.

Generalized-Content Reference Application

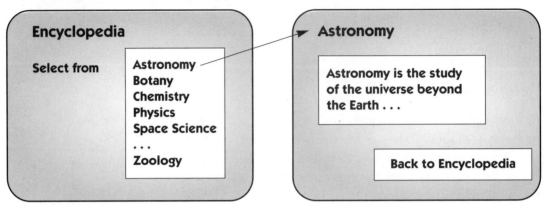

Detailed-Content Reference Application

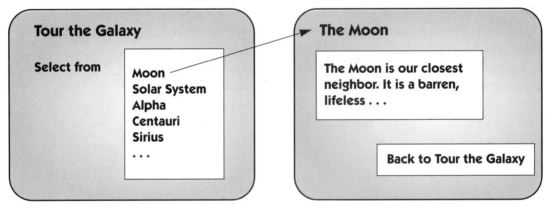

Figure 2-2 An example of generalized-content application versus a detailed-content application

- Back or "return to" functions quickly allowing the user to go to the last hit.
- Search or find capabilities to look for specific words or expressions within all of the content.
- "Main Menu" functions that quickly return the user to the topmost layer of the product from any point in the product.
- Print and export functions for copying information into other products or printing to hard copy.

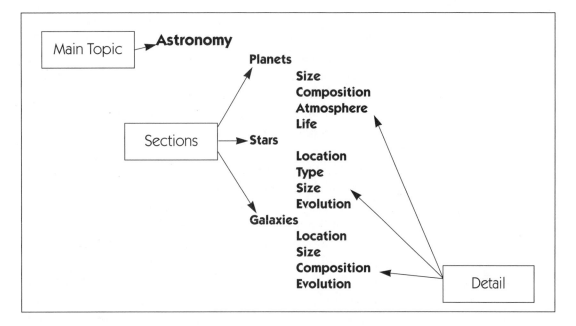

Figure 2-3 Organizing content information of a multimedia product

Content for reference systems include text, pictures, audio, and video. Content organization, as shown in Figure 2-3, is based on how the information itself is organized. The main body of information is subdivided into logical groupings of information or topics, which can then be broken down into more detailed groupings of information. For example, a reference product for a tool vendor could organize information about tools by their use and purpose such as metalwork, woodworking, or even types of screwdrivers to deliver a comprehensive product guide. Logical groupings may be alphabetical, numerical, or similar method for organizing information. Encyclopedias are organized alphabetically with each topic described at levels consistent for the type of user. For example, a children's encyclopedia under the letter "C" presents information on "cat," which describes a furry household pet that is fun to play with. An encyclopedia for older users would provide extensive information on the biology, behavior, and care of cats—information that is much more suitable for that type of user.

History products are usually organized by timelines. Historical reference products on modern authors might be organized along a timeline from 1900 to the present, while other reference products use more complex or exotic techniques for organizing information. For example, a reference work on animals might use a zoolike setting to organize groups of animals by habitats.

The usability and success of a reference product depends on the developer understanding the body of information and how end users will want to access it. Reference products are most often used for answering specific questions or for general browsing of information. The question-and-answer format of a reference product requires that information be logically organized with adequate search facilities to locate specific information content. Furthermore, the software must be able to anticipate the phrasing of questions from many different users. For example, one user might ask "What is size of the object?" while another asks "How big is the object?" Both questions are the same but the wording is different and the product must be able to understand both versions.

Question-and-answer products are often used to get information to use in another product such as a report or homework assignment. Browsing is free-form searching and usually has an entertainment element associated with it. Users simply look through the information without a specific purpose in mind until they focus on a piece of information or they quit because they are bored.

Database

Database products are similar to reference systems in that large amounts of information are made available to the end user. They are different because they focus on storing and accessing the actual data. Examples of database products include:

- Collections of fonts, pictures and art, and sound and video clips

- Large repositories or libraries of similar materials such as Shakespeare's plays or Edgar Allen Poe's stories
- Map, chart, and imagery collections
- Scientific survey information
- Phone number and zip code listings

In most database products, the information is stored and accessed for its own sake, not necessarily because it fits within a larger context. Like reference products, database products are usually delivered on CD-ROM or other media capable of storing large amount of data. Database products may also require multiple disks to store very large volumes of information such as phone numbers or street listings.

Database products, like reference systems, depend on support functions such as the following:

- A search and find engine to locate key words or descriptions of specific data. Graphics, audio, and video components are given text-based detailed descriptions including key words so that users can locate these elements quickly and efficiently.

- Presentation function to properly display the data elements. This includes font selection, graphic zooming, and the ability to randomly access content in audio and video clips.

- Export functions to extract data into other products.
- Print facilities for text and graphics.
- Conversion utilities for changing the format of data files.

The type of support functions will vary depending on the anticipated use of the product. For example, a repository of famous paintings may include features for tagging graphics with descriptive text such as the artist's name and year it was painted. The user can then use a search engine to locate a painting by entering the artist's name. Database products are sometimes used as foundations for building reference products or for educational products that depend on large amounts of supporting information or content.

Education and Training

Education and training products make up a significant share of the multimedia market ranging from pre-kindergarten to postgraduate offerings to technical and corporate training products. Education and training products often mirror textbooks and training manuals, and are often developed using resources cross-purposed from these text-based sources in addition to audio and videotapes. Education and training products fall into three general categories:

1. Instructor support products

2. Standalone or self-paced products

3. Combination products

Instructor Support Products

Instructor support products are used by teachers and trainers in conjunction with textbooks, lectures, and other activities within a classroom environment. Similar in some respects to reference and database products, they provide resource materials for instructors. They may include curriculum guides, study notes, lecture slides and handouts, and testing and assessment materials.

Standalone or Self-Paced Products

Standalone or self-paced products, also called **computer-based training (CBT)** are designed for students to use in lieu of an instructor-led environment. Learning objectives, course content, and testing materials are built within the product so that the student, usually at his or her own pace, can complete the course without external intervention.

Combination Products

Combination products fall between support and standalone. They are used by students at the direction of the instructor or to augment classroom activities such as lectures and exercises. Combination products may provide specific reinforcement of instructor teaching and are used in assessing student learning and comprehension. Typical of this are textbooks that include CD-ROMs to provide supplementary or additional material such as this textbook. The CD-ROM could be used to provide examples described in the textbook including content that is much better described through the use of digital audio and/or video. Of the three types of education and training products, combination products require a significant effort on the part of the teacher to integrate them into the learning environment.

Education and training systems are built with three things in mind:

1. The background and abilities of the students. What is the prior experience or knowledge of the students on the subject? Furthermore, are the students computer literate, do they have access to computers, and have they used computer-based training systems in the past?

2. The learning objectives and purpose of the training. What do the students need to learn or be able to do? For example, a computer-based training system could be used to explain the theory or why something is done, explain detailed processes, or even show how to do very specific tasks.

3. Assessment or testing of the students to make sure they have learned something. Since computer training can be accomplished with little or no intervention by an instructor, the system must ensure that the student did learn by testing the student.

Education and training systems are difficult to produce because they are dependent on the skills and abilities of the end users. At a minimum, the product's functionality should not impose significant learning requirements. You want the student to spend more time learning the material instead of the software. Navigation controls and support features such as Help should be clearly identified and easy to use. The content, as it relates to the course objectives, should be easy to follow and comprehend. Finally, testing mechanisms should rigorously measure content retention and comprehension but should not be difficult to use. One advantage of software-based testing is the ability to provide immediate feedback to the student and give reinforcement for incorrect answers.

Education and training products, like reference and entertainment products range from simple to complex and contain content that requires relatively little storage space to multiple CD-ROM disks. Many products are designed by educators and developers with the help of instructional designers who are versed in the practical application of learning theory. It is the instructional designer's job to ensure that the end user can learn from the product in a way that is self-motivating with long-term retention of knowledge and skills.

Kiosk

Kiosk products, ranging from bank machines to mall information centers to point-of-sales systems, are finding their way into many aspects of our lives. Kiosk products are characterized by having a relatively simple function and by being very easy to use. For example, a kiosk found in a shopping mall may be used to identify and locate mall stores. The user of the kiosk may range from a child to an elderly person with the broadest possible range of computer skills and physical abilities. Therefore, the kiosk must be simple and easy to use, comprehensive and nonthreatening, and it must run constantly, even days at a time, with little or no maintenance.

Kiosk products are one part entertainment, one part utility, and one part workhorse. The entertainment value will vary, but generally they are attractive and appealing to the eye. Pictures, sound, and video are often used to assist the user in finding information, provide information, or augment the delivery of information. For example, a voice-over may be used to read text making it easier to use for those with poor reading skills. The utility aspect is that the product does a relatively simple job, like dispensing cash and a bank statement, with as few keystrokes as possible. Finally, the workhorse aspect means that the product must be able to run for extended periods and reset itself periodically to a starting state after extended periods of not being used.

Kiosk products are unique in that they are delivered as integrated software and hardware solutions. They may include environmentally rugged touch screens, numeric keypads, built in speakers, microphones, and printers. Kiosk systems are often built as custom solutions in which the product depends on specific hardware features such as a touch screen to select program options. The kiosk hardware design must account for the surrounding environment: kiosks require access to power outlets and they cannot be too loud or distracting to the rest of the environment.

From a design perspective, kiosks consist of a top-level menu with usually no more than two or three layers of subordinate menus. Menu choices are kept very simple, and depending on the hardware environment, a touch screen for instance, navigational objects are boldly presented so there is no doubt in the user's mind about the purpose of an on-screen button. In informational kiosks, text, pictures, and videos must be presented in a way that requires minimal intervention from the user. This often means limiting the amount of text, making sure font sizes are large enough for those who are visually impaired, and presenting graphics that are useful without being overly detailed or too small. Returning to the top menu functions must be available for users to quickly reset the product. Finally, a timing mechanism may be required to reset the kiosk to a starting point following periods when it is unused. This ensures that the next user starts from a the beginning of the product and uses it quickly and efficiently.

Entertainment and Games

Entertainment and game products are among the most popular, especially for those people who may never use a computer for any other reason. Entertainment and game products may be accessed on standard computer workstations via CD-ROM or networks or on special purpose game machines that connect to television monitors for display. Like kiosks, entertainment and game products often have a relatively limited audience or use; however, the entertainment or game function may be quite complex and challenging for the user. These systems often forge the way for new technology and hardware development, which is later adapted into training or reference products.

Multimedia-based entertainment and game products depend on the use of graphics, audio, animation, and video to augment their operation. A game may include complex graphics taking the user on a treasure hunt on a deserted island. Audio is used for sound effects while video and animation are used for transitions or special effects.

Entertainment and game products rely on fairly simple navigation controls to enable the user to participate in the product. Joystick and track ball devices are often used for moving character objects, pointing guns, or flying aircraft while mouse buttons and keystrokes are used to trigger events or fire guns and missiles. Most game products depend on a timer and a scorekeeping system that may also track top scores between sessions. Finally, entertainment and game systems offer multiplayer features in which competition is managed between two or more players.

Entertainment products, like briefing reference, database, education, and kiosk products all have their unique place in supporting end users. They fill needs for learning or getting a job done, or they are simply used for fun and pleasure. Regardless of how they are used, multimedia products should be seriously evaluated by end users and developers to ensure they meet the needs for which they were produced.

Evaluation

With the broad range of multimedia products that can be created and/or purchased, it is critical that users and developers understand how to evaluate the quality or usefulness of a product. With this in mind, there are two perspectives for evaluation of multimedia products: the user and the developer.

Those who use multimedia products are primarily interested in:

- A product serving a need or solving a problem. This need could be for entertainment, education, or presenting the corporate financial bottom line.
- Information in the product being timely, accurate, and well organized.
- The product being easy to use.

  Those who develop multimedia products face:
- A variety of multimedia technologies and tools to build products.
- An assortment of specialized multimedia development strategies to effectively organize content.
- The need to find or develop content that is current, relevant, accurate, and of value to the end user.
- Budget, schedule, and resource constraints.

Given the various types of multimedia products, it is essential that users and developers understand and have strategies for evaluating products. These strategies will be discussed in greater detail in the following sections.

The User's Perspective

The user's perspective is often not considered a feature of multimedia evaluation. For the purposes of this discussion, we will treat multimedia products as **products.** Products typically are purchased or developed for a specific end user in mind. The assumption is that if a product is developed well it will be widely used. The end user, on the other hand, must be able to determine what product to choose, how this product will help, and whether the product is workable or usable given the set of skills. User issues can be generally categorized as:

- Subject/content
- Platform (hardware and software)
- Usability
- Cost

Install and run the product demonstrations to become familiar with how various products work.

Check the Web site for current information on multimedia vendors, products, and market trends.

Subject and Content

Most multimedia products are initially selected based on subject and content value. Criteria and examples include:

- Area of interest—Products that support specific interests such as astronomy, gardening, or physical training

- Entertainment value—Multimedia games and sports-related products

- Education, training, or learning objectives—How-to and subject-related products for mathematics, languages, arts, and history

- Need for information—Encyclopedias or similar reference products

Subject and content are evaluated in a straightforward fashion. Is the material complete or thorough, is it current, and is it accessible? Accessibility can be a subjective consideration based on how easy it is to find specific facts or details.

Platform

Platform issues focus on what type of equipment the user has and if it is compatible with a specific product. These criteria will be discussed in greater detail in Chapter 3; however, for the purposes of evaluation, the criteria includes:

- Hardware platforms

- Computer processor speed and data bus requirements

- Memory sizing

- Data storage requirements

- Disk and CD-ROM storage and capabilities

- Video display requirements

- Digital audio and video

- Network capability

- Special hardware such as a joystick, track ball, and touch screen monitor

- Operating system

- Related or support software

End users, depending on their knowledge of computer systems, hardware, and software, can find these criteria daunting. In fact, end users will often assume that a product is poorly designed when the culprit is actually an underpowered computer. For example, if a product has video and the sound is choppy or the images do not keep up with the sound, then the user will feel that the program is faulty when, in truth, the hardware is not up to the performance requirements of the product. If end users expect to evaluate multimedia products, they must be aware of the limitations of the hardware and software systems that support the multimedia product.

Usability

Usability is the measure of how good a program is in terms of the end user's expectations and abilities. It is based on how well the program works and whether the user can operate it. The assumption is that a successful program works with no internal errors that cause it to fail on its own. In other words, the programmers did their job. At this point usability determines if the user can learn, remember, and efficiently apply the program. The key criteria of usability include:

- Learning or training time—How long does it take to learn how to use the product? Kiosk systems should require little or no learning curve if they are to be useful. The same is also true of entertainment and game products to avoid frustrating a user who is more interested in having fun than reading the user's manual.

- Error rate—How often and how severe are mistakes made by the user? Education and training and reference systems can be frustrating if users are constantly making mistakes in operating the program. Mistakes should be limited to failed answers in tests rather than confusing sequences of buttons to press to properly run the program.

- Task-time—How long does it take to accomplish a task and how efficient are the steps? Database and reference systems should be designed to allow the user to find information rapidly and efficiently.

- Retention—How difficult is it for the user to operate the program in future sessions? This is an important question for education and training products so that users are more focused on learning rather than remembering how to use the product.

- "Look and Feel"—A subjective viewpoint based on cultural, ethical, and similar criteria; in other words, does the user find the program attractive, exciting, or entertaining? This criteria is often critical for entertainment and game products.

Usability applies to both the operation of the product and the content. These two perspectives often create conflicts when, for instance, a poorly designed interface makes it difficult to access and use much needed information.

Cost

Multimedia product cost is often the last factor considered by many people and the first for others. For example, a well-done multimedia-based typing tutor program may be purchased with cost as a secondary issue if there is confidence that the user will learn to type. Conversely, many games and educational products are often purchased with price as a primary consideration. Generally, the key criteria for costing from a user's point of view is the return on investment; in other words, how much is gained for how much is spent.

The Developer's Perspective

Developers of multimedia products should view evaluation as the tool that makes each product better than the last. In addition, by evaluating other products from other developers, you can improve your own products. Evaluation of multimedia products is important so that we do not repeat the mistakes of past efforts.

There are a number of issues when evaluating multimedia products. Some of these issues are similar to those applied by users in evaluating products while others are specific to the specification, design, and implementation of a multimedia product. Many of these issues should be considered throughout the development process:

- Content
- Performance
- Delivery
- Interface

Content

The developer must look at content in terms of its value to the user. Just because it is interesting or of value to the developer does not mean that others will feel the same way. Content should be judged by:

- Product domain or subject matter—Is the material useful for the end user?

- Message—How does the product communicate the information? Will it be understood by the users?

- Comparison to comparable products—Compare the product to similar products on the market. Is it comparable in terms of content, operation, performance, and cost? If not, will the differences be a problem or a benefit? For example, if your product is 30 percent more expensive due to more and better content than similar products, this will have to be considered in product marketing to point out that the extra and better content is worth the cost.

Performance

Performance is a tricky problem for developers because they tend to develop on platforms using as much processing power and storage as they can afford in order to maximize productivity. Developers must be careful because products they develop will most likely be run on hardware that is less capable than their own. Once again, developers must be aware of the user's technology and how it impacts the product they produce. Key considerations include:

- Behavior on the end user's hardware—How will the product behave on a variety of hardware systems? A common mistake for new multimedia producers is the use of high-end hardware for development and the failure to consider that end users often have equipment that has much less capability. Products should always be tested on a range of platforms before they are released to a general user population.

- Graphic presentation and quality—Is the product appealing to the user?

- Audio and video playback quality—How does the product perform on hardware that is underpowered for audio and video products?

Delivery

A successful multimedia product is more than software and a CD-ROM. Success depends on how the product is packaged and distributed. It depends on how fast the user is able to install it and become productive or entertained. Delivery is a function of:

- Installation—Are instructions straightforward and easy for the least skilled of users?

- Operational features—Will the user be able to figure out how to use the product without asking others or calling the developer every time it does not behave as expected?

- Packaging—Is the packaging and marking appropriate for the target market?

- Documentation—Are the user, installation, and troubleshooting guides thorough and adequate for the users?

Interface

The interface is what the user remembers most about a program. Starting from the beginning, was it easy to start the program? Was it easy to look up an encyclopedia entry? The interface must be evaluated for:

- Ease-of-use for novice users—Will the product be as easy to use for beginners as for advanced users?

- Depth for experienced or expert users—Will the product be useful for advanced users?

- Navigation features all work and are all useful—Are the buttons, graphic hot spots, and similar product functions user friendly? Will users be able to figure them out?

Strategies for New Developers

There are a great number of good and bad products on the market. New developers should always learn from past mistakes and good ideas. The following is a list of suggestions for honing your developmental skills:

- Select and evaluate multimedia products that are similar to those you wish to create.

- Analyze how these products work by considering the content, user interface, performance, and other characteristics. It may be useful to document the analysis to develop your own set of requirements and features for your product development effort.

- Analyze what works and does not work for each of the characteristics you have described. Design changes or improvements as necessary to correct these shortcomings.

- If you have programming and authoring skills, determine how you would implement them.

Apply the principles of product evaluation to the multimedia products on the CD-ROM.

You find current trends in multimedia product development as hardware, software, and user sophistication evolve on the Web site.

SUMMARY

There are a variety of multimedia products that include briefing, reference, database, reference, education and training, kiosk, and entertainment and game. The variety of products means that various features are required to make them useful and, for marketing reasons, profitable. In each type of product, the user must be considered in terms of his or her computer skills, need for the product, and under what conditions he or she will use it.

Understanding the various types of multimedia products is the basis for evaluating multimedia products from both the users' and developers' perspectives. Evaluation of multimedia products will enable users to get the best product for their money. For developers, evaluation of competitor products and past experiences are the first steps in creating the best products for the future.

REVIEW QUESTIONS

1. What types of multimedia products have you used?
2. What are the differences you have noted in how multimedia products are used? For example, the difference between a reference product and an educational product.
3. What issues for evaluation do you apply in selecting and purchasing multimedia products?
4. What are the differences in how you would evaluate the various types of multimedia products?
5. Evaluate a multimedia product that is similar to one you might build. What features would you mimic or adapt into your product? What would you do to improve the product?

CHAPTER THREE

Hardware, Operating Systems, and Software

Computer Architecture

The ability to produce and present multimedia is one of the most demanding activities placed on computers. Understanding how computers work is essential to both multimedia developers and, to some degree, consumers. There are a wide variety of computer systems ranging from wristwatch-sized personal information managers to multimillion-dollar supercomputers. This chapter will deal primarily with personal computers since they comprise most of the hardware used for multimedia production and distribution.

The most basic definition of a **computer** is a machine that is capable of gathering, processing, storing, and disseminating data. Computer data can range from a single bit, with a value of 0 or 1, to bytes (each containing 8 bits) to data files containing millions of bytes. A computer must interface with the world to collect and convert text, pictures, audio, and video, into ones and zeroes. The data is then stored and processed within the computer. Finally, data is converted back into some human-computer form (again, text, pictures, audio, and video) for viewing. With this in mind, there are five basic elements to a personal computer's architecture:

1. Processor
2. Memory
3. Input
4. Output
5. Control

After completing this chapter, you should know:

- How a computer works.
- How computers handle multimedia.
- The relationship between the hardware, operating system, and software for multimedia products.
- What devices are needed to create and present multimedia products.

Using the generalized computer architecture as shown in Figure 3-1, let us associate a computer's components with each of the architectural processes:

- Input: keyboard, mouse, modem, network
- Output: computer display or monitor, printer, speakers, modem, network
- Memory: short term RAM (random access memory); long-term hard disk, removable disk (e.g., floppy), magnetic tape, optical media, and CD-ROM.
- Processor: a parallel data bus ranging from 8 bits in early computers to 128 bits for handling data and instructions; the processor is capable of executing instructions at very high speed.
- Control: BIOS (Basic Input Output System), DOS (Disk Operating System), and **GUI** (graphical user interface manager also called Windows in Intel-based computers), word processors, spreadsheets, and other software.

Input and Output

The **input** and **output** functions are responsible for collecting and disseminating data. Input and output typically convert data between some analog format (keystrokes, pictures, audio and video signals) and the internal digital format that is most easily handled by the computer and then back to an analog form suitable for the end user. Input and output are the parts of the computer that are most apparent to human users and include the keyboard, monitor, mouse, scanner, and audio and video devices. Input and output are also responsible for networking two or more computers, which enables data to be transmitted and shared between computers.

Memory

Memory provides the means for a computer to store data for both the short and long term. Short-term memory is used to support the processor, input, and output with temporary

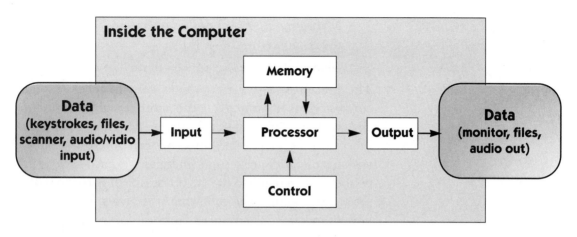

Figure 3-1 Overview of computer architecture

storage while data is moved around or as a scratch pad during calculations. Scratch pad memory is important so that the computer can keep track of interim calculations before final answers are stored permanently. Typically, short-term memory is only available when the computer is turned on and it comes in the form of silicon-based computer chips providing segments of memory in megabyte multiples (one megabyte equals 1024 bytes).

Long-term memory provides relatively permanent storage of data that can be used to transport data between computers. Long-term memory can take on many forms including floppy disks, hard disks, CD-ROMs, tape, and silicon-based chips. Long-term memory capacity ranges from a megabyte to gigabytes (billions of bytes).

The Processor

The **processor** is the heart of the computer. At the most basic level, it is a very fast and very powerful arithmetic machine capable of millions of calculations per second. The processor is based on the comparing, adding, and subtracting of ones and zeroes. Beyond arithmetic, basic processor functions include:

- Processing control instructions that tell the computer what to do

- Managing input and output operations that connect the computer to the world
- Managing the storage of data in memory

The processor, a single computer chip in most personal computers, is mounted on the motherboard within the chassis of the computer so that it is rarely seen by most users. Processors are usually measured by their speed in terms of millions of cycles per second (megahertz). Each cycle is the period of time required for the processing of partial or complete instructions. The following will give you an idea of how processing has advanced from the early 1980s to the mid 1990s:

- 1981: 8 bit data bus operating at 4.7 megahertz
- 1986: 16 bit data bus operating at 12 megahertz
- 1990: 16 bit data bus operating at 33 megahertz
- 1992: 32 bit data bus operating at 66 megahertz
- 1995: 32 bit data bus operating at 133 megahertz

As you can see, data capacity and processing speeds have improved and are expected to dramatically continue improving into the twenty-first century.

Integrating the Functions

The heart of all computers, as shown in Figure 3-2, is the interface within and between the various functional processes called the **bus. Data buses** are used to move data as ones and zeroes around the computer. These buses are parallel in nature and for personal computers move data 16, 32, and even 64 bits at a time. Obviously, the "wider" the data bus, the faster and more efficiently the computer can process data.

The **motherboard** is the device that integrates the processor and other components including the memory, disk drives, keyboard, and display. It includes the central processor chip, BIOS (Basic Input Output System) chip, and the data bus interface that allows disk drives, video, memory, and processor to communicate with the central processor. Typically, devices that connect to the mother-

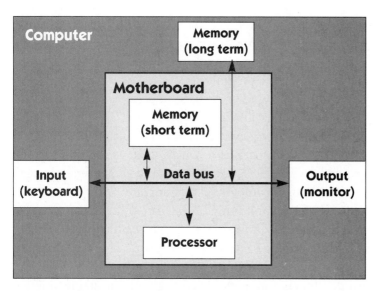

Figure 3-2 **Internal relationship of computer functions**

board directly, that is, directly into the data bus, are platform specific, which means they can only be used for the specific equipment they were created for.

Control

The **control** function shown in Figure 3-1, enables a computer to perform various actions. These actions are defined by programs or sets of instructions called software. Software instructions are defined and assembled at various levels of abstraction including:

- Machine language codes—ones and zeroes that the processor can interpret and execute; usually consists of very primitive processing steps.

- Assembly language—English-readable codes for machine language.

- Higher-level programming languages—higher level groupings of machine language instructions.

Computer programming can be accomplished at all of these levels. Machine and assembly languages are used to implement a fine level of control for computer operations. For example, using assembly language, you can manipulate individual bits and bytes; however, a great deal of effort is required to program even the simplest of operations. That is why higher level programming languages such as FORTRAN, BASIC, and C are used to achieve a more productive means to develop complex computer applications such as word processors, spreadsheets, and multimedia.

Software programs are usually designed and implemented for specific processor types and are not interchangeable, although compatible versions are often created for cross-platform applications. Similarly, data formats for text, graphics, audio, and video, and even the file formats themselves are unique to different platforms. This separation of file formats, data, and software has created many problems for developers and users in exchanging information and developing applications for all potential end users. For example, early graphic file formats for different computer platforms were not directly interchangeable, making it necessary to create programs to convert data from one platform to the next.

Control processes also include various levels of managing and controlling computer actions. Personal computers have a hierarchy of control levels that include:

- BIOS (Basic Input Output System)—provides low level activities such as accessing disk drives, display, and the keyboard. The BIOS is used at computer startup to initialize basic hardware functions such as accessing disk and keyboard components.

- Operating System—following the execution of the BIOS software, the operating system is loaded and provides more complex control over input and output devices, memory management, display operation, and program operations.

- Programs—specific executable instructions that perform various tasks, usually under control of an end user or computer operator.

Computer Architecture Standards

The large number of vendors developing Intel-based hardware and software products has created a problem in hardware and software standardization. Standards determine what is and is not compatible. For example, a processor may only be compatible with certain types of memory chips. In theory, standards are established so that components can be interchangeable and will work together in a completed system. However, computer standards have often been driven by the need to get to market first, and whoever built and sold it first has ended up defining the standard. This has created some good and some bad standards. Standards have generally yielded simpler approaches making it easier for other vendors to copy or integrate their components. For example, audio capture and playback hardware have standardized so much that software and hardware from various manufacturers are interchangeable. This has resulted in cheaper prices for components and systems because of widespread competition. Unfortunately, these standards have sometimes been less than optimal in terms of the fastest or most efficient solution. Furthermore, other problems would often arise when end users would try to mix and match components that did not always work well within the "agreed upon" standards.

The Apple Macintosh took a different view of the standards situation from the Intel-based systems. From the beginning to the mid 1990s, Apple owned and controlled all rights to the hardware and software; all components were designed and integrated by a single source. This meant that processors, disk drives, keyboards, and other components always worked well together. For the most part, Apple systems performed very well under most conditions and had few, if any, problems with end users such as having to deal with disk drives that could not or did not work with the particular version of computer they were using.

From the processor perspective, and based on market share in the 1980s and 1990s, Intel-based computers and Apple Macintosh virtually own the personal computer hardware market. Beyond that, components for memory chips, disk drives, CD-ROMs, audio and video hardware, and software programs are developed by a wide variety of sources. The Apple Macintosh, due to its single vendor source, offers the advantage of a tightly integrated hardware system that assures compatibility with any software created for it. Intel-based, also referred to as IBM-compatible computers, while sometimes suffering from compatibility problems, are based on open standards, which has encouraged competition from many vendors often resulting in generally lower prices for hardware components and computer systems.

Operating Systems and Software

Personal computer operation and function are based on a layered approach to running software programs. These layers of computer programs operate the computer from the most primitive level, such as collecting keystrokes, to carrying out advanced processing required for multimedia products. Figure 3-3 provides an overview of the relationship between the lowest level programs (BIOS) to application software.

Software architecture for the operating system and application programs has grown complex since the earliest personal computers. This is especially true with Windows and Macintosh environments that added a graphical layer to applications as well as support for multitasking (multiple applications running simultaneously) and clipboards for sharing data between applications.

Disk Operating System

The operating system is implemented at various layers that provide support for computer hardware and software capabilities. The basic layer is the disk operating system in which the computer is able to read and write data to various media.

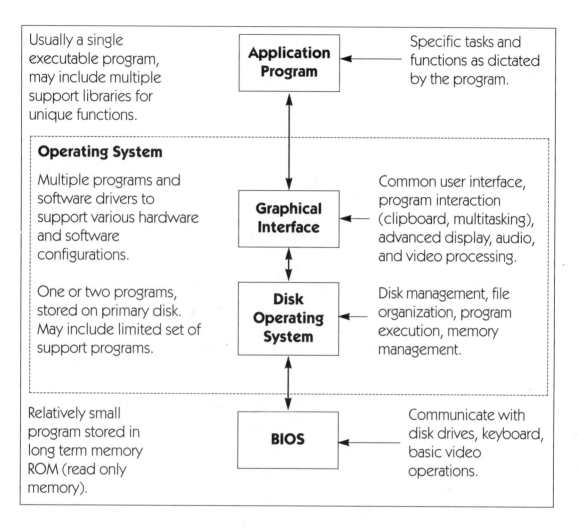

Figure 3-3 The relationship between different computer software layers

The disk operating system establishes a scheme to organize data as files and groups of files as components of folders or directories. This allows computers to easily store and transfer data between computers. The operating system enables the computer to:

- Present information on the monitor
- Output information to a printer
- Communicate with other computers via modems and networks

- Share information and functions among various programs in a computer (the clipboard is an example)

Graphical Interface

Personal computers have seen a significant evolution in the various hardware and operating systems. The first personal computers consisted of processors of limited speed, low memory, and relatively small and often slow disk drive storage capabilities with operating systems that were designed to support single programs. Typically, the software program was completely responsible for managing access to the disk, displaying information on the monitor, and managing its memory. As processor power, memory capacity, and disk capacity all increased, the operating systems started providing many of these features. These features were managed in "windowing" systems that provided standardized functions for accessing the disk, displaying textual and graphical information, printing, communicating with networks and modems, and managing memory resources. These advanced operating systems typically offered "graphic user interfaces" that enabled multiple programs to run simultaneously, although in early versions of these windowing systems, only the program in the active window was running until another window was selected.

As the window-based operating systems evolved, the functionality and support for software programs increased dramatically. Windowing systems now provide a common framework of functions for software applications that run within them. These functions include:

- Advanced disk management for organizing, naming, file compression, and rapidly accessing files.

- Common user interface features (e.g., pull-down menus, list boxes, and picture containers) across programs making it easier for end users to learn and apply new applications.

- Display support for graphics, including dynamically modifying the screen resolution and changing the number of colors available for applications. Multiple text fonts, sizes, and characteristics are also available for a variety of applications.

- Memory management to support multiple programs running simultaneously.

- Advanced printer support for the wide variety of printers that are commercially available.

- Managing communications resources including networks and modems.

- Common support for input devices such as mice, joysticks, touch screens, and serial and parallel ports. Also, operating systems will provide a common means to support sound and video capture and playback devices.

The advantage of the Windows approach is that individual applications do not have to worry about how to display information or access the hard drive. This reduces program size and enables developers to focus on unique functionality. Developers can also create applications with confidence that the operating system will always know how to get data from a network-based disk or write to a printer.

Multimedia Computer Architecture

Multimedia tools and products depend on the ability of the computer to capture, process, and present text, pictures, audio, and video. As you would expect, when compared to other software programs such as word processors, multimedia applications offer significant challenges to computer architecture in terms of its ability to:

- Input various data formats, including converting analog data to digital format. Input may be as simple as typing in characters from a keyboard, scanning images, or capturing analog audio and video.

- Store and retrieve digital multimedia data—a very significant effort considering that digital audio and video files can require megabytes of storage space or that some multimedia products may depend on accessing hundreds of data files to create a compelling product.

- Manipulate and edit multimedia data; for example, editing graphics, audio, and digital video files. Manipulation also includes the creation and editing of complex multimedia products.
- Output multimedia data including converting digital version into an analog format suitable for the end user. This includes placing graphics on the screen, sending sound to a speaker, or generating television signals for display on large screen projection systems.

Multimedia-specific hardware, as shown in Figure 3-4, includes a number of components with very special features:

Input

- Keyboards— also special layouts for limiting and controlling user input
- Mouse—also track balls, joysticks, and similar devices
- Graphic tablets—used in drawing and painting applications
- Scanner—capable of capturing images ranging from black and white to millions of colors
- Digital camera—capable of capturing and converting images and video directly into a computer-digital format
- Touch screens for kiosks providing simplified input where a keyboard is not practical or desirable. Touch screens are built with capacitive, pressure, infrared, and similar technologies that can be adapted to sense pressure on the screen.
- Analog audio input from microphones and audio player sources
- Analog video input— raw and processed video input. Some hardware systems even decode television signals for display.
- Network support for distribution of multimedia files
- Modem

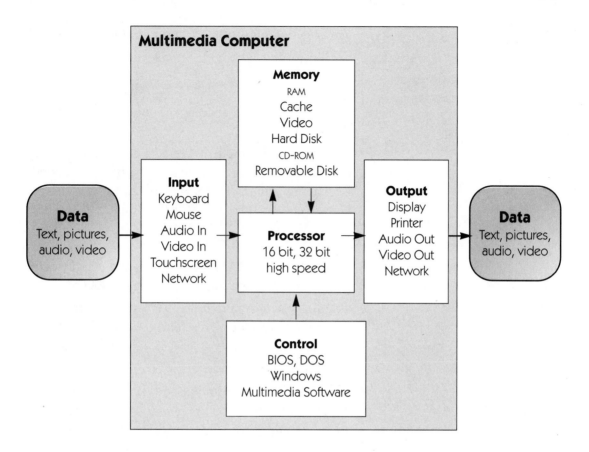

Figure 3-4 Hardware elements found in a multimedia computer

Output

- High resolution monitors capable of displaying black and white to millions of colors. A 256-color display is considered the minimum requirement for multimedia display.

- Specialized projection devices to replace or augment single user monitor/displays for larger audiences. These devices usually function in lieu of or simultaneously with a computer monitor.

- Audio output to speakers or to other audio devices such as amplifiers or tape devices.

You will find standards for multimedia computer hardware.

- Raw video output for television monitor display—the computer typically creates a television video compatible signal.
- Network support—networks typically provide communication speeds between computers up to 10 million bits per second.
- Modem—analog modems connect computers via telephone lines at speeds up to 28,800 bits per second. Digital modems via ISDN (Integrated Services Digital Network) offer speeds up to 128,000 bits per second.

Memory:

- Large amount of RAM for graphics, audio and video production, and writing multimedia products.
- Graphics memory, also called VRAM (video random access memory), for high resolution/color displays.
- Large, relatively fast hard drive systems for processing graphic, audio, and video data.
- CD-ROM—long-term storage and delivery of multimedia programs and data.
- Tape and similar long-term storage media.

Specialized Multimedia Hardware

Multimedia hardware focuses on the ability to capture, store, and present text, pictures, audio, and video. For each type of data, the computer must be able to convert it into digital format and store that data in a file. This file can then be edited and/or applied into a multimedia presentation product. The presentation software, in conjunction with the operating system, then converts the data back into an analog format that can be viewed, heard, or experienced by an end user.

CD-ROM

The **CD-ROM**, short for **Compact Disk-Read-Only Memory**, is considered the most common form of packaging for multimedia products. CD-ROM started out as a read-only technology in which you could store data once and access it many times. Advances in CD-ROMs have led to multi-session versions in which you can add to the content of a CD-ROM and even fully writable CD-ROM systems. CD-ROM is capable of storing between 500 and 680 megabytes of data in a reasonable sturdy environment. The downside has been the relative slowness for data access of CD-ROM devices because they access and retrieve data much more slowly than hard drives. CD-ROMs are governed by a set of industry standards which include:

- Red Book (ISO 10149)—describes the **CD-DA (Compact Disk-Digital Audio)** format. This is the original CD format used for digital audio and provides for 500 megabytes for 63 minutes of music or 680 megabytes for 74 minutes.

- Green Book—describes the **CD-I (Compact Disk-Interactive)** developed by Philips. This standard provides for up to two hours of stereo music or 20 hours of monaural (single channel) voice-quality audio. CD-I allows audio, video, and data tracks to be combined by interleaving for complex multimedia presentation.

- Orange Book— describes the **CD-R** (Compact Disk-Recordable) as a means to easily store large volumes of data in either write-once or read-write modes of operation.

- Yellow Book—describes the **CD-XA (XA for eXtended Architecture)** which allows for compressed audio to be added to other multimedia data.

In addition to these standards, there are other emerging standards such as CD-TV (television), PhotoCD, and a number of little used and even defunct standards for older products. The mid 1990s saw the emergence of Digital Video Disks (DVD) with increased storage capacity and additional features for storing multimedia information.

CD-ROMs store data using the **ISO 9660** format. ISO 9660, originally called the High Sierra standard, uses a format similar to the Microsoft DOS file system. Filenames use the 8.3 format and consist of alphabetic characters from A to Z, numbers from 0 to 9 and the underscore. Note that ISO 9660 does not use lowercase or special characters like @, &, -, and ~ as in DOS systems. The obvious advantage of this formatting scheme is how easily it will interface with most personal computer disk operating systems making it easier for applications to access data on CD-ROM media.

CD-ROMs depend on special purpose drives to access information. These drives, although similar, are more capable and functional than audio CD drives in that they handle larger error streams, are faster, and can be accessed and controlled at a much finer level. A CD-ROM drive operates by spinning the CD at a very high rate and moving a laser-based optical assembly across, but not touching, the disk. The efficiency of a CD-ROM is measured by how fast it is able to transfer data to the computer.

CD-Audio drives transfer data at 150 KB/sec (kilobytes per second), a rate significantly slower than hard drives. By speeding up the rotation of the CD-ROM drive, data rates are doubled (2X or 300 KB/sec), quadrupled (4X, 600 KB/sec), and even more. Another issue that impacts CD-ROM players is access time, which is based on how fast the data read-device—the laser-based optical assembly—is able to move across the disk. Typical access times for CD-ROMs are 100 to 200 milliseconds, which is still significantly slower than hard drives.

CD-ROM drives can be interfaced to a computer via SCSI (small computer systems interface), IDE (Integrated Drive Electronics, also known as the AT attachment), parallel, and proprietary. SCSI and IDE are the fastest and most standardized interfaces. Parallel interfaces are very slow and are only used as a last resort. Proprietary interfaces are more common with CD-ROM drives packaged with audio capture/playback boards or similar devices. CD-ROM drives can be used to play audio CDs by using internal circuitry to generate an analog audio signal accessible through an audio capture/playback board or headphones connected to the CD-ROM drive.

Digital Audio and Video

Digital audio and video typically require specialized hardware and software for capture and playback. As shown in Figure 3-5, there are three aspects of the digital audio video operation.

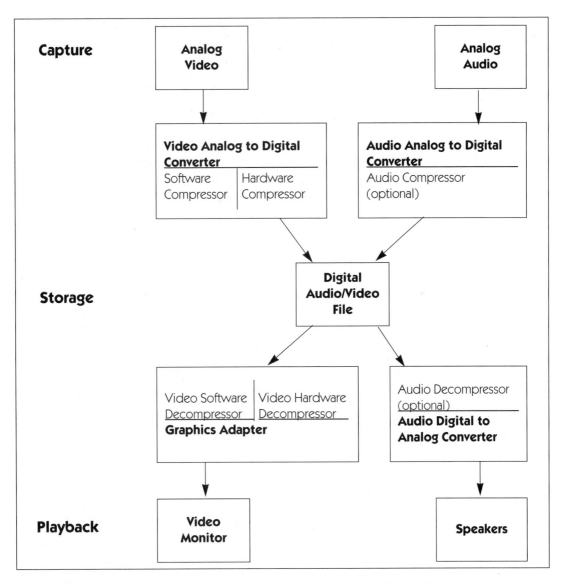

Figure 3-5 The three stages of audio and video capture, storage, and playback

1. Capture—raw analog sources are digitized; data may be compressed via hardware (audio and video) or software (video).
2. Storage—files are stored and/or transmitted.
3. Playback—playback based on hardware or software digital to analog conversion.

Since this chapter focuses on hardware and software for multimedia, we will discuss the specifics of audio and video devices here. The specifics of what the data is and how it is used are discussed in Chapters 6 and 7.

Audio Hardware

Digital audio requires special hardware for both the capture and playback of sound. The hardware may be part of the motherboard or in the form of an add-on board. Audio is usually input into the computer via a microphone or a line-in connection from external audio devices such as tape or audio CD players. Audio is output to speakers or as a line-out to an external amplifier or other recording device. Digital audio systems for computers include specific hardware to convert analog audio signal into a digital audio stream of bits and bytes and then reverse the process.

Video Hardware

Video hardware consists of devices to display and capture video. Video display devices, often called graphics adapters, enable the computer to present information on monitors capable of displaying up to 16 million colors. The VGA (video graphics adapter), most common for personal computers since the late 1980s, provides a 640 by 480 pixel display. A **pixel** is the smallest sized space in which unique information is presented on a display, usually as a unique color. VGA is capable of displaying a range of colors from two to 16 million. Super VGA extends the display from 640 by 480 pixels to 800 by 600 and 1024 by 768 pixels. In all cases, note that the aspect ratio, the width versus the height, of the display for VGA is 4:3.

Video capture devices enable the computer to connect to video cameras and video cassette recorders (VCRs) to record analog video as digital video. These devices can handle various types of television signals including American NTSC and European/Japanese PAL. Video capture devices are capable of converting analog video directly into a raw digital video stream that can be stored on a computer hard drive in both raw and/or compressed formats that significantly reduce the size of the video data stream.

Communications

The key issue for multimedia communications is **bandwidth;** that is, the amount of information that can be transmitted across a network of computers within a fixed period of time. Bandwidth is often measured in kilobits per second (Kbps) or megabits per second (Mbps) that can be carried by a network. Multimedia data file sizes, especially for graphics, audio, and video, can be quite large. Communication speeds for real-time presentation of audio and video in a computer network must be as fast as that for direct disk access within a single computer. Primary communications devices and functions include:

- Modems: Analog modems to 28,800 bits per second (bps), digital modems (ISDN—Integrated Services Digital Network) to 64,000 bps.

- Networks: up to 10 megabits per second (mbps) including shared bandwidth systems (multiple users share total bandwidth to 10 mbps).

- Digital Audio: audio files are downloaded or streaming audio systems for real-time communications; quality good for voice with insufficient bandwidth for higher quality music.

- Digital Video: similar to audio; video files are downloaded or streaming video for near real-time presentation; quality limited to very low frame rates.

- Remote application sharing: multiple users sharing a single application across a network.

Communications systems have created two classes of multimedia products: **synchronous** or real time and **asynchronous.** Synchronous applications are able to transmit and receive data in real time allowing the end user to view or hear data as it is being captured or created. Asynchronous applications use a store and forward method in which data is transmitted and stored for future presentation.

Let us consider two user scenarios for connectivity based on communications services:

1. Office-based with network up to 100 mbps, typically 1 to 10 mbps
2. Home users with modem 14,400 to 28,800 bps

The communications bandwidth for each scenario depends on:

- Network—configuration of the network, number of machines on the network, and amount of activity
- Modem—speed of the modem and line noise

In all cases bandwidth is also dependent on point-to-point connectivity. Generally:

- The slowest communications links in the network will bring overall speed down.
- High number of users will slow down access.
- Amount of traffic (file sizes) can slow down network.

Table 3-1 provides sample content sizes and associated transmission times. Note that the speeds listed here are under ideal conditions (actual performance may be 2 to 5 times less).

Real-time transmission and presentation are effective for text and graphics. Unfortunately, real time transmission of audio and video, even with networks, is problematic at best. Lower bandwidth, voice quality audio and video at single to low frame rate, is the best that is typically achieved on fast modems. With dedicated network access, that is, each user has a significant piece of 10 megabit/second bandwidth, faster video frame rates can be achieved with higher quality audio. The bottom line on multimedia and communications is that until significant bandwidth (in other words, higher data transmission speeds) is available to end users, remote multimedia products will be limited primarily to text and graphics.

Data Type	Typical Sample	At 28,800 bits per second (3600 bytes/second) Assumes ideal conditions
Text	Page of text (100 characters/line, 30 lines) = 3000 bytes	<1 second
Pictures	Full screen (640 x 480 pixels), 256 color bitmap = 330,000 bytes	91 seconds
	Compressed graphic format = 75,000 to 200,000 bytes (depends on type, detail, colors)	Compressed file, 20 to 55 seconds
Audio	Voice, one minute = 600,000 bytes (at 11 KHz sampling, monaural)	Voice, 166 seconds (nearly 3 minutes)
	Music, one minute = 10.5 megabytes (at 44 KHz sampling, stereo)	Music, 3000 seconds (50 minutes)
Video	One minute, uncompressed = 414 megabytes (image size of 320 x 240 pixels, 24-bit color, 30 frames per second)	Uncompressed, 115,000 seconds (1.9 hours)
	One minute, compressed = 10–15 megabytes (image size of 320 x 240 pixels, 24-bit color, 30 frames per second and depending on the compression scheme)	Compressed, 2777 seconds (46 minutes)

Table 3-1 Data types and transmission time

Multimedia Software

Multimedia products generally have two functional modes: development and delivery. In the development mode, multimedia products depend on a variety of functions to create and edit text and graphics, capture and digitize audio and video, and assemble content into comprehensive products. Delivery depends on the ability to present text, graphics and video, generate sound, and respond to inputs by users to control the flow of a presentation. In both cases, the multimedia product must be able to access hardware to locate content or store applications, control a sound board, or manage a video capture and compression device. Control-

Descriptions of advanced hardware technologies for multimedia computers.

Check the Web site for multimedia computer and hardware vendors.

ling these devices to develop and deliver multimedia products is, for modern operating systems, a function of both the application software and the operating system.

Operating systems were originally designed to provide basic support for the keyboard, disk drive, and video display. As these systems evolved with graphical features, additional functionality also emerged for memory management, video display control, additional user interface devices, and application multitasking. Desktop computer operating systems consist of a set of cooperative software programs that manage hardware and application operations. This same approach is used in supporting multimedia products.

Software Executables and Libraries

There are two classes of software that make up desktop software and multimedia products: executables and libraries. Executables can be completely self-contained executable programs that provide for all functionality of a particular application. More commonly, especially with complex window-based applications, executable programs are supported by libraries that provide functionality that is either shared between applications or has functions that are only used in rare occasions. These libraries, shown in Figure 3-6, are often called dynamic link libraries, object libraries, or hardware and software drivers. The last type, drivers, are typically used in multimedia systems to support very specialized functions with audio and video hardware or graphics conversion and display.

Software Drivers

Software drivers for multimedia are used to control specific hardware functions. The drivers must be able to interface the operating system, and ultimately the application program, to the specific hardware. Drivers are usually specific to hardware devices although some *de facto* industry standards have emerged that make drivers much more universal. Software drivers for multimedia devices include:

- Video display drivers

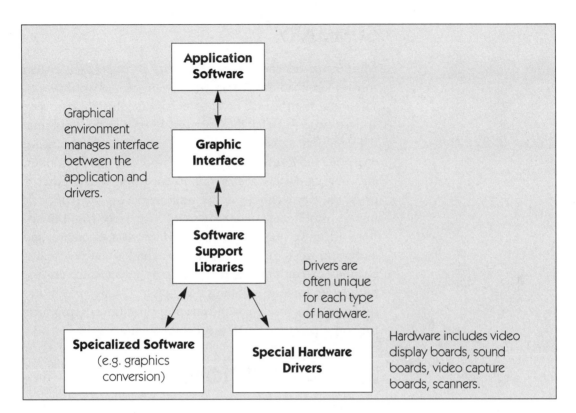

Figure 3-6 Software drivers for multimedia support

- Video capture
- Sound capture and playback
- Scanners
- Mouse, joysticks, and track balls

In each of these cases, the application accesses specific functions of the device (or is controlled by the device) via calls to the operating system. Functions such as "record audio, record video, and play audio" are standardized by the operating system making it easier for application developers to take advantage of many devices without worrying about specific control operations or characteristics for any one device. An additional benefit is that end users can also switch devices such as sound boards without having to worry whether or not the application software will still work.

SUMMARY

Multimedia depends on the hardware and operating system much more than other types of software such as word processors and spreadsheets. This chapter has described the hardware and software that enable computers to operate and multimedia products to be developed and delivered. The standard computer platform provides the the processor, memory, input, and output devices that a multimedia-capable computer is based on. Key technologies for multimedia capability include high density storage such as CD-ROM; high speed communications to move graphic, text, and video data elements; and audio and video capture, edit, and playback systems. The discussions of computer and multimedia architecture are the foundation for learning about text, graphics, audio, video, and understanding the design and creation of multimedia products for both CD-ROM and Internet deployment.

REVIEW QUESTIONS

1. A computer is based on a set of functions that define its operation. What are these elements? How are these elements related?

2. Computer control is determined by software. What types of software control the various operations of a computer?

3. How do computer standards impact the design of computer systems?

4. Multimedia hardware enables the computer to perform some unique functions. Describe some of these functions in terms of multimedia products that you have seen.

5. What are the performance limitations of the CD-ROM for delivering multimedia products?

6. What are the various CD-ROM formats? What formats are most commonly used in everyday applications?

7. How are the three aspects of digital audio and video related to the hardware platform?

8. How does bandwidth impact the delivery of multimedia data and applications?

CHAPTER FOUR

Text

Text in the form of words, sentences, and paragraphs is used to communicate thoughts, ideas, and facts in nearly every aspect of our lives. It is no surprise then that multimedia products depend on text for many things: to explain how the applications work, to guide the user in navigating through the application, and to deliver information for which the application was designed. Text technology forms the basis for many multimedia systems. How text is created and edited, how it is stored, and how is it used are all critical to the development and successful delivery of multimedia products and systems. This chapter describes the features of text, how it is stored, and how to use it in a multimedia product.

Elements of Text

Multimedia applications depend on text for many things, some of which includes:
- Page titles
- Delivering information in the form of multiple sentences and/or paragraphs
- Labels for pictures
- Instructions for operating the application

Text elements can be large and expressive or small and subtle. Depending on the purpose of the application and the intended audience, text is the most common form of information delivery. In addition, text often accompanies

OBJECTIVES

After completing this chapter, you should know:

- What text is.
- How text is stored in the computer.
- How text is created and stored in the computer.
- How text is used in multimedia products.

pictures, audio, and video. Generally speaking, text is a key component of every application ever created and plays a key role in most applications yet to be conceived.

Text Technology

Text technology is based on creating letters, numbers, and special characters such as periods, commas, and dollar signs to build words, sentences, and paragraphs of information. Text elements fall into a number of categories:

- Alphabet characters: English—A to Z, includes both upper- and lowercases depending on the language

- Numbers: 0 to 9

- Special characters: punctuation (. , ; ' "), signs ($ + = -), and nonprinted characters (carriage return, line feed)

Text, as an information media, was originally defined by printed media such as books and newspapers that used various typefaces to display the alphabet, numbers, and special characters more pleasingly.

Typefaces are the graphic representations of the alphabet, numbers, and special characters and usually vary by type sizes and styles. A **font** is a particular size of typeface; for example: "14 point Times New Roman" is a typeface of a particular size. Size is determined by measuring from the top of a capital letter to the bottom of a descender found on a "p" or "y." Size is determined by points with a single point being 1/72 (0.138 inches).

In addition to typeface and size, Figure 4-1 describes a number of characteristics that are also used to physically describe text:

- Ascender is an upstroke on a character, and can be found in the letters "h," "b," and "d."

- Descender is the downstroke below the baseline of a character; for example "p," "q," and "y" all have descenders.

- Leading (pronounced "ledding") is the spacing above and below a font: that is, the line spacing.

- Tracking is the spacing between characters.

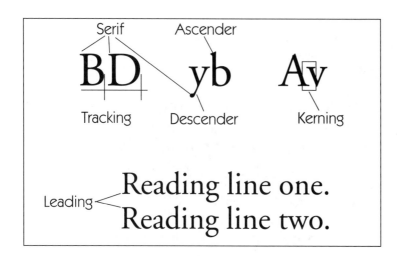

Figure 4-1 Text characteristics

- Kerning is the space between pairs of characters, usually as an overlap for improved appearance.
- Serif is the flag or decoration at the end of a character
stroke.

Fonts also take on a number of effects that are useful for
bringing the viewer's attention to content:

- Case: UPPER and lower versions of each letter; case is
usually set by the shift or caps lock function of the
keyboard.
- Regular: used in most situations; this is the standard
version of a font such as Times New Roman or Arial.
- **Bold: provides standout emphasis for highlighting
and titles.**
- *Italic: similar to bolding, used to draw attention.*
- Condensed and expanded: narrowing or e x p a n d i n g
the overall width of text characters.
- <u>Underline: used for highlighting.</u>
- ~~Strikeout:~~ usually indicates text has been removed; for
example, ~~He~~ She went to the ~~8~~ 7 o'clock show.

Font effects as just described are usually selected within a
word processing program by accessing a dialog that allows
the user to select the desired effects.

Times New Roman, Regular, 10 point
Times New Roman, Italic, 10 point
Times New Roman, Bold, 10 point

Times New Roman, Regular, 14 point
Times New Roman, Italic, 14 point
Times New Roman, Bold, 14 point

Courier, Regular, 10 point
Courier, Bold, 10 point

Courier, Regular, 18 point
Courier, Bold, 18 point

Figure 4-2 Examples of serif fonts

Types of Fonts

There are two classes of fonts: serif and sans serif. Serif fonts use decorative tips or flags at the ends of strokes; sans serif fonts do not have these features. Serif fonts are used in printed media because the serifs help to guide the reader's eye along the text. However, for computer displays, sans serif fonts are considered better because of the sharper contrast. Figures 4-2 and 4-3 show different examples of serif and sans serif fonts. Serif fonts include:

- Times and Times New Roman
- Courier
- Schoolbook
- Bookman

Sans serif fonts include:

- Arial
- Helvetica
- Avant Garde

Fonts come in many varieties when used in computer graphic environments. It is common for personal computers to be able to access and use dozens of fonts in a variety of ap-

Arial, Regular, 10 point
Arial, Italic, 10 point
Arial Bold, 10 point

Arial, Regular, 10 point
Arial, Italic, 10 point
Arial Bold, 10 point

Helvetica, Regular, 10 point
Helvetica, Bold, 10 point

Helvetica, Regular, 18 point
Helvetica, Bold, 18 point

plications. Graphical systems are able to create and use fonts due to a process called **rasterization.** Rasterization occurs when the computer draws the font onto the display one pixel at a time. Fonts, depending on the size and the number of pixels used to draw them, can appear jagged making them more difficult to read and follow. A technique called **anti-aliasing** is used to blend the font into the background by transitioning the color from the font color to the background color. This technique minimizes the jagged edges making for a smoother overall appearance. Anti-aliasing is commonly used in paint and drawing software packages where it is desirable to make the transition between the image background and text elements look smooth and seamless.

Figure 4-3 Examples of sans serif fonts

Fonts and Operating Systems

One of the major problems with so many fonts is that they can be platform and even machine specific. A basic set of fonts is usually supplied with graphical operating systems and additional fonts may be added later as a result of installing a printer or a new application, such as a desktop publishing or even a software-based font collection. These additional fonts often offer unique features such as a typeface or special graph-

Examples of
ASCII-encoded text

ical characters. For example, there are fonts that simulate handwriting or elegant character faces that can dramatically add to the look of an application or a document.

Word processing applications, paint and drawing software, and multimedia authoring tools use the fonts that are native to the machine being used for creation and editing. If special fonts have been installed on the computer and an application uses these fonts to create a product, then those special fonts will have to be installed on any other machine that displays the same product. If the data file is moved to another computer and the fonts are not installed on that computer, then the fonts will be mapped to other fonts. Font mapping is a process in which fonts are substituted for other fonts that are similar in format, size, and other characteristics. Alternatively, some applications will store fonts within the program data that can be temporarily used on the computer that is displaying the text.

Text Data Files

Text is maintained in computers as data files that can be stored for long periods of time, shared between applications, or transmitted to other computers. At the most basic level, text can be stored in desktop computers as letters, numbers, and characters using ASCII encoding. Beyond that, text can be stored with formatting to define font type, font size, bolding, italics, and other features. Text can also be stored as data by applications such as word processors and multimedia products. The following sections describe the more common data encoding schemes for text.

ASCII

The simplest form of data encoding for text is **ASCII (American Standard Code for Information Interchange)**. It is a 7-bit coding scheme for text yielding 128 characters that includes lower- and uppercase characters, punctuation, numbers, math symbols, and 32 control characters. Figure 4-4 lists the 128 characters found in the ASCII character set.

0–32: Special Characters	33–127: Letters, numbers, symbols		
7 Bell	33 !	48–57: 0–9 (numbers)	65–90: A–Z (uppercase alphabet)
10 Line Feed	34 "	58 :	91 [
12 Form Feed	35 #	59 ;	92 \
13 Carriage Return	36 $	60 <	93]
14 Strike Over	37 %	61 =	94 ^
27 Escape	38 &	62 >	95 _
32 Space	39 '		96 `
	40 (		97–122: a–z (lowercase alphabet)
	41)		123 {
	42 *		124 |
	43 +		125 }
	44 ,		126 ~
	45 -		127 Del
	46 .		
	47 ?		

As you may recall the basic unit of data in desktop computer systems is the byte, which consists of 8 bits. ASCII, which only requires 7 bits for 128 characters, uses the extra bit to create the extended character set. The extended character set consists of the **ANSI (American National Standards Institute)** standard characters. Depending on the platform, the extended character set may vary. For example, desktop systems in the 1980s used the extended character set to store line-drawing characters for creating boxes on text-only computer displays.

The ASCII character set is the most common way to encode, store, and transmit text between applications and computers. It is often used to exchange text between applications because it does not offer any formatting at the character, word, or paragraph level and any formatting is a function of the container holding the text. Furthermore, the

Figure 4-4 ASCII character set. *Note:* **Only a few of the special characters are shown that are commonly used in multimedia application.**

extent of formatting for ASCII text is usually limited to the use of carriage returns and line feed codes (ASCII code 13 and 30 respectively).

Encoded or Formatted Text

Encoded or formatted text uses embedded codes to determine the appearance of the text. In most cases, the text data format is ASCII with explicit codes embedded in the text. The codes are separated with special characters such as line feeds or bracketed by symbols such as "<" and ">." The encoding is used to determine text formatting at the character or string level and often includes font selection and encoding for paragraph alignment and spacing.

The hypertext markup language (HTML) used in World Wide Web pages is an example of text-based encoding. For example:

<H1> This is a Title *</H1>*

<P> This is a line of text in a paragraph format… *</P>*

The tags determine what formatting is used to present the text. In many cases a start and finish tag is used to surround the text that is being formatted. For example, the text between <H1> and </H1> is presented in a larger-sized (usually 14 point), bolded, sans serif formatted text font. Tags may also be separated by carriage return/line feed sequences. For example:

.title

This is a Title

.paragraph

This is a line of text in a paragraph format.

In both examples cited, the text would be viewed as follows:

This is a Title

This is a line of text in a paragraph format…

There are a number of encoding schemes that may be used to present text. Codes may be used to define:

- Selection of fonts including typeface and size

- Font features such as bold, italic, underlining, and color

- Paragraph start and finish, indenting, bullets, and alignment

- Page layout including header and footer, page numbering, and background color
- Document level encoding for chapters, indexes, and tables of contents

Examples of RTF formatted text

Rich Text Format

Rich text format (RTF) has gained significant acceptance as a means to store and manipulate text. It is a proprietary format owned and controlled by Microsoft Corporation for use with word processors. RTF provides a number of font formatting features including font typing, sizing, and bolding as well as paragraph formatting functions such as alignment. Many multimedia development applications have incorporated features to import and export RTF data to maintain formatting established in other documents.

Proprietary Text Formats

Word processing applications typically use a proprietary format to encode text. The formatting covers characters, words, paragraphs, and layout of the entire document. Unfortunately, the formatting tends to be unique from one word processor vendor to another making it difficult to transfer data from one word processor to another. Conversion is accomplished by:

- Using the word processor to convert the data into a common format. ASCII and RTF are common formats for conversion and transport. ASCII is useful for copying the raw text data (characters only) while RTF enables some level of formatting to be maintained between word processors.

- Special functions exist within the word processor to convert directly to or from the format of another commercial word processor.

Due to the large number of proprietary formats, multimedia development applications typically do not import and export proprietary word processor formats.

Using Text in Multimedia Applications

Computer systems have always relied on text for the user interface and information delivery. Even with graphic user interfaces, text is the primary delivery mechanism for captioning, menus, and directing user interaction. Although multimedia products include pictures, audio, and video, text may be the most common data type found in these applications. Text is used for a variety of purposes that include:

- Providing identification of objects such as pictures or program labels
- Delivering information in the form of captions and bulk text
- Assisting the user in navigating around the application

The following sections discuss typical uses of text within multimedia products and offer suggestions about how text might be implemented.

Labels and Captions

Labels are usually found in title bar windows or as identifiers for input functions such as text input boxes. Captions act as logos and identifiers for other information. For example, a caption may be used to identify the relationship of a picture to other information. Labels and captions tend to be short and to the point. They should stand out from the background and the font should be easy to read–sans serif fonts are usually best for readability. Captions often lay over pictures and anti-aliasing should be utilized to help the font blend in smoothly.

Informational Text

Informational text consists of a number of words, sentences, and paragraphs that convey a message. Multimedia authoring systems often use text container objects to hold large amounts of text that can be positioned appropriately on the display. Large amounts of text can be difficult to read on a computer display. As with captions, there should be a significant contrast in color between the font and the background. Scroll bars should be used for large amounts of text rather than shrinking the text to fit on the display. Depending on the resolution of the display, sans serif fonts are used for lower resolution displays, whereas serif fonts are used on high resolution displays.

Informational text for multimedia products is usually prepared in another program such as a word processing application, and then imported into the multimedia product. To accomplish this two techniques are generally used:

1. Text is stored in files that are external to the application. Font type, size, color, and other features are set for all text in the text container within the application. If the file contains feature information such as that found in RTF formatted data, the text container will display the text accordingly.

2. Text is stored within the application data file. Font type, size, color, and other features can be set for individual letters, words, and segments of text.

Some multimedia products have built-in word processors that can be used to format text for the specific multimedia authoring tool. These built-in word processors can be used to import text from other applications and word processors.

Navigation and User Support

Text-based controls for computer applications include buttons, list boxes, drop-down lists, and window menus. Although the operation of various controls depends on the use of a mouse for clicking or pressing the "enter" key, text is critical as an identifier or a selection element in the case of a list box. As with other multimedia objects, text in buttons and list boxes needs to be clear and concise. Contrast between the font and background is critical for making the control easy to see and use.

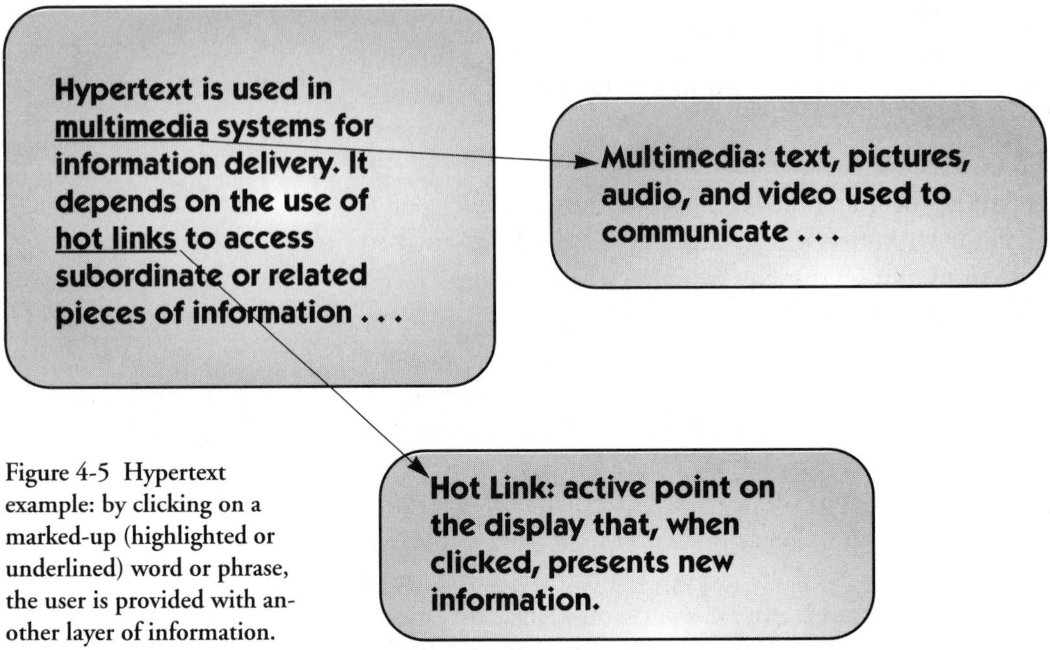

Hypertext is used in <u>multimedia</u> systems for information delivery. It depends on the use of <u>hot links</u> to access subordinate or related pieces of information . . .

Multimedia: text, pictures, audio, and video used to communicate . . .

Hot Link: active point on the display that, when clicked, presents new information.

Figure 4-5 Hypertext example: by clicking on a marked-up (highlighted or underlined) word or phrase, the user is provided with another layer of information.

Applying Text to Multimedia Projects

Use of text in multimedia products often depends more on common sense than on hard and fast rules. However, there are a number of general guidelines for using text in multimedia products:

- Since computer screens can be difficult to read, be careful when selecting fonts for readability. Generally speaking, sans serif fonts are the most readable.
- Keep the number of font typefaces in a presentation to a minimum. Too many fonts can be distracting.
- Watch the spacing between characters, lines, paragraphs within text, and the proximity of text to other objects such as pictures. Text too close to a picture or video can be difficult to read.
- Be careful when placing text over graphics, especially with color, font, and sizing.
- Vary size, style, boldness, and so forth to the message you are sending. For example, if you are trying to get someone's attention, use a larger, bold font.

- Use white type on a black background or reverses (opposite colors) for emphasis; also avoid similar colors or bleeding (colors that blend into each other).

- Use novel approaches (warped, curved, shadowed) in lettering to get the user's attention. Avoid novel text formats for informational text because it can be difficult to read.

Examples of how to use text in multimedia products

Hypertext

Hypertext systems use text that is indexed or "marked-up" to navigate through large volumes of information. Hypertext, as shown in Figure 4-5, is a navigational device that is very popular in multimedia and World Wide Web applications because it allows the interface to combine information and user control.

Hypertext systems can be used to navigate through large amounts of information. There are two general strategies for hypertext systems:

1. Indexed Retrieval

2. Linked or Hyperlink

These strategies are described in further detail in the following sections.

Indexed Retrieval Systems

Indexed retrieval systems consist of text that is keyed or indexed to other words. In most cases, these systems are automated so that a software program is used to build the indexes from the raw text resource. Help programs use this approach to create lists of terms to make finding help topics easier. In some cases, manual indexing may be used to identify special words or phrases or to eliminate trivial indexes; for example, the words "and," "or," and "the." As previously stated, indexed retrieval systems may be fully or partially indexed. In partially indexed systems:

- Text is usually highlighted indicating a link to another word or another part of the document containing related material.

- Sets of words (key words) are identified and automatically linked to other key words or terms.

In fully indexed systems, text is fully categorized; in other words, all words are indexed for fast retrieval. This is usually very processor intensive and may require significant storage space to track all links.

Search mechanisms may be applied to either type of indexing system:

- Search mechanisms can be used to search all words or indexed words.
- Searches can also be made using complex Boolean constructs (AND, OR, NOT, and BOTH). For example, a search construct could be: "auto AND car" or "engine OR transmission OR chassis."

Types of searches:

- Categorical—limiting documents, pages, fields.
- Word relationship—word proximity or order.
- Adjacency—finding words near other words; for example, look for the word "doctor" within five words of "medicine."
- Alternates—use "OR."
- Association—use "AND."
- Negation—use "NOT."
- Truncation—search words with pre- or suffixes.

Linked or Hyperlinked Systems

Linked or hyperlinked systems use specific linkages between text elements and **bookmarks** within a document or between documents. Bookmarks are predefined locations in a document that can be referenced by hyperlinks. These systems are usually produced manually—every link is defined and set by an author. Hyperlinks consist of two elements:

1. A text expression that is highlighted or set apart by underlining, bolding, or other means to differentiate its appearance from other text.

2. Link information that is correlated to the highlighted text and the destination.

The key to the use of linking systems is the operation of the application for displaying and manipulating the text. For example, World Wide Web browsers use information in the text file to determine which words are hyperlinks; when the user selects a link, the browser is able to jump to another part of the document or another document entirely. This is accomplished by setting a bookmark in the text in the form of an embedded tag. The "hypertext" link is also a tag that identifies a specific book or external document by its filename or location (for example, an Internet Web site). Hyperlink systems are also used in multimedia products to access other parts of the application or to present supporting information. Help file systems also use hyperlinks to link information that are often keyed to external applications for quick access to Help information. For example, when you select Help in a software application, the user is taken to the specific information in the Help file that will provide information for the user.

SUMMARY

Text is the basis for much of the information found in multimedia products. It is displayed in a variety of styles called fonts that, in turn, come in a variety of sizes. Fonts can also be bolded, underlined, and colorized to differentiate their appearance. Text is stored in files in a variety of formats of which ASCII is the most simple and useful for transport between applications and computers. Multimedia products use text to display titles, captions, and large pieces of information. They also use text, as hypertext, to link information together within and between documents.

REVIEW QUESTIONS

1. How many different font types are you familiar with? What fonts are available on your computer?

2. How do applications such as word processors manage fonts for displaying text?

3. Look at a multimedia product. What ways is text used to present information or manage operation of the program?

4. What are the difficulties in developing indexed and hypertext based systems?

5. What is involved in developing and using hypertext systems?

CHAPTER FIVE

Graphics

Graphics are the backbone of any multimedia product. In order to use them, developers must understand what they are and how to create them. Graphics, in the form of pictures, clip art, photographs, and line art, are used to provide backgrounds, informational content, and navigational controls for multimedia products. Graphics are created using a variety of tools including paint and drawing software, image scanners, and digital cameras. Graphics are stored in files in a variety of formats and sizes that support ranges of quality and use in various applications. This chapter explains the technical nature of computer graphics, how they are stored in data files, and how to use them in multimedia products.

Element of Graphics

Pictures as a form of communication can be traced back to the dawn of man. Computer-based graphics, like primitive cave drawings, are used to transmit messages or make statements of importance to both the sender and receiver. There are as many types of pictures as there are ideas on how to convey them:

- Pictures of people, places, and things including both artwork (drawn images) and photographs
- Diagrams of buildings (floor plans) and equipment (blueprints)
- Charts and graphs where figures are depicted through lines, curves, and color

In each of these examples, the picture may send a simple message such as what someone looks like, or complex information about economic reporting and forecasting.

Pictures and Images

Let us consider two levels of abstraction for graphics: pictures and images. Pictures are found in the world external to the computer, while images are the two-dimensional representations of pictures found in computers. Why create such an artificial separation? Pictures are often the product of the medium as well as the message. An oil painting of a person has a certain "look and feel" that results from the artist's interpretation of the subject and his or her use of the oil paint and canvas. Similarly, a photograph is subject to interpretation because of the skill of the photographer and type of camera and film. However, an image in a computer is a "realistic" version of the picture that is dependent on the quality and capabilities of the computer and the graphic artist's ability to use the software. The computer, in most cases, attempts to duplicate the "look and feel" of the picture using the abilities of the computer to store and process an image.

What about digitally created art or graphics created in the computer as the tool and medium? The product of an artist using a computer is still a picture. The picture, because it was created by an artist, and even though it was created in the computer, is really no different than an oil painting or a photograph. It is still an original creation that has meaning for both the artist and the viewer. The only advantage is that it is much easier to store and process in a computer because it already resides there.

Pictures are prepared on a variety of media ranging from paper and canvas to camera film. For use in the computer, the picture must be translated into a digital format or image that the computer can store, process, and transmit. There are two basic strategies applied when putting pictures in the computer:

1. Raster or bitmap images
2. Vector or metafile images

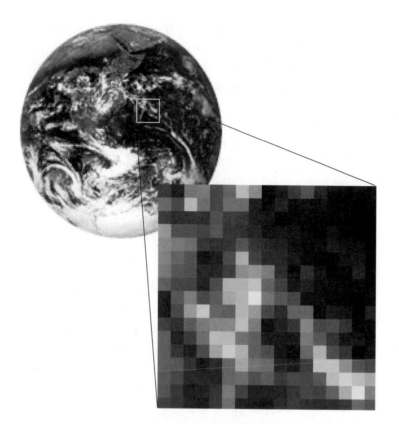

Figure 5-1 **Bitmap image example. Note that the cut-out section illustrates how a bitmap or raster image is made up of many points.**

Raster or Bitmap Images

The most common and comprehensive form of storage for images on a computer is as a **raster** or **bitmap** image. The terms raster and bitmap can be used interchangeably as they refer to images that are created as two-dimensional sets of points on a computer display. Depending on the hardware capabilities, each point can display from two to millions of colors. The use of the word "comprehensive" means that an image looks as much as possible like the real-world or the original product. This means that the proportion, size, color, and texture must be as accurate as possible.

Consider Figure 5-1, where a piece of the image has been enlarged over 15 times to show the individual points that make up only a small portion of the total image. In this image, a scale of 256 shades of gray, from black to white, is used to create an image of Earth and, in an enlarged cut-out

Look on the CD-ROM to find examples of raster images.

You will find samples of images in various color depths.

section of the image, the various shades of gray are shown that make up a cloud cover. In the enlarged cut-out section, the cloud cover is very difficult to distinguish; however, the cloud cover is an identifiable feature within the context of the larger image.

As mentioned earlier, a raster or bitmap image is composed of a matrix of elements called pixels. Each pixel consists of two or more colors. The color depth is determined by how much data, in bits, is used to determine the number of colors; for example:

- 1 bit yields 2 colors.
- 4 bits yields 16 colors.
- 8 bits (1 byte) yields 256 colors.
- 16 bits (2 bytes) yields 65,536 colors.
- 24 bits (3 bytes) yields 16,777,216 colors.

Figure 5-2 illustrates how image is created on a pixel by pixel basis. The number of pixels is related to the size of file that is required to store an image. To determine the size of a raster image, multiply the number of pixels in the horizontal plane (x) by the number of pixels in the vertical (y), then take this value and multiply it by the number of bytes per pixels (divide the number of bits used for color by 8, the number of bits in a byte). The equation is as follows:

$$X = \text{width of image in pixels}$$

$$Y = \text{height of image in pixels}$$

$$\text{image size (in bytes)} = x*y* (\text{bits per pixel}/ 8)$$

A standard computer VGA display is 640 by 480 pixels for a total of 307,200 pixels. A two-color or monochrome display image consists of 38,400 bytes, while a 256 color display image consists of 307,200 bytes. Finally, a full-screen VGA display image using 24 bit color would require 921,600 bytes. As you can see, the more colors used, the more bytes are required to encode the image, and the more bytes required for an image, the larger the file to store the image.

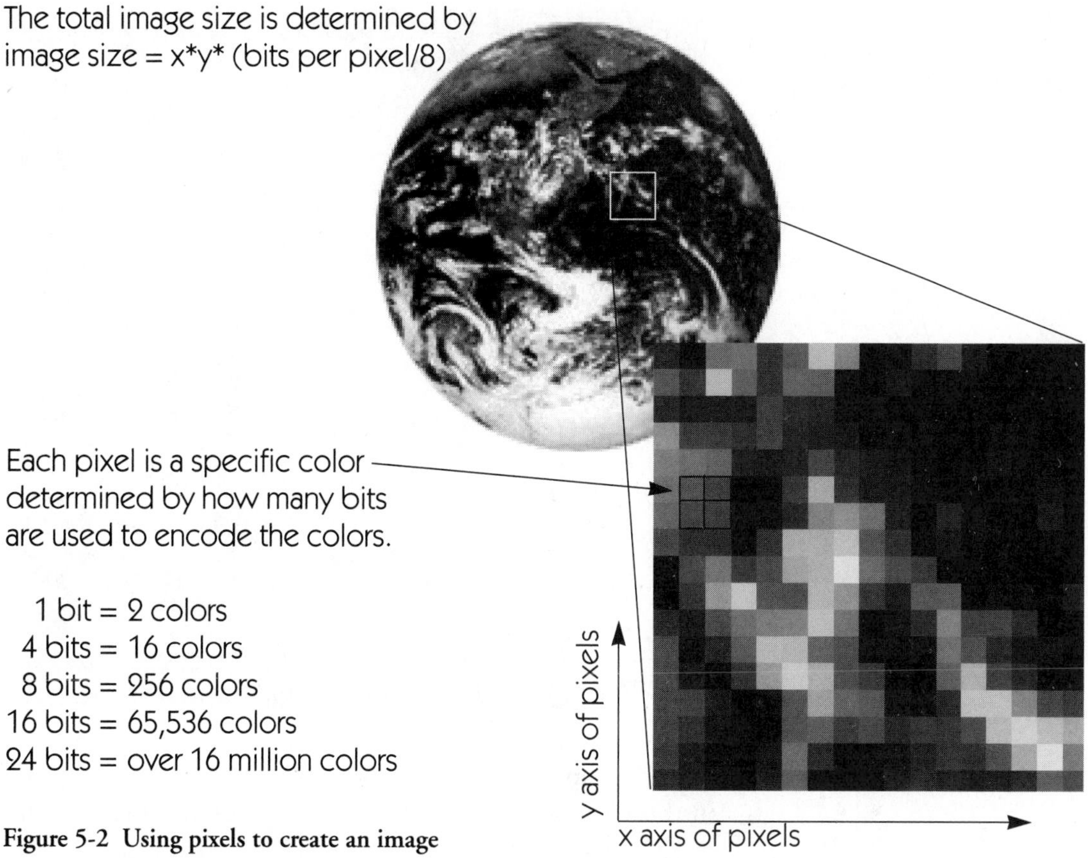

The total image size is determined by
image size = x*y* (bits per pixel/8)

Each pixel is a specific color
determined by how many bits
are used to encode the colors.

1 bit = 2 colors
4 bits = 16 colors
8 bits = 256 colors
16 bits = 65,536 colors
24 bits = over 16 million colors

Figure 5-2 Using pixels to create an image

y axis of pixels

x axis of pixels

Vector Images

Vector images are based on drawing elements or objects such
as lines, rectangles, circles, and so forth to create an image.
Vector images are actually stored as a series of commands
that define the individual objects. For example, the following commands are used to define various objects:

- Line: line x1, y1, x2, y2, color

- Rectangle: rectangle top, left, width, height, color

- Circle: circle top, left, radius, color

Figure 5-3 provides an example of an image created by
a vector image. Each element of the image is built by using
commands to draw lines, circles, rectangles, and so forth to
create the image.

Figure 5-3 Vector image. The image is constructed with a series of lines, rectangles, and circles.

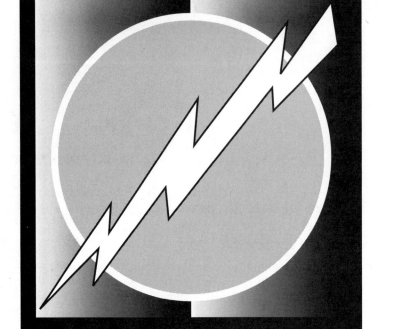

Check the CD-ROM for samples of vector images.

Bitmap images can be resized by stretching the image in the x and/or y axis, but the image is often distorted due to the replication of pixel elements. Vector images are created by larger objects (squares, circles, polygons) that can be proportionately resized without losing the integrity of the original image. By applying a scaling factor, as shown in Figure 5-4, an image can be easily resized.

The advantage of a vector image is the relatively small amount of data required to represent the image and therefore it does not require a lot of memory to store. The image consists of a set of commands that are drawn when needed. While a bitmap image requires the number of pixels to produce the appropriate height, width, and color depth, the vector image is based on a relatively limited number of drawing commands. The disadvantage of vector images is the limited level of detail that can be presented in an image. Simple vector images do not lend themselves to detailed images like photographs unless raster images are stored as component objects that are part of the vector image.

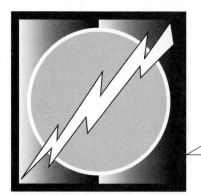

Figure 5-4 Scaling vector images. Scaling and sizing can be accomplished along both the x axis and the y axis.

Images and Color

Computer image color ranges from simple black and white to millions of colors. Line art illustrations are an effective use of a black and white image while a photographic image of a flower garden is ideally presented by systems that support the display of over 16 million colors. The use of color in multimedia depends on two factors:

1. The subject or content of the image
2. The technical capability of the computer hardware and software

The key to using color in the computer is to understand what color is. Color is based on the perception of light, which is part of the electromagnetic spectrum. Specific frequencies of the electromagnetic spectrum offer colors including red, orange, yellow, green, blue, indigo, and violet. Interestingly, computer-generated white and black are a function of the presence of all colors or none at all. White is created by combining all colors and black is created by the absence of color. Computer color is based on adjusting combinations of additive primary colors: **red, green, and blue (RGB)**. Printed colors, based on reflective light, use subtractive colors: cyan, magenta, yellow, and black.

The perception of color is the function of the eye. Receptors, called cones, in the cornea of the eye are sensitive to red, green, and blue frequencies of the electromagnetic spectrum. The eye is sensitive to millions of colors or hues based on combinations of the three colors: red, green, and blue. Combining these colors yields a basic set of working colors:

- Red + Green + Blue = White
- Green + Red = Yellow
- Blue + Red = Magenta
- Blue + Green = Cyan
- No color = Black

Computer Display Resolution

Computer display resolution is the number of pixels that make up the height and width of the display presented by the computer monitor. Early monochrome display-based computers relied on two-color displays that were measured in lines and characters, typically 25 lines by 80 characters. Early (Intel-based graphic) systems used pixel width/height measurements and color ranges from 2 to 16 colors while Apple-based graphic systems were capable of up to 16 million colors. Later Intel-based systems commonly used 640 by 480 pixels and 16 colors.

Multimedia-based computer systems since the early 1990s have established minimum capabilities when it comes to presenting graphics: 640 by 480 pixels and 256 colors. Depending on the capability of the graphics display hardware including both the monitor and the graphics adapter (the computer video board that processes the image), graphics capability includes:

- Image size of:
  - 640 by 480 pixels
  - 800 by 600 pixels
  - 1024 by 768 pixels
- Color depth of:
  - 256 colors
  - 32,768 colors
  - 65,536 colors
  - 16,777,216 colors

The ability to display large numbers of pixels and colors is dependent on the amount of video memory to handle storing the image display as well as refresh images. Refresh images are important because they enable computer display systems to create responsive and lifelike presentations by cycling the images.

Computer-Generated Color

Computer monitors display color by shining an electron beam off phosphorescent color dots (red, green, and blue) at very high speeds. The creation of visible color is a function of three characteristics: hue, saturation, and brightness (HSB) or lightness (HSL). Saturation, brightness, and lightness are defined by percentages—lightness of 100 percent is white while 50 percent is a pure color. Hue, saturation, and brightness are further defined as follows:

- Hue is based on a vector value moving from 0 to 360 degrees on a color wheel.

- Saturation is the intensity of the color in a percentage scale: 100 percent is a pure color, 0 percent is black, white, or gray.

- Brightness and lightness are a function of how much black or white is mixed with the color. A pure color has 50 percent lightness (or brightness) with 100 percent being white and 0 percent being black.

Color Palettes and Color Look-up Tables

Computers manage color via palettes or color look-up tables (CLUT), which are mathematical tables that define the color of any particular pixel displayed and the total number of colors that can be displayed on a system. Most multimedia systems are based on ranges from 256 to 16 million colors. Although most people can never distinguish 16 million separate colors, the richness of the palette ensures that any hue is possible for any type of image.

Color palettes are defined by indexing values correlated to red, blue, and green colors. The value range for multime-

Red Value	Green Value	Blue Value	Resulting Color
0	0	0	White
255	255	255	Black
255	0	0	Red
0	255	0	Green
0	0	255	Blue
255	255	0	Yellow
128	0	128	Purple

Table 5-1 Color Indexing Table

dia computers is 0 to 255, for 256 possible hues for each of red, blue, and green for a total of 16,777,216 color combinations. Using the indexed values, Table 5-1 shows some of the colors that can be created.

Computer images store colors in a palette with each image having a unique palette. The palette keeps track of the indexed color values used by the image. Computer graphic systems depend on the ability to display pixels within a specific number of colors (ranging from 2 to 16 million colors). The computer display has a "system palette" that manages the display of images for the computer. When an image is displayed, its palette is mapped into the system palette. The system palette is limited to the number of colors that the system is capable of displaying depending on its hardware and software configuration. Palettes are defined by the number of bits required to generate colors:

- 1 bit: two colors
- 4 bit: 16 colors
- 8 bit: 256 colors
- 15 and 16 bit: 32,768 and 65,536 colors
- 24 bit: 16,777,216 colors

Color Dithering

Scanned or digitized images are often captured at 24 bit, 16 million color depth. If the image is subsequently displayed on a computer monitor and system that is limited to less than 16 million colors, say 256 colors, the image must be transformed for display in the lesser color environment (palette). **Dithering** is the process through which colors are changed to meet the closest available color based on the available palette. The image palette is mapped into the new palette dimensions with colors substituted with the closest available values. The quality of the dithering will depend on the algorithm used but most systems provide close approximations of the original. An example of dithering is seen in some World Wide Web browser applications that use a limited palette of colors—typically 256 or less. Images with formats that include millions of colors are dithered to the limited color palette of the browser application.

Color Flashing

Color flashing occurs when images change the basic color palette. This happens most often with animation or consecutively displayed images with different palettes in each successive image. When the new image is loaded, the palette is mapped into the new set of colors and a momentary flashing can be observed that can be distracting to the viewer. Color flashing can be resolved by:

- Creating a shared palette; that is, using a common palette for all images.
- Fading images to black or white, which are common colors for most palettes.

Graphics File and Application Formats

There are a large number of graphic file formats available for storing various types of images. Graphic file data is often compressed to reduce storage space and to satisfy specific

Check the CD-ROM for examples of graphic files.

vendor requirements. The following sections provide overviews of various file formats. Common file extensions are given where appropriate.

Bitmap Formats

Bitmap file formats are one of the most common file formats for graphics across most computer platforms. Bitmap files offer a very accurate reproduction of an image based on its color depth and resolution. They are also the easiest files to import and export across platforms. Coded within the file, bitmap files contain specific information including file encoding, size, palette information, and pixel by pixel data values. Common bitmap formats include:

- Windows Bitmap (BMP) and Device Independent Bitmap (DIB) with color depth ranging from two to millions of colors.
- Windows Run Length Encoded (RLE) Bitmap: compression is used for 4- and 8-bit color depth images to reduce file size.
- Apple Pict.

Vector Formats

Vector files are common across many operating systems and a number of vendor specific applications. The Windows metafile is a common vector type image which is generated by processing vector commands by graphic functions in the Windows operating system. The commands are processed as a series of records that are loaded and executed in sequence. File formats include the type of file, sizing, number of objects, and the data. Metafiles can contain bitmaps as objects as well as other metafiles. Clip art files for various applications such as word processors are often stored as metafile images.

Compressed Formats

Bitmap and raster images in raw form can consume a considerable amount of file space. **Compression** can be used to dramatically reduce the file size, which can be useful for speeding transmission for networked applications or to store large numbers of images on CD-ROM or other media. Unfortunately, image quality can suffer and is typically correlated with the amount of compression needed. Compressed images often store images in files as follows:

- File header—stores various information about the type of compression, file size, color depth, and amount of data.

- Image data—image information that has undergone some type of algorithmic processing to reduce the amount of data while retaining some level of image quality. Many compression schemes can be controlled to increase quality and sacrifice file size or vice versa.

Although there are a number of common compressed file formats, the following are popular formats with widespread acceptance and use:

- **Graphics Interchange Format (GIF):** developed by Compuserve for moving images in dial-up situations; it has become a popular format for use in World Wide Web pages. GIF files use LZW compression, which is a Unisys-owned algorithm that requires royalties by program developers who use software that creates or reads GIF-formatted files. GIF files are limited to up to 256 colors. The file data includes information about the file format, layout of the data, image characteristics (height, width), color depth, color table (palette), and the image data. GIF files can also contain multiple images, which can be extracted and presented in sequence by special software to create simple animation presentations.

- **Tagged Image File Format (TIFF):** very high compression capability, good for black-and-white images. Used extensively in publishing and fax applications.

- **Joint Photographic Experts Group (JPEG and JPG):** packs a 24-bit color image into a relatively small file size. Microsoft has published the standard, which gained popularity for its use in World Wide

The CD-ROM includes a number of examples of graphic files in various formats.

Check the Web site to find out about emerging graphicfile formats and their uses.

Web applications. The JPEG file includes specific information about the image in the file header (including image size, bits per pixel, and number of colors used), the color palette, and compressed image data.

Proprietary Formats

Many commercial software paint and drawing packages use proprietary formats for storing graphic images. These same software packages often support other file formats for importing and exporting images.

Obtaining Images for Multimedia Use

Multimedia developers have a number of options for creating images. These options allow for ranges of quality, file size, and compatibility with multimedia authoring applications. Paint and drawing applications, image scanners, screen capture, and video digitization can be used to create images from many different sources including photographs, books, magazines, and live-image cameras. Each of these applications offers developers the ability to create images for backgrounds, buttons, and content.

Paint and Drawing Applications

Paint and drawing applications range from simple applications for beginning computer users to very powerful, complex tools for computer-based graphic artists. Capabilities of these applications range from simple two-dimensional drawing to three-dimensional images with texture and lighting effects. Paint and drawing applications include a number of features such as:

- Creating and editing graphic files; ability to import and export multiple graphic file formats.
- Free-form drawing, object drawing (lines, circles, rectangles, polygons), erasing, color-filling effects, and creating text.

- Object creation and manipulation (lines, geometric shapes, text).

- Image manipulation including image sizing, color level (brightness and contrast), color depth (converting between 2- to 24-bit color), perspective, and special filters (sharpening, softening, blurring).

- Rendering or converting a model, including lighting, shading, color, and perspective, into an image.

There is a range of paint and drawing applications available to multimedia developers. Generally, ease-of-use and cost are directly related to capability and function of these applications. Most tools can be generally assigned to one of the following categories:

- Simple/Beginner Tools: very inexpensive and often bundled free with other applications or as add-ins with operating systems; limited to simple drawing functions and limited color effects.

- Mid-range Tools: Low-cost tools capable of performing most graphic creation and editing functions; handle multiple-file formats. Basic operation is easy to learn with more complex features often left unused by beginners.

- Professional Development Tools: higher-cost tools intended for professional graphics development. Handle all basic functions with advanced features for editing images; include three-dimensional effects for shading, color adjustments, perspective, and compositing (combining two or more images).

- Conversion Tools: actually a subset of most mid-range and professional tools, conversion tools are utilities for graphic file format conversion with some tools having limited features for adjusting image color depth, color level, and image size.

- Screen Capture: tools that enable the user to capture images from application windows or the entire screen. This feature is sometimes built into other applications such as mid-range and professional development tools. Images

Check the CD-ROM to try out graphics tools.

The Web site can act as resource to identify vendors and tools for graphics production.

may be captured individually or as a series of images over a period of time similar to frames in a movie.

The selection of the appropriate paint and drawing tools often depends on the individual. Higher cost professional tools are the mainstay of professional graphic artists although they have many easy-to-use features for those individuals using them on an *ad hoc* basis. Simple beginner tools are of limited use in multimedia production environments except to build prototype images (backgrounds, place holder images). Mid-range tools can be very effective for developers as a means to manage scanned and digitized images or to convert images from clip art collections.

Scanners

Scanners are quite popular for capturing images from hard-copy sources such as books, magazines, letters, photographs, and even camera slides. Scanners operate in similar fashion to photocopiers in that images are electronically captured with an array of light sensors (the scanner). The sensors convert light into color and light intensity one line at a time until the complete document is viewed. Scanners depend on a bright light source to enhance the image for capture. Scanners come in three basic varieties:

- Hand-held: the scanner is physically moved across the image by hand. This is simple to use with limited fields of view and is subject to the steadiness of the hand and skill of the user. Hand-held scanners are relatively inexpensive.

- Drum: the image is mechanically moved across the sensor. It is easier to use than a hand-held scanner but scanning is limited to thin, flexible documents (paper). Drum scanners are very useful for scanning large numbers of documents.

- Flat-Bed: similar to a photocopier, the document is placed on a window and the scanner is mechanically moved across the image. Flat-bed scanners are best suited for larger documents as well as books and other odd-shaped source images. Generally speaking, flat-bed scanners are most popular among multimedia developers because of their quality and ease of use.

Scanners range in capability from black-and-white to full-color with resolution capability ranging from less than a hundred to over 1,000 dots per inch (DPI). Some flat-bed scanners scan in one pass while others scan in multiple passes, depending on the desired quality of the final product.

Scanners are controlled by software that interfaces the computer to the scanner device. The software manages the warm-up of the sensor array, controls the mechanical action (drum or flat-bed) of the scanner, and transfers the image from the scanner to the storage of the computer. Scanner software comes in two varieties:

1. Standalone application: the scanner software is a separate application from the scanner that operates the scanner and manages the image creation and saving-to-file process.

2. Embedded application: the scanner is operated via program commands from a secondary application such as paint and/or drawing software program. The image is transferred directly to the software for final manipulation.

Check the Web site to learn about scanner technologies.

Video and Image Digitizers

Video and image digitizers are related to scanners in that they both capture images from fixed objects such as books and photographs. However, digitizers also include digital cameras and video capture software. Video capture devices will be discussed later in Chapter 4. Digitizers use light-sensitive devices to sense color and intensity and convert it into an image. Unlike scanners, image digitizers can operate with limited light, which also limits the quality of the image.

Digital Cameras

Digital cameras have emerged as a popular means to capture images and move them directly into the computer. Digital

Check the Web site for information on video digitizers and cameras.

cameras include both still and motion types. In either case, the images are stored digitally on media within the camera. The user can then transfer the data to the computer via an interface device such as a serial or parallel interface port.

Using Graphics in Multimedia Applications

Multimedia applications use still images, pictures, photographs, and line art for a number of reasons ranging from aesthetics to information delivery. Most images are created or obtained from:

- Scratch: the image is drawn by a skilled technician such as a graphic artist.

- Scanning or digitizing: the image is captured from another medium. Depending on what the original medium is, the image may be subject to royalty fees.

- **Clip art:** the image is part of a larger collection; clip art often consists of groupings or collections of images by subject that can be incorporated into a project free or at cost, depending on royalty arrangements with the original owners. Multimedia developers often rely on libraries of images found on CD-ROM media that can store hundreds and even thousands of images for a variety of uses.

Selecting Graphics for Multimedia

There is a basic strategy to follow when selecting graphics for multimedia products based on purpose, quality, and cost. These factors are interrelated in that the purpose of a graphic, determined by the application itself, will require a specific quality. The quality will drive the image cost in terms of the quality of the original image and how it is adapted for a particular application. For example, a multimedia product on art history depends on higher quality graphics in keeping with the expectations of those end users of the application that appreciate fine art.

Consider the following basic ideas when using graphics in multimedia products.

Purpose

Images used in a multimedia product should be useful and meaningful to the application. Avoid using images for "filler" or when they have little in common with the overall message or purpose. A common mistake is to trivialize products with cartoons that can be distracting to the viewer. Another mistake is using too many images for a single display. If multiple images are used, make sure they reflect a common message such as providing the user with an example or an illustration.

Quality

Any image used in a multimedia product should reflect the overall quality desired of the entire product. Be careful of image color depth, especially for applications that will be displayed on systems using a lower color capability. Be aware of image size and avoid using loud or very vibrant colors because they can be distracting. Mixing images, especially color bitmaps, can exceed palette limits for various systems. Images should be produced for the lowest common platform that they will be displayed on. For example, 24-bit color images require higher graphics processing capabilities and their image quality can suffer on systems limited to 256 colors. If the majority of end users have systems limited to 256 colors, the graphics should also be kept to that color during their production.

Cost

The cost of a graphic is directly related to its purpose and quality. Copyright and ownership of graphics will determine who is to be paid. In some cases it may be required to give credit to the source of the image in addition to, or in lieu of payment for using the image. Costing is often negotiated at a flat rate or is based on how many units of the product are sold.

See the CD-ROM to find examples of graphic images including backgrounds for multimedia products.

Check the Web for resources of graphics images on the Internet.

Backgrounds and Transitions

Backgrounds and transition screens provide the color foundation for everything else that is found in a multimedia product. Backgrounds have fairly simple characteristics:

- They fill up the available display space.
- They complement, but do not overwhelm, content placed on top of them.
- Colors are chosen carefully so as to avoid color or palette flashing or conflict with other media.
- They are used consistently throughout the application. The entire application may use a single background or segments within an application may use a common background.

Transitions are used between "pages" or events in a multimedia product to maintain continuity. Like backgrounds, they should fill up available space and complement content. Colors should also be used carefully to avoid palette flashing. Transitions often come in solid colors, such as black, white, or a "neutral" color, that blend the preceding and succeeding images.

Information Delivery

Images are used to convey information in multimedia products. For example, a picture of an automobile engine is much more effective than text that merely describes it. Graphics for information delivery include:

- Drawn images
- Charts and graphs
- Maps
- Scenery
- People

In each case, the image must be relevant to the overall product. Image size, color in respect to the application and other images, and positioning must all be considered when using images.

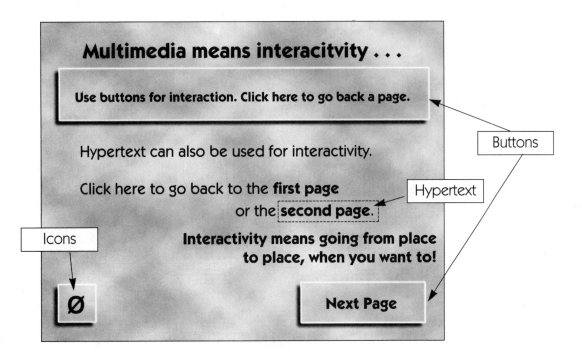

Figure 5-5 Types of objects used as navigational controls

Navigation

If a multimedia product is to be interactive, the user must be able to locate and activate "objects" to move from screen to screen. These objects, as shown in Figure 5-5, can take the form of buttons, "hot spots," icons, or other graphical elements that cue the user in to identifying and selecting them. Beyond buttons and icons, images for navigation may occur as part of informational images or as backgrounds. For example, by clicking on part of an image, you may be taken to another screen and presented with additional information.

The function of navigational images should be clear and concise. The use of arrows and other graphical symbols in lieu of text should be considered carefully so that their meaning is clearly understood.

SUMMARY

Pictures are stored and used in computers in two basic formats: bitmap or raster and vector. Bitmap or raster images are created by a two-dimensional array of pixels, with each pixel ranging from two to millions of colors. Vector images are created by a series of commands that draw images onto the computer display. Bitmap and vector images are stored in a variety of file formats with compression schemes used to reduce the file size. Multimedia products use graphics to deliver information, stage the appearance of an application (backgrounds), and control the flow of the application. Understanding graphics provides multimedia developers with the key to developing interesting and useful multimedia products.

REVIEW QUESTIONS

1. In what situations would two color images be used effectively in lieu of higher color depth (256 or 16 million color image) or vice versa?

2. What experiences have you had with graphic production tools? How would you compare the various tools that you have used?

3. Given the various types of graphic production software, what criteria would you use in selecting the appropriate paint and drawing application for the casual image producer or a graphic artist?

4. What are the drawbacks of the various types of scanner mechanical systems?

5. Identify examples of effective use of graphics in multimedia products that you have used.

6. Based on your experience, what are good and poor examples of background and transitional graphics?

7. Describe at least six different types of navigational images.

CHAPTER SIX

Digital Audio

OBJECTIVES

After completing this chapter, you should know:

- What sound and digital audio is.
- How sound is digitized.
- How digital audio is processed and stored.
- How digital audio is used in multimedia products.

Sound gives multimedia products a dimension that transcends other computer applications. At a basic level, sound acts as a notice or a warning that something is happening, a feature that has been commonly found in computer applications since the first desktop systems. Multimedia products have since extended the classic computer "beep" to door knocking and realistic train whistles. Beyond the trivial, though, is multimedia that contains soothing background music or a voice-over explaining the operation of a program. From a content perspective, sound is offering music and voice to explain Beethoven or inspire the user with John F. Kennedy's inaugural speech from history.

Applying sound to multimedia products means understanding a little bit about the nature of sound itself and how it is converted into bits and bytes. How do the bits and bytes represent voice and music in both stereo (two channels) and monaural (mono or one channel)? Once sound is captured, how can it be changed? Finally, how is it effectively used in developing multimedia products? This chapter will address and answer all these questions.

Characteristics of Sound and Digital Audio

Sound comprises the spoken word, voices, music, and even noise. It is loud and quiet, it is deep and shrill, and it can even be felt (have you ever stood in front of a large speaker

Figure 6-1
Graphical display of a sound wave

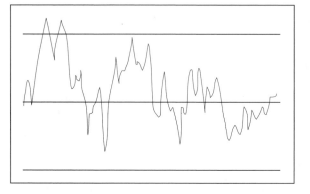

and felt the vibrations?). Sound is based on two things: energy and a transport medium. Energy from a banging drum is converted into pressure that is transmitted by the air. Sound is actually created when air pressure is varied. The change in air pressure is detected by the ear drum and a vibration occurs that is sensed by nerves that carry electrical signals to the brain. The vibration of the ear drum can be represented by a wave over a period of time as shown in Figure 6-1.

There are two characteristics of sound waves as shown in Figure 6-2: amplitude and frequency. **Amplitude** is the power or intensity of the sound. The louder the sound, the larger the amplitude. **Frequency** is the rate at which sound is measured. It is measured in cycles per second or Hertz (Hz). The higher the frequency, the clearer and sharper the sound. Human hearing is capable of detecting sound vibrations ranging from 50 Hz to 20,000 Hz. A 50 Hz sound is very low and deep like a distant background hum while a sound at 20,000 Hz is very high pitched like a drill or the highest notes of a soprano singer. It is a well known fact that dogs and bats, as well as other animals, are capable of hearing at much higher frequencies. Even with humans, the ear is an organ that is subject to age and injury, so it is common that hearing range often falls well above 50 Hz and well below 20,000 Hz.

To effectively record sound, you need to record at twice the frequency that sound is heard. Therefore, if human hearing ranges up to 20,000 Hz, the sound must be recorded up

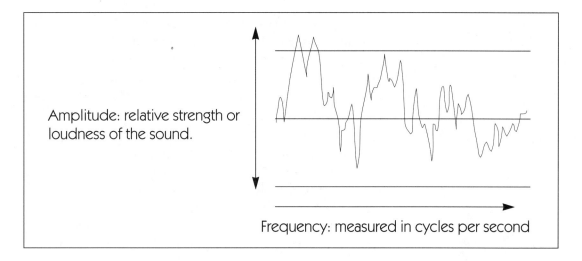

Amplitude: relative strength or loudness of the sound.

Frequency: measured in cycles per second

Figure 6-2 Measuring sound amplitude and frequency

to 40,000 Hz. This means that the amplitude of the sound must be sampled at these rates for effective capture and eventual playback. Obviously, the higher the sampling rate, the better quality of sound will be recorded. At lesser rates, subtle changes in pitch and tone will be lost. This loss of quality can be significant for some sounds and not as critical for others. For example, human voice is effectively sampled at ranges of between 5,000 and 15,000 Hz, whereas music requires much higher sampling rates up to 40,000 Hz.

Voice and Music

Let us consider three classes of sounds: voice, music, and sound effects. Voice is defined as talking, not singing, while music can be created from human singing or musical instruments. Human voice, while distinctive, does not have great fluctuations in pitch and tone. Music, on the other hand, can have rapid changes in tone and pitch within very brief periods of time. Music is usually recorded and played in stereo, or multiple playback tracks, to capture the richness and fullness of many singing voices or the instruments of an orchestra. Sound effects can be voice or music, but are more often created by natural events such as a door slamming shut or a thunderclap. Sound effects vary in tone, pitch, and time.

Why are three classes of sound important? The capture of sound into a digital format requires that a measurement of sound (the amplitude) be made at specific intervals of time (the frequency). Higher capture frequency means more data sampling, which requires more data storage space and greater resources to play back the recorded sound. Three classes of sound means we can consider different frequency ranges for capture in order to manage data sizes.

Voice can be captured at a much lower frequency rate than that required for music, which is usually captured in stereo. The lower frequency rate requires less data. In addition, because the sound is monaural, or a single channel of sound, the amount of data is halved from stereo. Music, being much richer in quality than voice, requires higher capture frequencies to ensure that all aspects of the sound are thoroughly recorded. Sound effects fall in the middle; sometimes it is possible to capture them with relatively low frequencies and with a single channel while other times it is necessary to use higher frequencies and stereo.

Digitizing Sound

Digitizing sound means capturing the sound amplitude at a specified frequency. Figure 6-3 illustrates the three characteristics for recording sound:

1. Frequency rate
2. Amplitude measurement
3. Sound channels (monaural and stereo)

For multimedia computers, standard frequency rates include:

- 11.025 kilohertz (KHz)
- 22.5 KHz
- 44.1 KHz

Other frequency sampling rates are also used, especially lower rates (5 and 8 KHz), for networked applications. Lower frequency rates, while they sacrifice some quality, will also significantly reduce the amount of data. Amplitude measurement is based on 8 bits (one byte) for 256 levels and 16 bits for 65,536 levels.

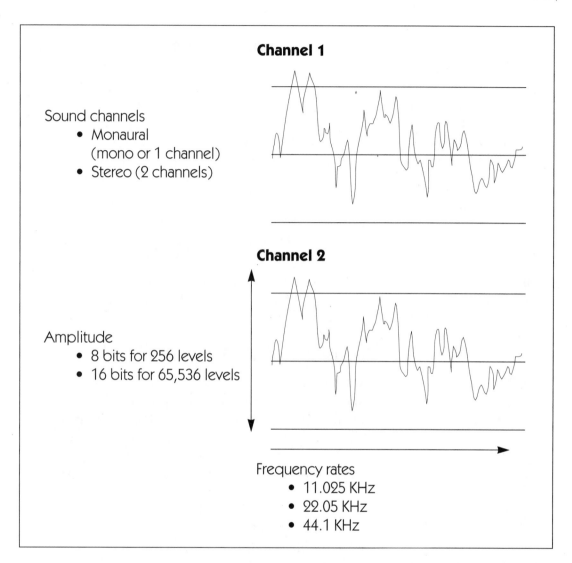

Sound channels
- Monaural (mono or 1 channel)
- Stereo (2 channels)

Amplitude
- 8 bits for 256 levels
- 16 bits for 65,536 levels

Channel 1

Channel 2

Frequency rates
- 11.025 KHz
- 22.05 KHz
- 44.1 KHz

Figure 6-3 Sound capture characteristics and standard frequency rates

The number of bits used for the amplitude measurement is based on how precise the level of sound is to be measured. Eight bits allows for 256 levels, which is adequate for many types of sound. However, 16 bits allows for 65,536 levels of sound, which provides a much finer level of precision. The advantage of capturing sound with greater precision enables very fine differences in sound to be recorded. For example, greater precision will enable differentiation between violins in an orchestral recording.

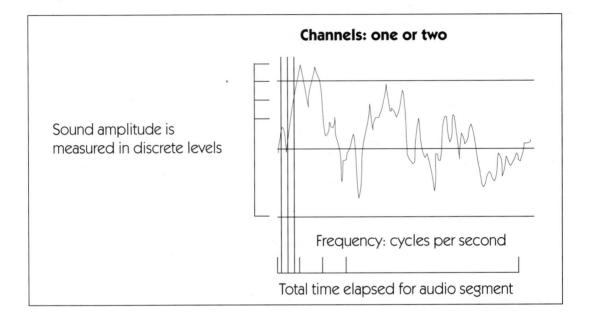

Channels: one or two

Sound amplitude is measured in discrete levels

Frequency: cycles per second

Total time elapsed for audio segment

Figure 6-4 Detailed perspective of sound digitization

Calculating Audio Data Size

Using the three characteristics just described for calculating audio file sizes, amplitude, sound channels, and frequency rates, let us represent them using the following variables:

c = number of channels (mono - 1 channel, stereo - 2 channels)

s = sampling rate in Hertz (cycles per second)

t = time (seconds)

b = bytes (1 for 8 bits, 2 for 16 bits)

File size = $c * s * t * b$

Figure 6-4 offers a detailed perspective on how these parameters are used.

For example, calculate the file size for 1 minute, 44.1 KHz, 16 bit, stereo sound:

c = 2 (two channels - stereo)

s = 44,100 (Hz - frequency)

t = 60 (time)

b = 2 (bytes, 16 bit capture)

File size = $2 * 44100 * 60 * 2 = 10,584,000$ bytes

Another example: calculate the file size for 30 seconds, 16 bit, 11.025 KHz, mono

Frequency Sampling	Data Size	Stereo or Mono	Size for 1 minute	Comments
44.1 KHz	16 bit	Stereo	10.5 MB	CD-quality recording (standard). This is the Red Book Audio standard (ISO 10149).
44.1 KHz	16 bit	Mono	5.25 MB	Voice or monoaural, high quality.
44.1 KHz	8 bit	Stereo	5.25 MB	Best quality for playback on low-end personal computers.
44.1 KHz	8 bit	Mono	2.6 MB	Good trade-off for voice quality.
22.05 KHz	16 bit	Stereo	5.25 MB	Decent quality, darker sounding because of lower frequency.
22.05 KHz	16 bit	Mono	2.5 MB	Good for voice, but the disk space requirement is high.
22.05 KHz	8 bit	Stereo	2.6 MB	Acceptable for good quality playback in low-end personal computer systems.
22.05 KHz	8 bit	Mono	1.3 MB	Thinner sound, lacks quality, television quality.
11 KHz	8 bit	Stereo	1.3 MB	Lowest quality for music audio, dark sounding.
11 KHz	8 bit	Mono	650K	Lowest reasonable quality for voice.

c = 1
s = 11,025
t = 30
b = 1

Table 6-1 Digital Sound Characteristics for Various Sampling Rates, Data Sizes, Channels, and File Sizes.

File size = 1 * 11,025 * 30 * 1 = 330,750 bytes
Typical file sizes for various frequencies are detailed in Table 6-1.

The table also provides commentary that is useful for developers who are capturing audio. Note that:

• Higher frequency, stereo, and 16 bits are used for best quality of capture.

• Lower frequency, mono, and 8 bits are acceptable for voice quality (talking voice, not singing).

• Using mid-range frequencies (22.05 KHz) with 8 and 16 bits, offer options for file sizes and quality.

The CD-ROM includes a number of samples of digital audio.

Although 44.1 KHz, 16 bit stereo, stereo recording offer the best quality, the file size can be of concern. A compact disk with a 650 megabyte capacity can store only a little over 60 minutes of digital audio. Combined with other content such as text and graphics, a significant amount of high quality digital audio would limit the storage space for other content. In many multimedia products, this is managed by varying the audio capture characteristics based on the quality needed to support the content and the amount of data to be stored.

Digital Audio Systems

Digital audio systems for multimedia computers are based on special circuitry that interfaces the computer to external audio components such as microphones, audio players and recorders, and speakers. The circuitry for digital audio systems are often found in special purpose add-on hardware (circuit cards) or as integrated parts of the computer system. As shown in Figure 6-5, the digital audio circuitry is responsible for:

- Converting the audio signal from a microphone or other audio source into a digital signal via a special component called an analog to digital converter.
- Transferring the digital data to the computer's storage media.
- Converting a digital data from storage into an analog audio signal via a digital to analog converter and, if necessary, amplify it for playback using speakers.

Digital Audio Software Support

The digital audio circuitry is managed by software that provides a number of user and software support functions:

- Playback: translate the audio data into sound.
- Record: capture audio data from an external analog source.
- Stop: halt playback.
- Fast Forward: move to a later point in the data stream.
- Reverse: move to a prior point in the data stream.
- Rewind: move to the beginning of the data stream.

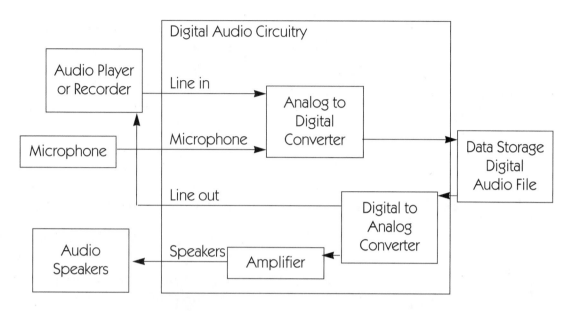

Figure 6-5 Digital audio hardware configuration showing input, output, and storage

Note that many of these functions are similar to controls found on standard commercial audio tape players.

Audio software for multimedia computers has evolved considerably since the 1980s. Digital audio systems originally operated by the program software interfacing directly with the audio system hardware. This meant that each program was responsible for all aspects of recording and playing sound. More advanced systems, based on Windows and Macintosh graphical operating systems, take a more efficient approach:

- Software modules, often called drivers, are loaded by the operating system to manage and control the digital audio circuitry.

- Software commands from various multimedia products send standardized commands to the operating system, which are processed to play, capture, and manipulate digital audio.

The advantage of this approach is the standardization of functions that are carried out by digital audio hardware when executed by different applications through the operating system. From a developer's standpoint, they can depend on a standardized software program interface that will work with digital audio hardware developed by many different vendors.

Tools for capturing and editing digital audio

Vendors for digital audio software

One of the advantages of digital audio system is **random access,** based on the ability of computer storage devices to jump to any point in the storage medium and access data. Unlike analog devices, such as tape players in which the tape must be physically advanced or rewound, digital audio systems can very quickly jump to any point in the data stream.

Editing Digital Audio

Digital audio editing consists of capturing and modifying an audio data file. Most audio editing software include a number of editing techniques such as:

- Trimming—removing dead spots from the beginning and end of a digital recording.
- Splicing and assembly—linking separate audio segments together, usually from different files.
- Volume adjustments—increasing the loudness or softening the sound level; also used to soften or eliminate distortions.
- Format conversion—changing the file format to move audio between computer systems or changing data formatting (file header and other information).
- Resampling or downsampling—changing by reducing the frequency or number of bits used for recording. For example, you would downsize a 44 KHz, 16 bit, stereo audio file to 22 KHz, 8 bit, mono to significantly reduce the file size, with a corresponding reduction in quality.
- Fade-ins and fade-outs—increasing and decreasing the volume within a segment of the audio data.
- Equalization—used to clean up noise by reducing spikes or levels within the audio data stream.
- Time-stretching—slowing down or speeding up the sound by removing or adding filler data to the signal.
- Digital signal processing—digitally adding sound effects such as reverberation, echo, inserting silence or sound level, and other effects.
- Reversing sounds—reversing the data stream to play the sound backwards.

At a minimum, simple audio capture/editing software allows:

- Recording of digital audio segments
- Trimming of digital clips
- Splicing of clips, usually by adding a segment to the beginning or the end of the original segment
- Volume adjustment of the entire segment
- Reversing the entire segment
- Copy, cut, paste, and delete segments of digital audio

Most audio editing systems also contain a graphical viewer for monitoring the audio waveform signal. The viewer can be used in editing the signal by letting you highlight sections of the audio signal and then cutting, pasting, copying, or deleting the segments. The viewer can also be used to identify specific sounds within the recording by matching the waveform to the actual sound produced.

Sound Controls

Multimedia computers usually have software that acts as a control for the computer's sound playback and recording. This software includes:

- Selection of components (microphone, speakers, line-in, line-out)
- Volume level, both monaural and stereo
- Recording input level
- Bass and treble controls

These controls are usually accessible for a user from the operating system of the computer as well as from within multimedia products themselves.

MIDI

The **Musical Instrument Digital Interface (MIDI),** is an encoding scheme for recording and playing musical instruments on a computer. MIDI was originally developed as a standard for interchanging information between music synthesizers. It has now become a recognized way of inter-

Check the CD-ROM for sample MIDI files.

changing information about complex sets of musical requirements between computer systems. MIDI synthesizers are provided on most computer sound cards. In addition, MIDI interfaces are available for connecting music synthesizers to a wide range of computer systems. This allows musicians to take advantage of computer processing to develop and enhance musical production.

MIDI, because of its broad acceptance by the music industry and the computer world, follows a specification that helps to ensure compatibility of components and systems. The MIDI specification organizes sounds into sixteen families of eight variations each. This organizing or grouping of sounds makes it easy to reorchestrate a piece using similar sounds. An Instrument Patch Map, part of the MIDI specification, lists 128 sounds, with corresponding MIDI program numbers. Most of these are imitative sounds, though the list includes synthetic sounds, ethnic instruments, and a handful of sound effects.

Microsoft Windows MIDI provides for a base level capability that plays three instrument parts with at least 6 notes at a time and a percussion track with 3 notes at a time. Extended level MIDI allows nine instruments with 16 notes, percussion track with 16 notes, which is found on very high quality audio cards. Each sound in the MIDI table can also be played for various durations.

Audio File Formats

Digital audio, depending on the platform, uses a variety of file formats to encode data files. There are two general categories of digital audio files: sound audio files and MIDI.

Audio Files

Sound that is captured into a digital format can offer a very high level of capture quality to reproduce the broadest range of sounds from human voice to music. Audio files can be compressed to reduce storage space and can also be exchanged between computer systems. Audio files come in a variety of formats depending on the operating systems they support. The following is a list of platforms and file formats that have gained acceptance since the late 1980s.

Apple

The Audio Interchange File Format (AIFF) is actually used across a number of platforms and environments. AIFF files contain a header with information about the audio sampling frequency, data size, number of channels, file size, and other information followed by the formatted audio data.

Microsoft

Waveform or wave files are commonly used in the Intel-based computer world. Wave files typically use a .wav extension and are based on the Microsoft Resource Interchange File Format (RIFF). RIFF files are comprised of chunks of information including file type, audio sampling frequency, data size, and number of channels, and the audio data.

CD-Audio

Red Book Audio standard: used for CD audio; format is called Linear Pulse Code Modulation. It typically provides 50 to 60 minutes of high fidelity stereo music captured to 16 bit, 44.1 KHz data.

MIDI Files

MIDI files offer the advantage of being quite small compared to captured audio files. They can be used to deliver relatively high quality synthesized music for a variety of applications. MIDI files are composed of chunks for a header and one or more tracks. The header chunk provides identification of the data, arrangement of the data tracks, and timing. The track chunks provide the timing and type of event or instrument to be played.

Using Audio in Multimedia Applications

Multimedia applications use audio primarily to enhance the appearance and function of a multimedia product or to enhance another form of data. It may also be used as a primary information delivery vehicle; that is, the digital audio can be

Descriptions of various audio file formats.

the primary content delivered by the application. For example, an application could include digital audio clips of words, expressions, and even complete paragraphs in various languages for a foreign language tutorial.

Audio Quality

The quality of digital audio depends on a number of factors:

- The quality of the original audio source.
- The quality of the capture device and supporting hardware.
- The characteristics used for capture (frequency, data rate, and number of channels).
- The capability of the playback environment.

As in any audio recording, the quality of the original sound is paramount. If the original sound is a scratchy phonograph recording, then the captured audio quality will suffer. Although digital editing techniques can be used to "clean up" a recording, the editing process will inevitably degrade the original information. Live recording of sound can also be difficult because of background noise and electronic static, which are difficult to remove in real time while recording.

The recording and playback systems also suffer from similar problems in order to achieve optimal digital audio quality. Sound capture and playback hardware range in capability and functionality on a scale most often based on cost. The more expensive devices offer more functionality and higher quality for playback and recording. Fortunately, as multimedia computer systems have become more commonplace, the quality found in lower priced systems has been very good and quite acceptable for most applications.

Frequency rate, data size (number of bits for capture), and number of channels (mono or stereo) are the key issues to consider when capturing digital audio. Although higher frequencies, 16 bit data sizes, and stereo offer the best quality, the prime benefit is often significantly increased storage space. Increased data size means more traffic for the computer data bus, which moves data between the processor, memory, and the rest of the computer, impacting other applications such as simultaneous loading of a graphic in a multimedia product. In many cases, the operating system will try to accommodate a number of data access requests and the lag time in data access can degrade the quality of the playback. Unfortunately, if the audio data file size is reduced by using a lower capture frequency or smaller data size (8 bits), the actual quality of the audio can be severely degraded.

Achieving audio quality for multimedia products is a process of trading quality for the storage space and performance of the capture and playback systems. Multimedia product developers often use smaller audio file sizes in order to save disk space for other data elements such as text, graphics, and video. Developers must also take into account what kind of system the end user has. Developers do not want to tax the capability of the hardware by using audio files that are too big.

There are a number of things developers can do to manage the quality of digital audio capture. Generally, the best option is to use the highest quality analog audio systems (tape decks, amplifiers, and mixers) and facilities including professional audio recording rooms. However, for smaller projects, there are some simple things a developer can do that will dramatically improve the quality of digital audio:

- Use scripts for live recordings. Voice ad libbing can be problematic; know what you want to say before you record it.
- Pay attention to the quality of sound needed for the application based on storage requirements and playback environment. If smaller file sizes are required, use the best quality source available.
- Use the best recording available for audio capture; take higher source quality over better equipment. When the source is of lesser quality, use external audio processing filters to minimize noise and flaws prior to digitizing.
- Microphones (for voice) can be tricky. Find a quiet room to help in reducing background noise. Take some time prior to recording to set the best levels for loudness and tonal quality.

The bottom line on quality is to balance the hardware and software with the application needs. How will the audio be used? What are the expectations of the end user? These questions are often critical in determining the best decisions on where and how to use digital audio.

Audio for Managing Software Function

Digital audio is often used as a background device to help an end user in navigating through an application. Audio may be used to indicate that a program selection has been made by providing a clicking sound when a button is pressed, or opening or closing a door when the screen changes to another view. Audio may be used to tell the user that input is required. For example, a program might announce: "Please select from the list on the screen," or go as far as to announce what each selection is as a mouse cursor passes over the choices.

Developers must remember that audio sounds can be both useful and annoying in applications. A constantly repeated instruction, however simple it may be, may be useful to one user and a distraction to another. A choice is often provided for the user to "turn off" audio or to mute it to a more desirable level. In some cases, different sounds can be attached to program functions depending on the whim of the end user. For example, some programs allow the user to add specific digital sounds to events such as opening and saving files.

Using Audio to Enhance Other Content

Multimedia products should be more than separate elements of text, pictures, audio, and video. Digital audio is an integral part of digital video and will be discussed more thoroughly in Chapter 7. However, for our purposes digital audio can also be used to significantly enhance text and graphics.

Audio can be used to repeat content and to enhance or augment it. Repeating content is most often used with text to provide a verbatim narrative of displayed text. For example, a written copy of the Gettysburg Address could be stored as a digital audio file for playback to help a student to understand it better by hearing it delivered. It could also be used to add background to a picture of Abraham Lincoln for a biographical presentation. Audio can also be used to narrate specific elements of a graphic. For example, a diagram could be described in significant detail through an audio presentation just as if a person were describing it in a live presentation.

Audio for Content Delivery

The most obvious use of digital audio is for delivery of sound-based multimedia content. Speeches and music make up a significant part of our daily experience. The number of multimedia products has dramatically increased as end users have acquired audio-capable hardware and software. The key issues to remember when using large amounts of audio for content delivery are the quality of the digital audio and the amount of storage space available for the application.

The quality of the digital audio depends on the nature of the sound and how it will be used. Voice quality audio normally requires much less storage space than music unless it is used for other purposes; for example, reproducing a specific voice such as a famous figure in history. In cases where specific vocal tones or inflections must be preserved, then higher frequency and data sizes are used to ensure better quality capture with a corresponding gain in data size. Digital audio for music reproduction can also consume large amounts of disk space unless lower quality can be used. Given a 650 megabyte capacity for a CD-ROM, the following provides a general idea of how much digital audio can be stored:

- Voice quality (11 KHz, 8 bit, mono, at approximately 600 kilobytes per minute) - 1083 minutes total.
- High quality music (44 KHz, 16 bit, stereo, at approximately 10 megabytes per minute) - 61 minutes total.
- In-between, very good voice or acceptable music (22 KHz, 16 bit, stereo) - 122 minutes.

The trade-off of quality versus storage capacity can also be influenced by the quality of the playback system. If the playback system is very good then a higher frequency or data rate may be desirable to ensure optimal quality.

The amount of digital audio to use may be a determining factor in designing the application, especially when there is a need for other content such as graphics. For example, a product that depends on high-quality graphics combined with musical content may be relatively limited for the amount of music it can use per graphic. The alternative is to be very selective when choosing audio content in terms of how much time is used, the quality of the digital audio in terms of frequency, data size, and channels, or the number of elements to be presented.

SUMMARY

Digital audio provides a voice for multimedia products. Recorded from voice, music, and other sources, digital audio is based on capturing sound at very high frequencies ranging from 5 KHz to 44.1 KHz, in single and stereo channels, and amplitude measurements at data rates of 8 and 16 bits. Digital audio can be edited in a number of ways to clean up defects or to add special effects such as echoing. Multimedia products benefit from digital audio as informational content such as a speech or voice-over and as special effects to indicate that a program is executing various actions such as jumping to new screens. Digital audio plays a key role in digital video, which will be discussed in the next Chapter.

REVIEW QUESTIONS

1. What are the various advantages and disadvantages of the various frequency, data size, and number of channels for digital audio recording and playback?

2. Compare the functions of simple and complex digital audio software editors. How are they similar and how are they different?

3. What are the advantages of external audio equipment such as filters and mixers in producing digital audio?

4. How would you use digital audio to enhance a graphic or text-based presentation?

5. How would you manage the quality and type (frequency, data size, and channels) of digital audio for a multimedia product on "famous classical music composers?"

CHAPTER SEVEN

Digital Video and Animation

Digital video combines features of graphics and audio to create dynamic content for multimedia products. Content for digital video may originate from video cameras or film that has been captured and digitized for the computer. It may also be created by putting graphic images together to create animation. This chapter depends on concepts that were covered in the previous two chapters on Graphics and Digital Audio. It carries these concepts forward by discussing how digital video is created, edited, and applied in multimedia products.

Background on Video

Video is simply moving pictures. At a minimum, the moving pictures offer momentary glimpses of time frozen from one frame to the next. If the interval between each image is short enough, then the playback of these images creates an illusion of motion that we call video. The most common forms of video are movies and television. Movies use film to present a series of images. Similarly, television uses a series of electronically transferred images. Digital video and computer animation are the computer-based counterparts to television and movies. In fact, digital video is often used to capture content from movies and television to be used in multimedia products.

Sources of Digital Video

Digital video can consist of much more than movie clips taken from existing film resources, it can also include:

- Recordings of live action, usually captured with a video camera

- A series of graphic images played in rapid succession similar to a cartoon

- Still images taken from film, videotape, or live action

As you can see, digital video takes on many more forms than a digital movie. Digital video:

- Is captured from television, VCR, and camera sources.

- Relies on devices called **controllers** which are used to control VCR, video disk, camera, and other video devices. Controllers, in the context of digital video, are electronic devices that enable computers to control the operation of video equipment.

- Is based on specialized **video capture** hardware that accepts video input and turns it into a digital format. Video capture is the process of transforming a video input signal (from a VCR or camera) into a series of graphic images that can be stored on a computer.

- Uses graphic **overlay** techniques in which digital video images are placed on top of other graphic data on the computer screen. Overlays are created when the computer turns over specific sections of video memory to video capture devices so that the video presentation is smooth.

In order to understand digital video, one needs to understand what **analog video** is. Analog video is video information that is stored using television video signals, film, videotape, or other noncomputer media. Analog video is important because it defines where the digital content will come from and what will be required for the computer to access it.

Types of Analog Video

Several methods are available for the transmission of video signals—the most common form being analog video in the form of television. In an analog video signal, each frame of the video is represented by a fluctuating voltage signal known as an **analog wave form,** also referred to as **composite video.** Composite analog video has all the video components, including brightness, color, and synchronization (or sync), combined into one signal. Due to the **compositing,** or combining, of the video components, the quality of composite video is considered marginal. Compositing results in color bleeding, low clarity and high generational loss. Generational loss, as it relates to video, is similar to photocopying—the best copy is always made from an original, but even that is inferior to the original. Furthermore, as copies are made from copies, each succeeding copy will be inferior to the previous copy.

There are a number of composite or analog video signal formats for television broadcast, some of which include:

- **NTSC (National Television Standards Committee)**—Format used in the United States and Japan for transmission of video. NTSC consists of 525 scan lines drawn every 1/30th second on a screen that has a 4:3 **aspect ratio**. Aspect ratio is the comparison of width to height for a viewing area. As shown in Figure 7-1, the scans are done in two passes, called interlacing, that cover even, then odd lines, at a rate of 60 cycles per second (60 cps).

- **PAL (Phase Alternate Line)**—Format used in the United Kingdom, much of Europe, Australia, and South Africa. PAL consists of 625 scan lines drawn every $\frac{1}{25}$ second. Pal is interlaced at 50 cycles per second.

- **SECAM** (Sequential Color with Memory [translated from French])—Format used in France. Like PAL, SECAM uses 625 scan lines and is interlaced at 50 cycles per second.

The creation of PAL and SECAM actually followed NTSC and therefore have superior color quality. A new standard is emerging called High Definition Television or HDTV, which is based on 1,125 scan lines at 60 cycles per second with a 16:9 aspect ratio. HDTV will provide a significant improvement in both image and color quality.

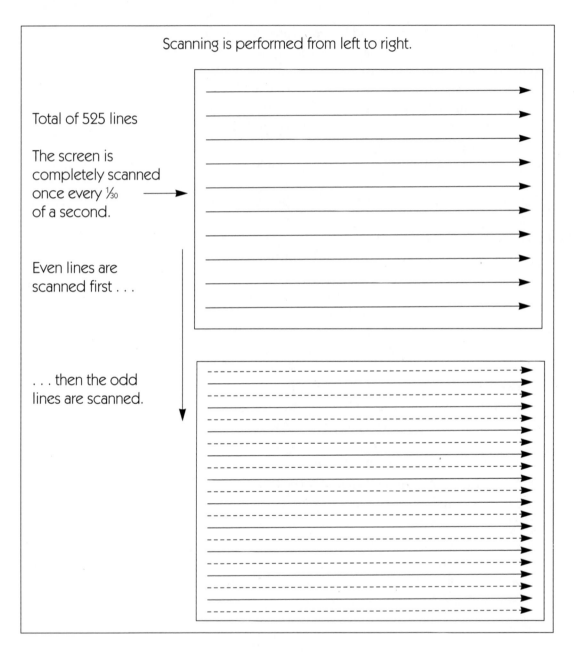

Figure 7-1 Interlaced scanning for NTSC video signals

Component Video

Component video is considered more advanced than composite video discussed earlier. Component video takes the different components of video such as color, brightness, and sync, and breaks them into separate signals. Through improvements to component video a number of formats, such as S-VHS Video and RGB have emerged. S-VHS Video is based on storing color and **luminance** (brightness) information on two separate tracks. RGB stores video on separate channels for red, green, and blue color components. Unfortunately, component video, like composite video, is also susceptible to quality loss from one generation to the next.

Digital Video

Digital video solves generational loss because it is a digital representation of the analog video signal. D-1 is considered to be the highest quality of digital video and is based on four component channels of red, blue, green, and luminance stored on 19 mm tape. D-1 requires a significant investment in hardware for production and editing, which has spawned development of newer versions of digital video including:

- D2—a two channel composite video signal based on color and luminance that is cheaper to produce than D-1
- Digital BetaCam—adds four channels of audio to the D-1 format

The main advantage is that digital video is not subject to generational loss because each copy is identical to the parent. Even though the video data is digital in nature, virtually all the digital formats are stored on sequential tape, and as a result, most video professionals are more accustomed to working with tape media.

There is a significant market for high quality digital video in the television and movie industries. Digital mastering means that quality will never be an issue. However, these industries usually rely on tape as the means to store and transmit digital video. In the following sections we will discuss how digital video can be stored and used in the computer environment.

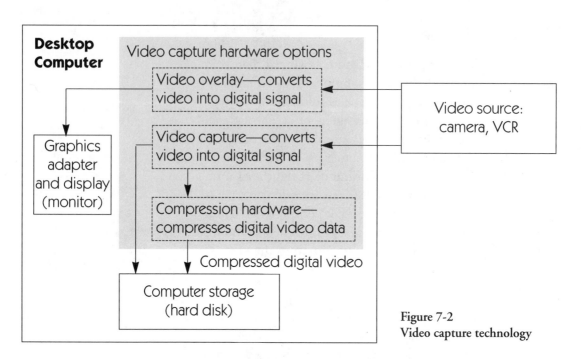

Figure 7-2
Video capture technology

Computer-based Digital Video

There are two significant advantages in using computer-based digital video:

1. The ability to randomly access the video

2. The ability to compress the video

These advantages are significant particularly when editing the video, transporting the video, and storing significant amounts of video for multimedia projects.

In the analog world, sophisticated, and often expensive, video equipment is used to capture and digitize the video into tape media. As shown in Figure 7-2, there are a number of ways that the desktop computer can be used to capture video and transform it into digital format:

- Video overlay board accepts video and places it over computer display image by mapping it to the image in the display adapter.

- Video capture board is able to accept and convert analog video to digital video at 1 to 24 bit quality up to 30 frames per second. Some video capture boards

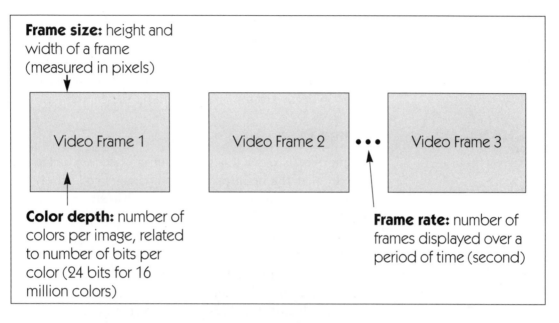

Frame size: height and width of a frame (measured in pixels)

Video Frame 1

Video Frame 2

• • •

Video Frame 3

Color depth: number of colors per image, related to number of bits per color (24 bits for 16 million colors)

Frame rate: number of frames displayed over a period of time (second)

also capture audio, others require standard audio capture and playback hardware.

Figure 7-3 Characteristics of digital video

- Compression hardware or circuitry on video capture boards that compress digital video in real time.

Characteristics of Digital Video

The **frame** is the basic feature of digital video and has some of the same characteristics as two-dimensional computer graphics including height, width, and color depth. A frame is a single image in a video sequence and is the same as a single cel of movie film. Figure 7-3 summarizes three basic characteristics of digital video:

1. Frame Rate—number of images displayed within a specified amount of time to convey a sense of motion. Frame rate is usually described in frames per second (fps).

2. Frame Size—the height and width of each individual frame or image.

3. Color Depth or Resolution—the amount of color for each pixel within each frame or image.

Being familiar with these characteristics of digital video is critical for successfully capturing, storing, and processing video content. The size of a digital video file is directly related to the frame rate, size, and color depth. The quality, while a more subjective factor, is dependent on these factors as well.

Frame Rate

Frame rate is based on presenting a series of images so rapidly that the brain processes the images collectively instead of as single images. Frame rate is usually measured in frames per second. The standard for displaying nonfilm video, such as videotape, is 30 frames per second while photographic movie film is displayed at 24 frames per second.

The frames of movie film, called **cels,** are moved past a light source for projection at a constant rate. Computers and television handle the display of video frames in very different ways. Television depends on electromagnetic scan lines called **fields** that are projected onto a phosphor tube for display. The phosphor tube when struck by different levels of an electromagnetic signal is illuminated to create an image. Television displays its analog video signal by presenting odd lines first, then the even lines next. As shown in Figure 7-1, one odd line and one even line form a pair of scans, which in turn form a frame. There are 60 of these fields displayed every second (or 30 frames every second). This is referred to as **interlaced video.**

Computer Frame Display

A computer monitor uses a process called **progressive scan** to update the computer display one line at a time, from top to bottom. It is important to note that the computer screen is not broken into fields like television. This entire frame is displayed 30 times every second and is referred to as **noninterlaced video.** This process only accounts for how the computer display functions. For digital video, a simpler technique is used to account for motion.

Digital video relies on the same process used in displaying film images. A series of images, called frames, are sequentially presented creating the illusion of motion. In full-motion video people and inanimate objects appear to move normally.

A key factor not to overlook when developing full-motion video is the association of sound with the images. The best way to test sound is to watch the lips of the speaker and listen to hear if the sounds of the words match the movement of the speaker's lips. Movie film provides an analog soundtrack on the film that is physically co-located on the film with the images being presented. As the image is projected, the sound is processed in real time. Digital video usually places chunks of audio within the data file at various intervals. Although the computer is a linear device, the computer processes the image for display and sound so quickly that the image and sound appear to be synchronized.

Depending on the computer system for video and audio processing can lead to difficulties particularly if the computer data bus, disk access speed, or processing are otherwise occupied or just slow. In this situation, the computer usually sacrifices images rather than sound causing noticeable problems. Poor image and sound synchronization can be distracting for the end user and degrade the quality of a multimedia product.

Frame Size

The size of the image determines the quality of the image displayed and the processing involved to display that image. Obviously the smaller the frame, the less of the image you are able to see or appreciate in terms of content. Larger images provide improved resolution. Unfortunately, there is a corresponding penalty for larger frames—the larger the frame the more processing required to present the frame.

Both the NTSC and PAL standards have a larger image perspective than standard desktop computer video frame size. The video graphics adapter (VGA) standard used in most computers since the early 1990s calls for monitors with resolutions of 640 by 480 pixels. Since the resolution between analog video and computers is different, conversion of analog video into digital video must take this into account.

The difference in resolution can often result in the downsizing of the video and the loss of some of the image resolution.

Digital video at 640 by 480 requires a significant investment in image storage and processing power, especially when frame rate is taken into consideration. Therefore, it is common that digital video frame sizes are less than 640 by 480 pixels. Common frame sizes utilized when presenting digital video in multimedia products include:

- 640 by 480, full screen VGA display
- 320 by 240, quarter of a VGA display
- 240 by 180, about a sixth of a VGA display
- 160 by 120, sixteenth of a VGA display

The larger frame size is obviously the best for resolution and image quality, although unfortunately, a significant penalty is paid for processing the image. Smaller frame sizes require less processing but the image quality is lessened. The key is to find an image size that is of acceptable quality and that is within the performance capabilities of the computer's processor.

Color Depth or Resolution

Digital video attempts to reproduce the highest quality image possible. Frame rate and size are critical for image resolution and a sense of motion, while color depth or resolution is critical in order to create a lifelike effect. **Color depth** or **resolution** refers to the number of colors displayed on the screen at one time. As you may recall, computers deal with color in an RGB or red-green-blue format that includes color resolutions ranging from 1 bit for 2 colors to 8 bits/pixel (256 colors), 16 bits/pixel (65,535 colors), and 24 bits/pixel (16.7 million colors).

As with frame rate and size, color resolution is a factor to consider for storage space and processing. It is common for digital video systems to use two color strategies:

- 24-bit color to achieve optimal color reproduction
- 8-bit black-and-white (**grayscale**) or 256 color for a reduction in file size while still maintaining an acceptable image resolution

Since 24-bit color offers a significant color palette, it is used more often than 8-bit color because it enables digital video to be transported across platforms with minimal loss in per frame image quality. However, 8-bit color has regained interest because it results in smaller data sets that are more suitable for transmission on the Internet.

Balancing Characteristics

Another important but often overlooked factor when developing digital video is quality. Quality is a subjective measure based on what you think looks and feels acceptable for your application. Quality is directly related to factors including size, frame rate, and color depth. For some applications, this may mean a 1/4 screen, 15-frame per second video, at 8 bits per pixel, while other applications require full screen (640 by 480), full frame rate video (24 or 30 frames per second), at 24 bits per pixel (16.7 million colors). For example, a multimedia training application that uses digital video to present the operation of equipment would require a high resolution, large display to effectively communicate critical information.

Frame rate can often be reduced to 20, 15, or even 10 frames per second with a significant level of quality maintained. Ten frames or less can be used to present video of scenery or other slowly changing events, while a person talking might be presented with a smaller image at a much higher frame rate per second.

Quality depends on content; for example, video with a great deal of motion, especially detailed motion, requires a higher frame rate to achieve an acceptable level of quality for playback. Video of the "great outdoors," in which the scenery is paramount, requires a larger frame size and 24-bit color to adequately present the desired effect. It is up to the developer to carefully consider the best frame size, frame rate, and color depth based on the type of content being prepared.

Multimedia developers must balance digital video quality, based on subjective look and feel, with the amount of digital video in an application. The amount of digital video is based on frame rate, frame size, color depth, and quantity of video (number of seconds or minutes of video). It is essential to understand how to size digital video in order to provide the best quality when producing digital video.

Digital Video Data Sizing

The amount of storage needed to capture and manage digital video can be staggering. As you may recall, a single graphic image that is 640 by 480 pixels with 24-bit color requires nearly one megabyte for storage. Applying some math shows that a one second, 24-bit color video, with a 640 by 480 resolution, at 30 frames per second, requires a 26 megabyte file for storage—one minute requires over 1.5 gigabytes. The data from this file must be able to move from a disk to the processor in one second in order to play it. Obviously, this file size surpasses the capabilities of the standard desktop computer data bus (typical bus speeds run around 400-800 KB/s), and it also can quickly overburden existing storage systems (one minute requires nearly 1,620 megabytes). However, before discussing how to handle large digital video files, let us look at how to calculate digital video file sizes.

Calculating the Size of a Digital Video Stream

The following can be used to calculate the size of a video data stream:

f = frame size (width * height)
r = frame rate (frames per second)
c = color depth (in bytes)
t = time in seconds

Raw video data size   = $f * r * c * t$

Add .5 to 1 MB for each minute of digital audio depending on the frequency (11 to 44 KHz), data size (8 or 16 bits), and number of channels (mono or stereo).

Using the above, consider the following example:

- Source: one minute of video analog video

- Goal: digital video at 30 frames per second (fps), 24 bit color (3 bytes), 320 x 240 (quarter VGA display)
- Data size: 60 sec * 30 fps * 3 bytes * (320 pixels * 240 pixels) = 414,720,000 bytes (plus audio - up to 1 MB+)

Now, let us look at how we size video data by looking at one minute of full screen (VGA) video at 30 frames per second:

- Multiply width times height: 640 pixels (width) times 480 pixels (height) equals 307,200 total pixels.
- Multiply this by the color depth (24 bit or 3 bytes). 307,200 pixels times 3 bytes per pixel equals 921,600 total bytes per frame.
- Multiply data size per frame times number of frames per second: 921,600 bytes times 30 frames per second equals 27,648,000 total bytes per one second of video.
- Multiply by the number of seconds: 27,648,000 bytes times 60 seconds equals 1,658,880,000 bytes per minute.
- Note that this does not include audio; add about 600,000 bytes for one minute of 11 KHz, 8 bit, mono quality audio.

As you can see, one minute of full screen, high quality, digital video would easily fill gigabyte-sized hard drives and would be quite difficult to process in an economical fashion.

Managing Digital Video File Size

To reduce the amount of data down to a manageable level, we must compromise on one or more of the video characteristics: frame rate, frame size, and/or color depth. Certain applications may not need a full 30-frame per second frame rate or a full-screen display. You can reduce the frame rate to 15 frames per second and the frame size to 320 by 240 pixels. This yields:

Height times width: 320 pixels times 240 pixels = 76,800 total pixels per frame x 3 bytes per pixel = 230,400 total bytes per frame x 15 frames per second = 3,456,000 total bytes per second times 60 seconds = 207,360,000 bytes

While these numbers are significantly less, they are still quite large. A one gigabyte disk could hold only about five minutes worth of video at this frame rate, size, and color depth. In order to make digital video easier to work with, the data needs to be compressed into smaller data files.

Video Compression

Compression methods use mathematical algorithms to reduce or compress video data by eliminating, grouping, and/or averaging similar data found in the video signal. Compression is required to make digital video manageable for storage, transport, and processing. Video compression is based on applying an algorithm to the raw video stream to reduce the data size. The type of algorithm used is a constant for the entire video data file in that it determines how the data is compressed for both capture and playback. There are actually a number of algorithms that have been developed for digital video and constant advances and improvements in efficiency and quality are being made all the time. The output data file is stored within a data file that can be processed by specialized video software for the operating system. There are several factors to consider when considering desktop digital video compression.

Real-time Versus Nonreal-time Video

The term "real-time" has created a considerable amount of confusion where video compression is concerned. At a minimum, it means that a compression system must capture, compress to disk, decompress, and play back video at the capture frame rate in real time with no delays. At higher frame rates, usually 24 to 30 frames, playback at this rate can be difficult for many desktop computer systems.

Symmetrical Versus Asymmetrical Video Capture

This refers to how video images are compressed and decompressed. Symmetrical compression means that if you can play back a sequence of 640 x 480 video at 30 frames per second, then you can also capture, compress, and store it in 30 seconds as well. Asymmetrical compression means just the opposite. The degree of asymmetry is usually expressed as a ratio. A ratio of 150:1 means it takes approximately 150 minutes to compress one minute of video. Asymmetrical compression can sometimes be more elaborate and more efficient for quality and speed at playback because it uses so much more time to compress the video.

Compression Ratios

A second ratio is often referred to when working with compressed video. This is the **compression ratio** and should not be confused with the asymmetry ratio. The compression ratio relates to a numerical representation of the original video in comparison to the compressed video. For example, 200:1 compression ratio means that the original video is represented by the number 200 and the compressed video is represented by 1. The more the video is compressed, the higher the compression ratio or the numerical difference in the two numbers. Unfortunately, the higher the compression ratio is, the poorer the video quality will be. Compression ratios vary from one compression method to another, but hardware and software that perform well on a PC or Mac may be less efficient on a different machine.

Lossless Versus Lossy Compression

The loss factor determines whether there is a loss of quality between the original image and the image after it has been compressed and played back or decompressed. The more compression, the more likely the quality of the video will be affected. Virtually all compression methods result in the loss of some quality. Even if the quality difference is minimal, these are still considered **lossy** compression methods.

Interframe Versus Intraframe Compression

The **intraframe** method compresses and stores each video frame as a discrete picture. **Interframe compression,** on the

Descriptions of video compression technologies

Emerging technologies for video compression

other hand, is based on the idea that although action is happening, the backgrounds in most video scenes remain stable—a great deal of the scene is redundant. Compression is started by creating a reference frame. Each subsequent frame of the video is compared to the previous frame and the next frame, and only the difference between the frames is stored. The amount of data saved is substantially reduced.

Bit Rate Control

The final factor to be aware of with video compression is bit rate control, which is critical if the playback system has a limited bandwidth from a slower processor or limited memory. Bit rate control is based on how much data can be processed in a limited period of time. More data means more content in terms of frame rate, size, and quality, but it also means more speed is required to access the data or to process it.

A good digital video compression system allows the user to control the compression hardware and software and to determine which parameters are most important for their particular needs. In some applications, frame rate may be of paramount importance, while frame size is not. In other applications, it may not matter if the frame rate drops below 15 frames per second, as long as the quality of those remaining frames is good.

Video Compression Algorithms

Uncompressed digital video files are too large to be practical, therefore they are compressed to manageable sizes for storage and playback. Digital video compression is based on applying an algorithm to an uncompressed file that applies many of the considerations that have been discussed. For example, an algorithm may implement a lossy compression strategy by comparing a frame with the following frame to determine the change in the image:

- The initial frame, called a key frame, is compared to the next frame.

- If there is great similarity between the key frame and the next, then the next frame is dropped; otherwise the next frame is kept and becomes the key frame.
- This process is repeated for the entire file.
- During playback, key frames are used to reconstruct dropped frames so that the complete number of frames is reconstructed.

If the source video is made up of gradually changing images, then the compression level can be very high.

Video compression is part of the overall picture of how digital video is captured, stored, edited, and used in multimedia products. Compression may be accomplished during or following capture, and depending on the playback system, decompression may be performed by the computer processor or require specialized hardware. The following section will describe how this hardware and software fit together to make digital video practical for multimedia products.

Video Capture and Playback Systems

Digital video is based on a combination of hardware and software to capture, store, edit, and play back digital video. This involves equipment including cameras and VCRs in addition to the computer systems that are configured to connect to these devices to produce digital video. Video capture systems, as shown in Figure 7-4, consist of a number of components:

- Video source such as a camera or video cassette recorder (VCR), capable of producing NTSC, PAL, or other compatible video signal.
- Analog to Digital Converter: circuitry for converting the analog video stream into a digital video stream. The digital video stream is a series of bits and bytes that represent the images from a video source.

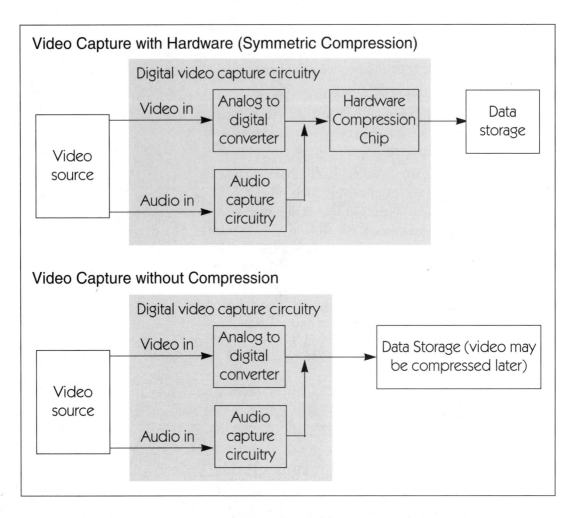

Figure 7-4 Digital video capture system process with and without compression

- Audio Capture Circuitry: sound capture device that operates concurrently with the video capture system. This produces digital audio data that can be integrated with the digital video data.

- Hardware Compression Chip: special hardware, usually a digital signal processing chip and associated supporting hardware, for implementing a compression algorithm on the raw video stream. The output is a compressed video data file.

Video playback, as shown in Figure 7-5, is accomplished one of two ways:

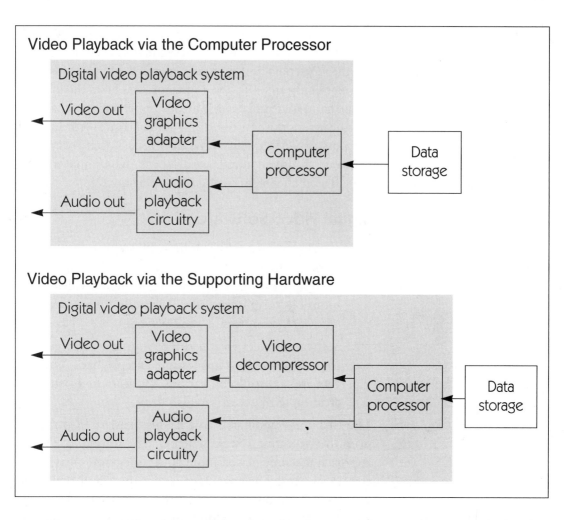

1. If necessary, video data is decompressed and processed into images that are displayed by the computer's video graphics system. The processing of the video data is accomplished completely by the computer processor.

2. In other situations, the video data is decompressed by additional hardware called a "decompressor." The video information is transferred directly to the video graphics system. The computer processor is only responsible for managing file access and related system functions.

In the first case, the video playback is very dependent on the power of the computer processor. If the processor is too slow

Figure 7-5 Digital video playback system via the computer processor and via supporting hardware

or busy performing other tasks, the quality of playback will be impacted. The second option offers the advantage of having the video data decompression performed by a specialized piece of hardware , the decompressor, that takes the load off of the computer processor. The decompressor also enables a significant increase in the frame rate and size with little, if any, loss of video quality. The downside is that specialized hardware is also required for playback, which may not be available on all systems using the application.

Digital Video Software

Digital video software, like audio software, is based on one of two approaches:

1. Each application that depends on digital video is responsible for all aspects of controlling video capture hardware, compression, and playback.

2. Software drivers within the operating system control the video capture, compression, and playback. The drivers are accessible by various applications to support creation of or access to video data.

The first case, popular in the 1980s, was based on more primitive operating system schemes. The second case is the approach taken by newer, more powerful, graphic-based operating systems. The advantage is that the newer operating systems can support various hardware configurations and applications by merely adding new digital video drivers as they are required. Digital video software comes in three basic forms:

1. Video capture
2. Video editing
3. Video playback for applications

Video Capture

Video capture software is often used to control video capture hardware. It includes the ability to control the video signal input characteristics such as color and brightness. It also controls how the video is captured, including the selection of a compression algorithm, frame rate, frame size, color depth, bit rate, and audio sampling. The output of video capture software is a data file that may be compressed if the video capture system offers that feature.

Video Editing

Video editing software is used to produce a finished digital video product. Video editing software is capable of:

- Compressing raw digital video to much smaller files
- Copying, cutting, pasting, and deleting video frames from a video file
- Combining frames from two or more video data sources
- Changing the size or frame rate of the video data segment
- Editing the audio by removing, copying, or adding to it
- Adding special effects to video clips such as titles or transitions between video segments

Video Playback

Video playback is dependent upon an application being able to display a digital video file within another application. The simplest capability is to merely play a video clip within a window or a full-screen application with controls to play, pause, stop, rewind, fast forward, and frame advance or retreat. Multimedia products usually present digital video data with other data placing the video segment on a part of the display integrated with other data in the application. For example, text describing space exploration could be accompanied by a digital video of Neil Armstrong walking on the moon.

One of the advantages of digital video is that the user can instantly jump around the video by moving the file pointer to the desired location and quickly access any frame in the video. This feature may be used by the end user or an application to display certain segments of a digital video file on demand.

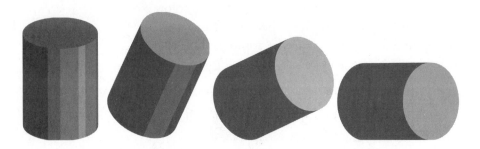

Figure 7-6 Animation is a series of images viewed sequentially. Each image depicts a position and when viewed in succession illustrates motion.

Computer Animation

Computer animation is the use of computer generated images to convey motion. Digital video is based on capturing video from a camera or other source and converting it into a digital video data file that can be played by a computer. The digital video is automatically created from an analog source that provides a steady stream of images. Complementary to digital video is animation that is originally created, one frame at a time, by the computer. A graphic artist or animator uses a set of tools to create a series of images that, when presented in rapid succession, convey a sense of motion to the viewer. Animation is created by:

1. Creating a series of still images that can be shown rapidly creating a sense of motion

2. Manipulating and moving an object along a vector or path

3. Storing animation information in a data file for later playback.

In the first instance, although similar to the capture of video into digital video (one frame at a time), the difference is that animation frames are created and assembled with software tools such as graphics software rather than using live or recorded video. In the second instance, animation is created by working with objects that assume capabilities through programming. Finally, regardless of how the animation is created, it can also be stored in a data file for playback in a viewer application or by a multimedia product.

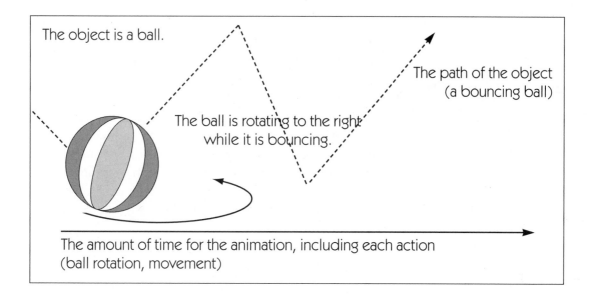

The object is a ball.

The path of the object
(a bouncing ball)

The ball is rotating to the right
while it is bouncing.

The amount of time for the animation, including each action
(ball rotation, movement)

Creating Animation

Creating a series of images is shown in Figure 7-6. Each image supersedes the previous image with a minute change that, over time and rapid playback presents an illusion of motion by the content of the segment. Animation software tools enable developers to rapidly build a succession of images by group objects and managing backgrounds. The final product is output to a file for later playback. In some cases, the output file is compressed using the same algorithms as used for analog video capture.

Object-based Animation

Another technique utilized when creating animation is the use two- or three-dimensional representations of real-world objects. These objects come in many forms from simple bouncing balls with limited behaviors to wire-frame representations of people that can walk, touch, and show facial expressions. Objects can be manipulated by modifying the behavior of the elements within the object. Figure 7-7 provides an illustration of object-based animation.

Figure 7-7 Example of object-based animation

Examples of animation

Objects are usually represented by "wire-frames" that identify the features of the object. The object itself, and even the features of the object, can have associated behaviors that can be called upon to create lifelike behavior. Object behaviors depend on the object itself but can include growing, shrinking, stretching, coloring, and numerous other behaviors. The object can also be moved along a predetermined path on the background. In more advanced systems, the object can have shadows that change as the object moves or as its behavior changes. The output of object animation software may be one of two data sets depending on the animation application used:

1. A set of commands that can be used by a "player" program to reproduce the animation

2. A digital video file similar to that created by analog video capture including compression to reduce the overall file size

Using Digital Video in Multimedia Applications

Multimedia applications use digital video primarily for information delivery. In limited cases, it is also used to support navigation or to help the user operate the application. Generally speaking, digital video and animation are powerful tools for presenting complex information in a way that is as close to "hands-on" as an end user of a multimedia product can get.

The most common use of digital video in multimedia products is for information; for example, historical events such as President Kennedy's going to the moon speech, or "talking heads" such as interviews of experts. Historical scenes can be taken from archival live video and film footage or from re-creations including commercial movies and television. Historical footage is often quite effective because it provides a context for many end users.

"Talking heads," videos of people speaking, are the most commonly abused application of digital video. Although it can be quite effective when the speaker is well known or presents the information very dynamically, the information is primarily audio and does not necessarily need to be conveyed through images. Furthermore, by using digital audio, a significant amount of data storage is saved over that required for digital video. Talking heads require higher frame rates to capture lip motion and can be problematic on playback particularly if the computer is slow or busy with other activities.

Animation can be a very powerful tool to use in educational applications but can be very expensive to produce because it is usually created from scratch. This is contrasted with digital video, which is often produced from stock footage that is cheaper to obtain and convert into digital form.

Samples of professionally created digital video

Resources to acquire digital video stock footage

SUMMARY

Digital video combines the best of graphics and audio to enable multimedia products to come alive. Digital video is based on capturing, storing, editing, and playing a sequence of frames. Capture and playback of frames are driven by the frame rate, frame size, and color depth. Digital video files tend to be very large based on the total number of frames, individual frame size, and number of bytes to store color information. Video file sizes are compressed using a variety of techniques to make them manageable for storage and playback. Video capture by computers requires a set of hardware that connects to video signals from cameras or VCRs to capture and compression circuitry. Playback of digital video is accomplished by either the computer processor or specialized playback hardware connected to the computer video system. Animation is a special kind of digital video that is based on computer-generated images viewed in rapid sequence.

REVIEW QUESTIONS

1. Why is the quality of analog video critical to digital video creation and editing?

2. Correlate the performance of digital video to the computer platform in terms of the processor, data storage, and video display.

3. Consider instances of digital video you have seen in multimedia products. What characteristics stood out in terms of content, quality, and presentation?

4. What digital video editing tools have you used? How easy or difficult were they to use compared with other image and graphics tools?

5. How would you use a talking head in a multimedia product? How would you replace a talking head in a multimedia product?

6. What are the advantages of rendered animation over digital video?

CHAPTER EIGHT

Product Design

OBJECTIVES

After completing this chapter, you should know:

- How a multimedia product works.

- What parts and pieces are found in a multimedia presentation.

- How multimedia products are organized.

- What story-boarding is and how it is used to create multimedia products.

How a multimedia product looks, feels, and works may be the most important factor in how well it sells and even more importantly, how much it is used. Look and feel are often subjective and driven by the content of the product or the quality of the artwork.

Product design is one part content, one part understanding the end user, and one part understanding the subject. To discuss product design, there needs to be agreement on some unit of presentation called a **page.** The page is the basic unit of a multimedia product. In some multimedia authoring environments the page may be called a frame, slide, or have some other designation. At a minimum a page is a single view of a multimedia presentation and includes some combination of text, pictures, audio, and video. The page is the basic element of the presentation and is combined with other pages for a variety of products and products.

Building Blocks

Behind the design of a multimedia product, one finds the use of "pages" that contain content and information supporting the structure and flow of a presentation. These pages are used to provide functions for navigation, information presentation, and support for the user. Pages can be categorized as follows:

- Introduction
- Splash
- Menu
- Content
- Help
- Credits
- Quit

These pages are not found in all multimedia products; however, most multimedia products depend on these pages or the functions they represent.

Introduction and Splash Pages

Introduction and splash pages are used to start a presentation. Splash pages are used to indicate that the product is loading, which is often useful if a great deal of multimedia content is being preloaded for better performance. Introduction pages provide many features such as:

- Identifying the product
- Identifying the source of the product
- Providing instructions on how to use the program
- Providing security features such as password protection

Menu and Content Pages

Menu pages are used to organize the content of a multimedia product and they make up the bulk of the pages in any multimedia product. They support linking to other pages, called branching, which enables a product to be layered for easier access to content. Menu pages usually contain little in the way of content beyond standardized background pictures and audio. Content pages are used to present the content of a multimedia product. They offer limited options for branching to other pages—usually to succeeding pages in a linear series, the previous page, and to support functions.

Help, Credit, and Quit Pages

Help, credit, and quit pages enable user support functions for the smooth operation of a product. Help pages provide information about how the presentation is organized and how controls work. Help pages can usually be accessed from any point in the presentation and the user can easily return to where they came from after accessing the Help function. Help pages may also be layered to provide levels of support for the user.

Credit pages provide information about the developer and content sources. They may also list related products and update information.

Quit pages are used to terminate the program and usually offer an option to return to the product just in case the Quit function is inadvertently selected.

Classes of Products

There are two basic design strategies that developers can employ when creating multimedia products:

1. Non-interactive: linear in nature, user has little control over operation.
2. Interactive: user dictates flow of information delivery.

Non-interactive products are the simplest because the content is presented in a linear fashion. The end user simply watches a sequence of pages in a predetermined fixed sequence. This format resembles a videotape or a television format because of the limited control that the end user has to vary the delivery of information. Interactive delivery, much more common in commercial multimedia, means that the end user can control the delivery by pressing buttons or hot links, or turning audio and video on and off.

Non-Interactive Multimedia

Non-interactive multimedia includes products such as animation and standalone presentations similar to a movie or a

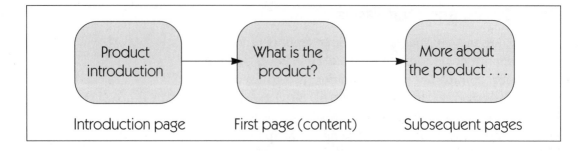

Figure 8-1 Non-interactive presentation format

video. These products may be used to present information to a large audience on a giant screen or to play on a television monitor. The product will usually play from start to finish or even loop to continually present information. However, the end user usually has some level of control over non-interactive multimedia, ranging from starting and stopping the presentation to actually controlling the pace of the presentation. The pace of the presentation may be managed by clicking the mouse or pressing a key to go to the next page. Non-interactive multimedia is by far the most basic form of multimedia and usually contains more than one data form, text, and pictures at a minimum.

Figure 8-1 offers the simplest layout for non-interactive multimedia presentations in which a series of pages are presented one after another. Non-interactive presentations are characterized by the following:

- Incorporation of text and graphics are a minimum. Audio and video components including background music and extended video and/or animation clips are also common.

- The program typically starts and ends under user control.

- The program proceeds under user control by clicking the mouse or pressing a key to add elements to a page or advance to the next page.

- Advanced features enable automatic page turning according to preset times and display of page elements when the user clicks on the screen or presses a key.

The non-interactive format is useful for a number of products such as:

- Corporate overview presentations
- Teaching and training presentations
- Sales and marketing presentations

In each of these cases, there are common characteristics for presenting information. Most importantly, information builds on more information. For example, a series of screens provides:

- The name of the company, followed by
- The company mission
- History of the company
- Organization
- Products

In each page, the user is led on a tour that provides a comprehensive description of the company. The user is given information in bits and pieces making it easier to understand and retain.

Training products often depend on sequences of information based on time-dependent processes. For example, a product to teach cooking would start with gathering the ingredients, mixing the ingredients, cooking, and conclude with the serving of the food. It would make little sense to order this presentation any other way. The non-interactive, linear format is most effective for this type of information because it keeps the end user from jumping ahead too fast and skipping important pieces of information.

If the end user is a salesman or a teacher, the non-interactive linear strategy is the easiest to organize and present. Facts, examples, and other relevant information are made available in a linear sequence that is shown on a monitor or projection system to a large audience. In cases where the presenter may be nervous with the material, the audience, or the technology, a simple, linear presentation is the easiest to deliver. The presenter simply pushes a button and the next slide appears with the content ready for discussion.

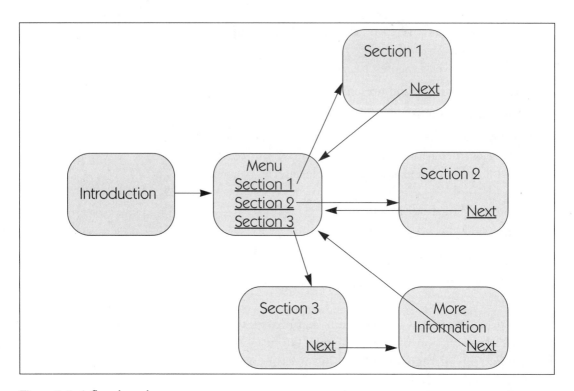

Figure 8-2 A flowchart showing the possible movement through an interactive multimedia presentation

Non-interactive presentations lend themselves to linear media such as videotape. For example, a video yearbook for a group of second grade elementary school students included the following:

- A musical introduction
- A video clip of the teacher and the principal
- Pictures and video of various class activities
- An alphabetical presentation of students containing a biography, self-portrait, and voice-over for each person

The entire presentation was developed on a multimedia workstation and then transferred to videotape for distribution to the students. In this fashion, all of the students were able to take home and view the final product without having a multimedia-capable computer.

Interactive Multimedia

Interactive multimedia is the more common model followed by developers when creating commercial products, which include training, entertainment, and educational products. Interactive multimedia is characterized by the ability to jump around or follow different paths through the information. Figure 8-2 represents a simplified perspective on how an interactive presentation works. Interactive presentations are organized as menus and content pages that allow the end user to make decisions about where to proceed. Buttons, graphic hot spots, text-based hyperlinks, menu lists, and similar techniques provide the user with choices. When a choice is made a new page or view is presented and the user continues through the information. There may even be sections of interactive presentations that act as page turners—the end user simply follows a linear sequence of pages before returning to a menu.

A great deal of complexity can exist in an interactive presentation. Depending on the product and the amount of content, there may be many layers for navigation. This potential for complexity has advantages and disadvantages. The main advantage is that very complex domains of information can be represented by developers of multimedia products. This can also be a disadvantage for end users who need to navigate these complex information sets to find specific information.

The interactive format lends itself to a variety of products including:

- Reference tools such as encyclopedias and dictionaries
- Education and training
- Electronic news and magazine delivery
- Entertainment

Reference products, due to their sheer volume of information and content, need to be organized to provide specific facts quickly. Education and training products may require interactive access to specific training tasks or may require their use to complete exercises out of order from other activities. Electronic news and magazines may be divided into sections such as current events, politics, sports, and confidentials that provide selectable content for the end user. Finally, entertainment products may be divided into various

The CD-ROM includes a number of samples of digital audio.

types of games, skill levels within games, or complex story elements that users may exit and return to different sessions.

Interactive Strategies for Organizing Information

Information can be structured a number of different ways depending on the amount of information and its complexity. However, there are some fundamental views of how information can be organized that are useful for designing multimedia products. These strategies, as shown in Table 8-1, include:

1. Linear—Information is presented in a straightforward fashion; as in books, it may be divided into chapters, sections, and paragraphs.

2. Tree or hierarchical—Information is broken down into subordinate layers based on logical structure.

3. Network—Information is linked to other parts of the product.

These are basic strategies that illustrate effective ways to manage information.

Interactivity and Presentation Strategies

Interactive systems are implemented in a number of different ways depending on the product, content, and development tools. In nearly all cases, the user controls how the information is accessed and there are three basic approaches:

1. Linear

2. Programmed branching

3. Hypermedia

Linear Products

The linear strategy is similar to non-interactive in that a sequence of pages or views of information are presented and the interface contains controls for advancement of pages. The user can typically advance to the next page or go back a page. Many of these systems also allow the user to jump to

Strategy Characteristics	Advantage/Disadvantage
Linear	
Series of multimedia pages or slides	Easiest to produce and simplest to follow
Navigation is to the next or previous page	Limits complexity of information by providing lengthy serialized presentations
Tree (Hierarchical)	
Layers of menus accessing subordinate pages with content	Difficult to create, test, and maintain if there are a large number of paths
Navigation is to subordinate layers with returns to prior layers	Need to have an easy return to top or to previous layers
Network	
Combination of linear and tree formats	Similar to tree-based systems
Navigation is to successive layers and across layers depending on the content	Good for large volumes of unstructured information
	Can be difficult to use and maintain with extensive cross-branching

Table 8-1 Strategies to Organize Information for Multimedia

pages out of sequence. Advanced multimedia lecture tools for instructors fit into this category. The instructor presents content on individual pages and, for the most part, the presentation is a sequential one. However, the instructor may go back a page to answer a question, jump ahead, or interact with the page by drawing over a graphic, adding text comments, or randomly accessing specific frames in a digital video clip. This type of product requires a presenter who feels very comfortable with both the content and the technology.

Programmed Branching Products
Programmed branching products are the most common type of commercial multimedia. Examples range from education and reference to gaming products. In a programmed

branching product, the user has limited control over the path that the product will follow. The control is via choices presented by the user interface such as buttons or graphic hot spots. Like all multimedia products, the developer specifies, designs, and implements the choices that are available.

In this model, each page of the product contains content and choices. The choices are used to take the user to another page in either another part of the product or to the next page in a sequence of pages. The choice may also be to go to a Help page or to exit from the product. Programmed products are fairly common in multimedia products because they allow the user to have a sense of freedom while viewing large sets of information.

Hypermedia Products

In hypermedia products, the sequencing is very nonlinear in terms of how the content is organized with the user having full control over sequence and pace of the presentation. World Wide Web pages and many Help file systems typify this type of model. **Hypermedia** products are usually implemented as text or graphic pages with the end user clicking on a word or graphic element. Clicking on the element takes the user to another part of the page or a new page entirely. In many respects, this format is very similar to the programmed branching format in that the user is given preprogrammed choices to navigate through the information. The key difference lies in the ability of the user to operate within the context of the presentation—to access new information or to step out of the presentation to access a search mechanism or "Back" and "Forward" commands or to move between pages of a presentation. Help file systems depend on hyperlinks to browse Help material. Help file systems also allow the user to search for key words or page through a series of pages for Help instructions. World Wide Web browsers enable programmed hyperlinks to access local and remote documents, provide a "Back" button to go to previous pages and views, and supply bookmarks so the user can jump to previously visited pages.

Content Organizational Strategies

The most critical aspect of designing and building a multimedia product is organizing its content. Key questions about the nature of the product must be answered to determine how the content is to be used. Does the content tell a story or does it describe a person, place, or thing? Various strategies can be applied to organize information for a product based on time, space, or function. These strategies are actually used to layer and manage large volumes of information. Organizational strategies for multimedia content include:

- Reference
- Temporal
- Geographical
- Systemic
- Organizational

Common to all of these strategies is a "drill down" approach that layers product content to best present the information. Like a power tool, the user drills down to successive layers to isolate specific information. The drilling enables better use of the display by not overcrowding it with too much information or content and it enables more intuitive and logical organization of information.

The following sections provide further discussion and examples of organizational strategies. Bear in mind that these are very simplified models, and in some cases two or more of these techniques may be combined in a single product.

Reference

Reference-based organization is probably the most common and straightforward strategy for encyclopedic works. It is based on structured lists or logical groupings from which the user can rapidly find a specific term. Figure 8-3 illustrates a simple example in which items are sequentially ordered, each item is subsequently divided into sub-items, which in turn lead to content. Typical ordering schemes for reference products include:

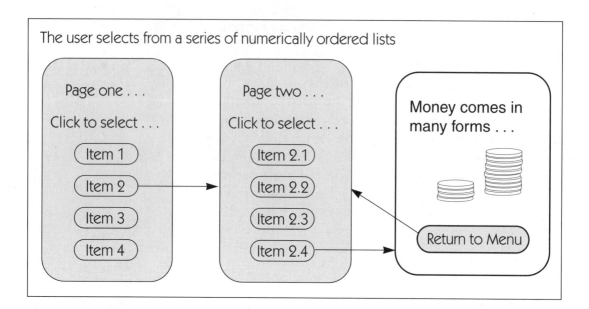

The user selects from a series of numerically ordered lists

Page one . . .

Click to select . . .

Item 1

Item 2

Item 3

Item 4

Page two . . .

Click to select . . .

Item 2.1

Item 2.2

Item 2.3

Item 2.4

Money comes in many forms . . .

Return to Menu

Figure 8-3 Reference application design using a numerically ordered list

- Alphabetical—A, B, C ordering.
- Numerical—1, 2, 3 or I, II, III ordering.
- Color—White to black and spectral sequencing; color may be used to create separations of information categories.
- Size—Small to large or vice versa; like color, object size may be used to create separations of information categories.

Temporal

History products, although sequential and similar to reference, deserve their own category because they are so common. Temporal or time-based present a series of events or identify specific moments in time. As in reference products, drill-down techniques are also used for historical context where detail is required. Figure 8-4 provides an example of a timeline-based organization that allows the user to select from a millennia to a specific year in history.

One of the key problems in temporal products is how to correlate time to events. For example, most people can easily recall an event such as the Revolutionary War but as-

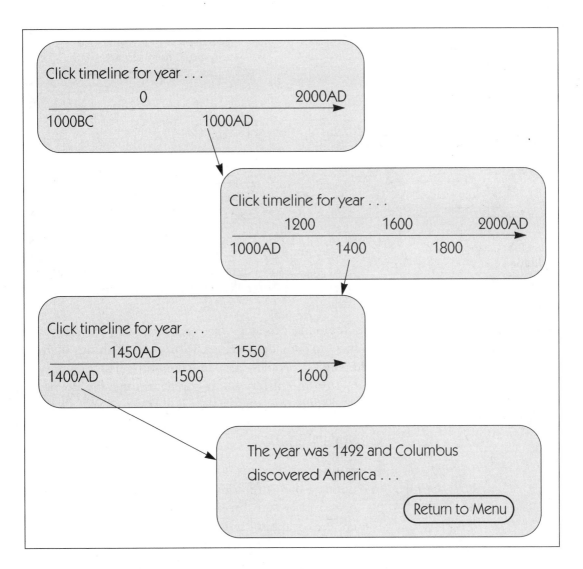

Figure 8-4 Temporal application design

signing specific dates can be problematic; therefore, various techniques are used:

- Presenting a timeline with event names in the fore-front. For example, "Revolutionary War" would overlap the 1776 to 1783 segment of the timeline.
- Using pop-up displays to show events as the user moves the mouse or cursor across a timeline. When the user moves the cursor over 1789, the words "Revolutionary War" would appear.

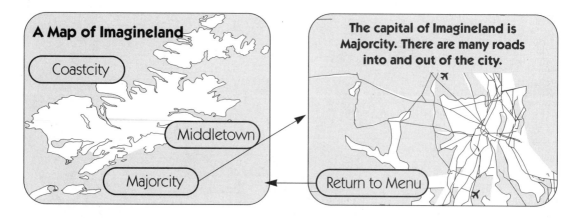

Figure 8-5 Geographical application design

- Using graphics to identify faces, locations, and things that are closely related to a specific point in history. A picture of George Washington would appear on the timeline.

Temporal products may be combined with reference products to provide timelines with physical things such as technologies, peoples, art, and literature. For example, a product on the history of art correlates different art mediums and styles to specific points in history.

Geographical

Geographical systems use two- and three-dimensional space to organize a body of information. They rely on maps, floor plans, and two- and three-dimensional charts to organize content. Geographical systems may also be layered to make it easier for the user to drill down and isolate specific information. For example, in Figure 8-5, the user is presented with a map of a country with various cities and when a city is selected, the user is given information about the city. Successive layers of maps could in turn be presented to identify specific neighborhoods, streets, and even houses.

Geographical products, like temporal products, correlate places with things and time. For example, a timeline might be placed next to a map of the United States to show westward expansion. The user could click on the map at a specific spot and the timeline presents information relating to when something occurred at or near that location.

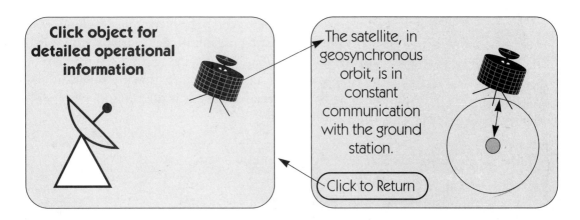

Systemic

Figure 8-6 Systemic application design

Systems define the structure and operation of our world. Hardware, software, mechanical, electronic, biological, and other systems are typically decomposed into subordinate systems called subsystems. Subsystems can be further decomposed until a desired level of detail is reached. This decomposition of a system is useful in organizing information so that it can be easily and quickly accessed. The example shown in Figure 8-6 of a satellite telecommunications system, illustrates how the user is presented with a picture of a satellite system and is able to select a component to obtain more information about that component. Systemic products are usually layered hierarchically so that successive layers offer information relevant and appropriate to the current layer.

Systemic products are risky because it is not always likely that the user will understand the nature of the system upon initial entry into the product. The designer must provide a frame of reference for the system, such as a component or device, that the user can relate to. The black box can then be decomposed into subordinate systems or components that the user relates to in locating information.

Organizational

Organizations are special cases of systems because they deal with people, organizations, or companies. Organizations,

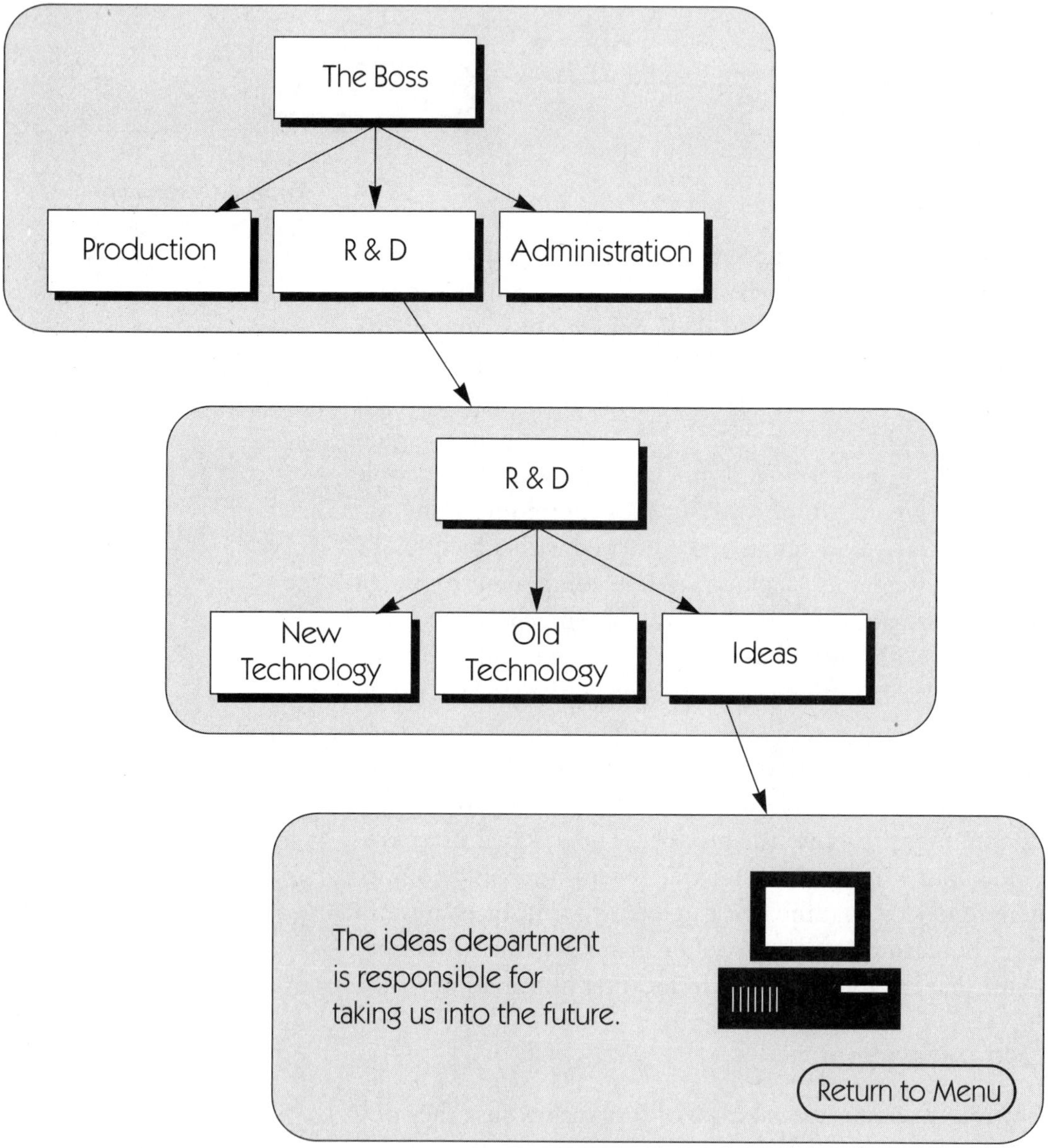

Figure 8-7
**Organizational
application design**

similar to systems, also tend to be hierarchical making them easy to map to existing organizational charts. With limited display space available as shown in Figure 8-7, it may not be possible to describe an entire organization in a single display. Drilling is an alternative since it is used to provide significant levels of detail.

Storyboarding

Now that the various types of products and the ways to organize information have been established, it is time to discuss building a multimedia product. **Storyboarding** is a process lifted from other media development including movie making, cartoon animation, and marketing. Storyboarding is literally building a story on paper that describes and details the message or story of the product. For multimedia, storyboarding is used to link content to the message so that it can be translated into product software. The storyboard exists on two levels, first the page and second, the product.

Storyboard Page

The storyboard page is used to describe a specific frame of time within a multimedia presentation. It is logically equivalent to the page term introduced earlier and used throughout this chapter. The storyboard page, as shown in Figure 8-8, describes:

- The message for the page
- The content of the page including the source and instructions for formatting
- Layout of the content for the page
- Layout of navigation controls for the page
- Specific interactivity for the page
- Designer information including who designed it, when, and where
- Comments or other information that may be useful for the programmer

There are no specific rules on how to lay out a storyboard page. Depending on the product, a storyboard may be as simple as a series of crude sketches or as complex as needed to help in managing a large body of information and multiple developers.

Product demonstrations illustrating various design strategies

Commercial products demonstrating various design strategies

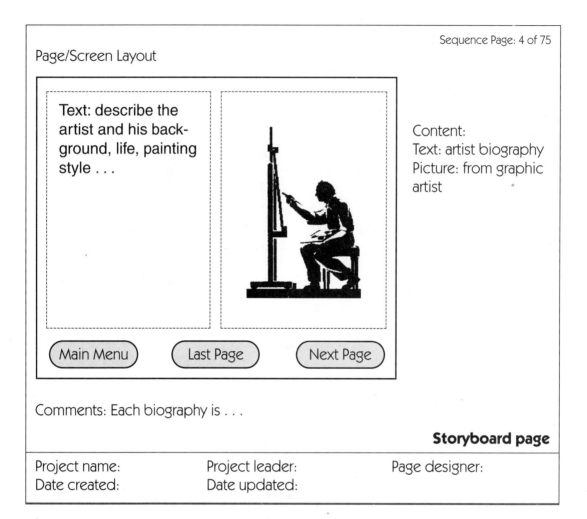

Page/Screen Layout

Text: describe the artist and his background, life, painting style . . .

Content:
Text: artist biography
Picture: from graphic artist

(Main Menu)   (Last Page)   (Next Page)

Comments: Each biography is . . .

Storyboard page

Project name: Project leader: Page designer:
Date created: Date updated:

Figure 8-8 Storyboard page

Product Storyboard

Since most multimedia products are more than a single page, it is necessary to link the pages together to present the entire story or project. The product storyboard is the "big picture" that describes how all of the individual pages or storyboards come together. As with a single page, the complexity of the product and information will determine how large the complete product storyboard will be. Figure 8-9 offers a limited view of a product storyboard with a very limited number of pages. Realistically, a product storyboard could consist of hundreds of pages. There are a number of ways to manage these pages:

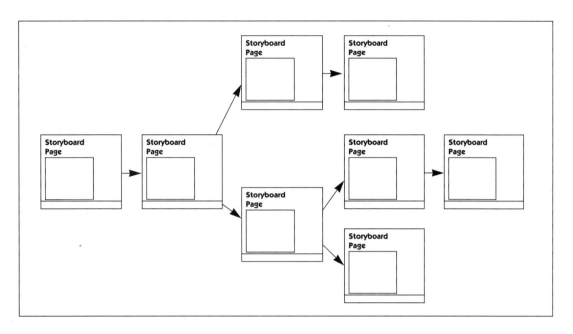

Figure 8-9 Application storyboard

- Use a loose-leaf notebook to contain the pages, organizing groups of pages by menu hierarchies.
- Place the pages on the wall, one following the other for a linear production.
- Place the pages on the wall or a large sheet of paper with links showing relationships between navigational controls and pages.
- Use reference cards correlated to storyboard sheets that can be organized on a larger board.

The Big Picture

A good storyboard, once agreed upon by all parties, is one of the most powerful tools for effectively managing a multimedia production effort. The purpose of the storyboard is to help the designers organize their ideas and contents—in other words set up the big picture. Even with short, simple, linear presentations, a storyboard is an effective technique to use when planning the project so that you do not spend a great deal of time sitting in front of the development software trying to be creative while generating the product.

Storyboards are often used to present initial ideas to users. They tend to be nonthreatening and can easily be modified to build a consensus among end users or the developers. Storyboards often start out as a few scribbled pages and end up as volumes of pages in a notebook or spread out across the wall of a room. In any case, the storyboard enables the designers, content producers, authors, and end users to all agree on what the final product will be.

SUMMARY

Multimedia product design is the platform for content and function that makes a product worthwhile or profitable. At a basic level, multimedia products are made up of pages with menus, content, introductory, and Help information. These pages make up the types of products: non-interactive and interactive. Various organizational strategies such as reference, temporal, geographic, systemic, and/organizational can be applied to structuring the information in a multimedia product. Finally, storyboarding is presented as the tool to put a product together by putting to paper the pages, organizational strategy, and content so that it can be authored into a product.

REVIEW QUESTIONS

1. A page is a basic element of a multimedia product. What are the types and characteristics of a page?

2. Compare and contrast interactive and non-interactive multimedia? What examples are you familiar with?

3. What are the issues involved in developing interactive versus non-interactive multimedia?

4. What strategies are used to organize information for a multimedia product? What examples have you seen of these strategies?

5. Select a sample product and describe the use of two or more organizational strategies to structure the information.

6. What is the benefit of storyboarding?

7. Build a storyboard for a simple product of at least ten pages.

CHAPTER NINE

Authoring Tools

The multimedia authoring tool is the glue that holds the data together in order to inform, educate, or entertain. As with many software tools, there are many variations and capabilities that depend on the needs of the end users and expertise of the developer. Authoring tools offer two basic features: first, the ability to create and edit a product; and second, a presentation scheme for delivering the product. Just as there are a number of comparable programs for word processing and graphics production, there is a large number of tools available on the market for creating multimedia products. Therefore, the selection of an authoring tool based on how it works and what it does can be one of the most critical elements of multimedia product development.

Authoring tools will be discussed from four perspectives:

- Tool—any software package that authors multimedia products. Tools include programming environments such as C++ or BASIC, graphical presentation software, and complex interactive multimedia authoring programs.
- Product (also referred to as an application)—the result of combining content and/or procedures by using a multimedia authoring tool.
- Developer—programmers, multimedia authors, and designers of a multimedia product.
- End user—the customer or viewer of a multimedia product.

OBJECTIVES

After completing this chapter, you should know:

- How multimedia products are created and authored.
- What kinds of multimedia authoring tools you have to choose from.
- How various multimedia authoring tools work.
- How to choose the best tool for a multimedia project.

Check the CD-ROM for fully functional multimedia authoring software and commercial multimedia authoring software demonstrations.

State-of-the-art authoring technologies, commercial multimedia authoring product descriptions, and links to vendors.

Understanding how tools work to build products for end users is essential in developing multimedia products for personal, corporate, or commercial use.

Multimedia Tool Selection

Authoring tools for multimedia range from relatively simple word processor applications to expensive multimedia authoring/delivery environments costing thousands of dollars. The selection of the appropriate tool for product development depends on a number of requirements typically driven by the end user or nature of the product. The criteria for selecting a tool include:

- Function—a complete understanding of how the product will work, especially from the user's point of view.

- Content—nature, volume, format, and types of data that will be incorporated into the product.

- Hardware—platforms expected to run a product; also unique requirements for displaying graphics and playing audio and video.

- Software—unique software requirements such as operating systems or interface to other software applications such as database managers.

- Performance—speed and efficiency expected; critical for gaming applications or fast-paced presentations. Multimedia authoring tools can be resource-intensive, using large amount of memory and disk space, that can result in multimedia products performing poorly on underpowered platforms.

- User Interface—screen layout, data presentation, positioning of controls, and visual and auditory cues for the end user. The user interface depends on the ability of the end user. Therefore, it is critical that the developer understands the end user's skill level. For example, a kiosk in a shopping mall can make no assumptions about the skills (or lack thereof) of its users. Therefore, the user interface must be simple and straightforward. On the other hand, if the end users have significant computer skills or will be extensively trained on the product, then more complex functions and capabilities can be designed into the interface.

- Database—will the product support access to large sets of relatively structured information that need to be queried or browsed by an end user or accessed by a software application?

- Reliability—critical for commercial applications; reliability is essential within the product itself and how the product behaves with other products.

- Maintenance and Update—many multimedia products evolve over time with updates to content and functionality. It is essential that a tool be supported for the lifetime of a product to avoid having to recast into another tool.

Other elements that play a significant role in tool selection include:

- Personnel Skills—many multimedia production shops have personnel skilled on a limited set of tool products. New tools require time spent on training and familiarization that may be beyond the scope of a project. Fortunately, many production houses have a reasonable array of tools at their disposal so that sound choices can be made.

- Cost—the cost of authoring tools range from less than $100 to well over $10,000. Presentation software sometimes requires license fees for mass distribution, which can further drive up the cost. These factors can be critical for commercial product pricing.

- Schedule—the amount of time allocated to develop a project is closely related to personnel skills and cost. A short schedule requires that personnel be familiar and competent with tools, whereas a longer schedule may allow another tool to be selected with ample time to train and/or orient the production team.

Given the needs and/or benefit to define a set of requirements for optimal multimedia tool selection, the reality is that most tools are selected based on personnel skills to

Check the Web site for information on current multimedia authoring technologies.

use a particular tool. From a practical point of view, this is not necessarily a bad situation. For example, a "one time use" product for a briefing would not be an appropriate candidate for a complex authoring tool and it may not be cost effective to hire such skills for this type of application. Furthermore, use of a simple authoring tool with limited features may be very appropriate. Many developers have a "tool box" complete with three or four tools of varying capabilities and, given the features these tools possess, they are often more than adequate for most multimedia products.

Multimedia Tool Features

Common to nearly all multimedia tool platforms is a number of features for encapsulating the content, presenting data, obtaining user input, and controlling the execution of the product. These features include:

- Page
- Controls
- Data
- Execution

In order to establish a common vocabulary for the types of tools discussed later, the following section briefly highlights these features.

Page

The page is an instant in time for a multimedia presentation. It is found in various development environments under various names such as frame, stage, template, or window. The page acts as a container for other features or objects such as text or graphic content or controls such as buttons. It is usually capable of various transitional effects such as fade in/out on the screen. The page may be the palette manager in some applications by controlling the main palette that subordinate objects such as graphics and video depend on for smooth graphics transitions.

Controls

Controls enable the user to interact with the product. Controls may be used to manage or direct sequences of events or

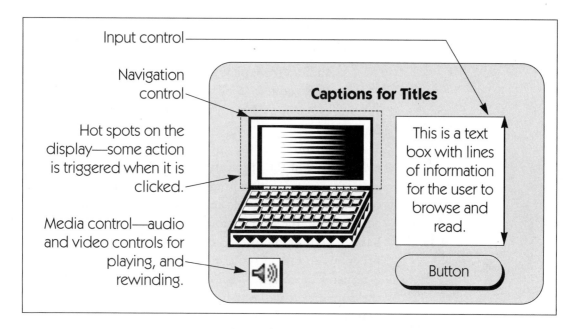

Figure 9-1 Types of controls for multimedia tools

to collect data, or to manage data objects (zooming, video controls). As shown in Figure 9-1, there are three general categories of controls:

1. Navigation: buttons, hot spots, hypertext. Many tools have a fixed set of objects, such as standard gray buttons, that can be modified (size, position, caption). Hot spots are used over graphic objects to allow the user to interact with the data. Hypertext is usually indicated by highlighting through changing the color of the text or underlining it. When the user selects the highlighted text, an action is initiated such as presenting a definition or related information.

2. Input: text, check boxes, radio buttons, combo/list boxes. These are used for collecting information from the user or controlling a sequence of the information presentation. Data collected from these may be directed to a file or other device for storage or transmission.

3. Media Controls: applies to managing or presentation of fonts, graphics, audio, video. Specific features for each of these include:

- Fonts: select type, size, bold, italic
- Graphics: zoom, scroll, mark-up/edit
- Audio/Video: play, stop, pause, rewind, step, volume, zoom

Data

Depending on the authoring tool, data may be stored internally as part of the application program or as external files that are accessed during program execution. Internal storage of data usually means faster data presentation and easier transport of the application and the data. On the other hand, external data storage usually means smaller executable programs and faster program startup. Another advantage of external data storage is that data can be modified to change the application without having to use the authoring tool. Data types include:

- Text: may be stored or accessed as ASCII, RTF, or other encoded format. Two general types of text presentation: captions, small strings for titles, headers, or other information, and text boxes; often with scroll bars, for presenting large volumes of text.

- Graphic: a number of formats are often used; however, bitmaps are the most common to minimize decompression during program operation and provide maximum quality. Graphic file size, combined with reuse or speed requirements (an image needs to be shown in a hurry), will usually determine whether the file is stored in the application or as an external file.

- Audio: number of file formats are supported; may be stored internally depending on size and whether it is reused more than once in the product. Wave files are very common in CD-ROM products followed by AIFF and RIFF audio formats because of the large number of these types of files on the Internet.

- Video: various file formats and compression standards are supported; files are usually stored externally to the product because of the large file sizes. Most authoring tools support a number of digital video types and compression schemes.

- Live audio/video: usually integrated into the product as an external function; requires specialized hardware for compatibility with the tool and product.

- Database: large sets of "structured data" that can be queried or browsed; often stored in commercial database applications. Many authoring tools have built-in interfaces for querying and formatting data for presentation.

On the CD-ROM you will find sample data files for developing your own multimedia projects.

Execution

Execution is the process that controls the presentation and sequencing of the application. It can take on one or more of the following mechanisms:

- Linear sequenced—presentation is controlled by the user; pages are presented via a scrolling or page-advance mechanism.

- Program controlled—code or scripting within the application controls program execution. Execution, in some cases, may be fixed or altered by the user.

- Temporal controlled—presentation is controlled by a timer that initiates events in a predetermined order. The presentation may pause and wait for the user to provide input prior to continuing.

- Interactively controlled—presentation waits for the user to select a function such as pressing a button before continuing. The selection determines the next part of the presentation.

Categories of Authoring Tools

Authoring tools consist of two basic features. First, an authoring facility for creating and editing, and second, a presentation vehicle for delivery. The authoring facility is usually based on a metaphor for organizing information and enabling interactivity. For example, a multimedia authoring tool might use a page layout format to place controls and data; interactivity is based on events created when the user clicks on a button or hypertext. The delivery vehicle enables an end user to view and interact with the product. For our purposes, authoring tools can be divided into four broad categories:

- Simple authoring tools such as word processors and presentation software.

- Programming tools, especially those with graphic user interface design and programming features.

- Simple interactive authoring tools that enable the developer to create applications with data and controls for basic interactivity.

- Complex interactive authoring tools that allow the developers to use programming constructs to provide a fine degree of application control.

Simple Authoring and Delivery Tools

Basic multimedia authoring starts with the premise that a product can be delivered as text on a screen using a simple word processor. Although few would seriously consider this "true" multimedia, the addition of graphics to the text starts to change this viewpoint. Graphical user interface (GUI) based word processors are able to incorporate both text and graphics, and with embedded objects and other methods, are now able to incorporate audio and video. A number of commercial graphics programs are available offering varying levels of interactivity, graphic manipulations, and embedded audio and video capabilities.

- Word Processors: At the most basic level, these tools provide the ability to display text in a variety of font types, sizes, and color. Graphics can be created or imported and placed inline with the text. Content can be augmented with embedded objects for sound and video. Word processors can enable anyone to develop very simple multimedia presentations that are surprisingly effective. Beyond the lack of interactivity, the primary limitation of word processors, as shown in Figure 9-2, is the vertical nature of a software document presentation requiring the end user to scroll

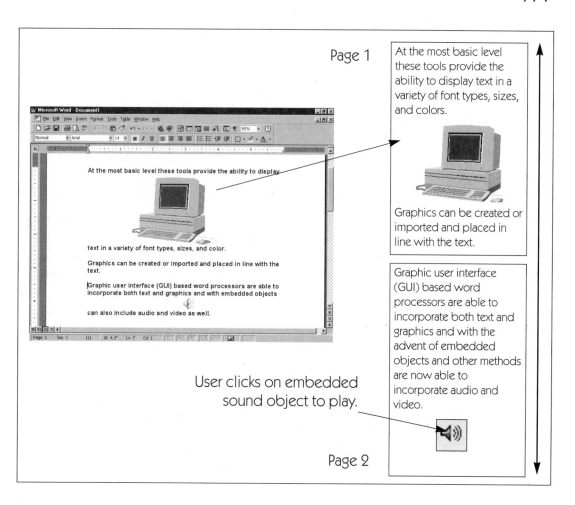

Figure 9-2 **Page layout and operation for word processors as multimedia authoring tools**

through the information. Also, embedded objects for audio and video depend on other system applications to run and may be confusing to the end user if they are unfamiliar with their use.

- Graphics Software: Graphics software ranges from simple to very complex and includes powerful paint programs. Simple paint programs are useful for creating graphics that can be placed in other applications but are very limited for more complex multimedia presentations.

- Presentation Packages: Presentation software packages typically provide a multiple page-based medium for text and graphics with content delivered as a sequen-

Check the CD-ROM for commercial multimedia authoring software demonstrations.

tial series of slides. These slide shows often contain complex text and graphics that can be animated to glide on or off the screen. Although the presentation is linear as shown in Figure 9-3, the end user usually controls the timing. Like the word processors, presentation packages can also contain audio and video as embedded objects.

Programming Languages for Authoring

At a fundamental level, computer programming languages form the basis for all other authoring languages. Therefore, it is conceivable that multimedia products can be developed and delivered using programming tools such as assembly languages, C, or BASIC. As with other programming tools there are advantages and disadvantages to this approach:

The advantages of implementing multimedia products using programming tools include:

- Languages such as C and assembly language tend to be very efficient and fast.
- A fine degree of control over the environment can be achieved enabling complex interaction by the user or the product.
- Easier integration with other software or the operating system to access data or manage resources such as memory.
- No dependency on a third party tool developer.
- The product may be ported to similar compilers on other platforms. This is very true for C and C++.

The disadvantages of implementing multimedia products using programming tools include:

- Multimedia products are complex software programs that display data and support user interaction; they are best implemented as a shell program written in the programming environment. This allows the product of the programming effort to be reused for a number of products. However, the shell is similar in functionality to commercial multimedia authoring

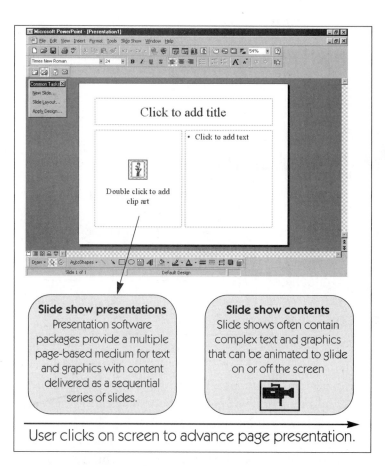

Figure 9-3 Linear nature of a slide show presentation

tools and, in many cases, developers have built their own shells with many of the same features found in commercial shells.

- Programming expertise is required to create and maintain the product.

- Much more code is required making long-term maintenance difficult and correspondingly more expensive.

- The product can become platform-dependent based on the choice of language.

While assembly language yields the most efficient executable code, it is not a common choice for multimedia products because of the resulting code complexity. Assembly language products are often used for high performance, special purpose functions, such as system interface program-

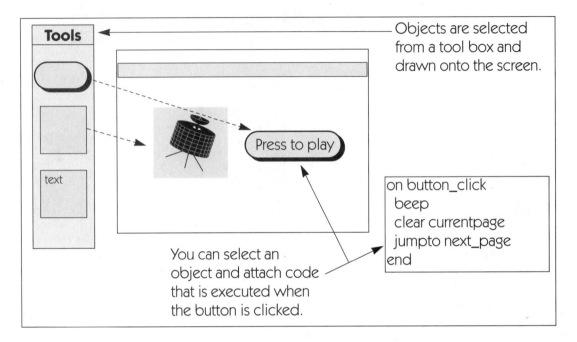

Figure 9-4 Programming using a fourth-generation programming tool

ming to access special purpose devices such as disk drives or analog devices. These assembly language modules are compiled and integrated with applications written in other languages such as C or Pascal.

Third generation tools such as C and Pascal provide a higher level of coding abstraction than assembly language. However, multimedia products tend to be graphic and presentation intensive making interface programming difficult. For example, the placement of a graphic and a button on a screen would require you to know how to use the programming language.

The difficulty in this approach to programming a multimedia product lies in the abstraction of the code to corresponding visual elements such as buttons or other display objects. Errors in written code, such as positioning of a button, may go undetected even through the most rigorous testing due to the interactive complexity of a multimedia product.

Fourth-generation languages with built-in graphical user programming tools have emerged with great success since the early 1990s. Fourth-generation languages, also called 4GLs, are programming environments combined

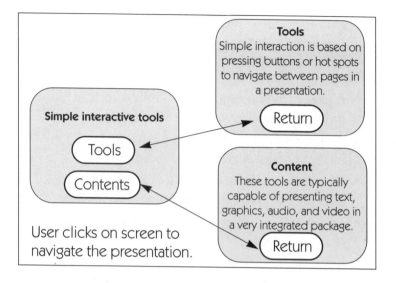

Figure 9-5 Simple interactive authoring tool application

with advanced tools to develop user interfaces and write software code. These tools, as shown in Figure 9-4, enable the developer to place objects such as buttons and image containers on a form using the mouse. Code for actions is directly associated with objects such as buttons based on events such as clicking or passing the mouse over the object.

Fourth-generation programming tools are commonly used for many multimedia products. Furthermore, they are often used to prototype new products or ideas because of their ability to easily integrate other applications like commercial databases or access system level functions such as graphics methods. The prototype can be used to assess the value of a new product or usefulness of a function, which can then be incorporated in a commercial authoring tool for use across a number of products.

Simple Interactive Authoring Tools

Simple interactive authoring tools provide the critical feature of being able to interactively navigate through a product. The qualifier "simple" refers to the fact that only limited interaction is available to the end user. Simple interactive authoring tools are typically capable of presenting text, graphics, audio, and video in a very integrated, easy-to-use environment. Simple interaction, as shown in Figure 9-5, depends on pressing buttons or hot spots to navigate between pages in a presentation.

Most simple interactive authoring tools include the following capabilities for creating and editing products:

- A page metaphor upon which objects such as buttons or image containers are placed.

- A number of objects including buttons, hot spots, image containers, text boxes, and captions.

- Objects for audio and video including integrated controls for play, stop, frame stepping, and rewind.

- The ability to vary font type, size, color, and other characteristics.

- Importing of text and graphic files. Most tools access audio and video files directly when they are played.

- Animation of objects such as moving graphics or buttons across the screen in a predetermined path.

- Assigning event-driven actions to objects such as buttons and hot spots. For example, when clicked the presentation displays a different page or starts an action on the current page.

- Many simple interactive authoring systems generate a delivery module that contains everything a user needs to play the product. In some cases, data files may need to be included as part of the delivered product.

Simple interactive authoring tools offer many advantages. They allow you to create what-you-see-is-what-you-get (WYSIWYG) applications; that is, where you put the data or control is where it appears in the completed product. They are often easy to learn as they build on concepts found in linear-based presentation packages. They provide a number of powerful, interactive features that satisfy most requirements for a product. Furthermore, they tend to be reasonably priced compared to many of the complex tools. The disadvantages lie in the inability to program buttons and hot spots and to integrate with other database applications. In other words, functionality is limited to "what you see is what you get" for the tool.

Simple interactive authoring tools are useful for corporate briefings and presentations where interactivity is used to present complex information sets. They are also useful for small applications or for prototypes of larger more complex applications. Generally, those who are not full-time multimedia developers, but who want to use multimedia presentations, will learn to use these products as the means to quickly create effective and interesting presentations.

Complex Interactive Authoring Tools

Complex interactive authoring tools combine features found in simple interactive tools with programming features. They also offer more complex creation and editing functions that go beyond simple page layout. Advanced tools generally fall into three categories based on how they are used for creation and editing:

1. Page-based layout

2. Temporal-based

3. Icon-based

Advanced authoring tools use many of the same techniques to create or edit applications. These include:

- A page metaphor upon which objects such as buttons or image containers are placed.

- A number of objects including buttons, hot spots, image containers, text boxes, and captions.

- Objects for audio and video including integrated controls for play, stop, video stepping, and rewind.

- The ability to vary font type, size, color, and other characteristics.

- Importing of text, graphic, audio, and video files for storage in the application.

- Assigning event-driven actions to objects such as buttons and hot spots. When clicked the presentation displays a different page or starts an action on the current page.

Programming, the ability to incorporate instructions into an application, is a key feature of advanced authoring tools. Typically, programming is accomplished by attaching code to objects such as buttons, graphics, or other elements of the application. Programming enables the developer to tie in system functions such as reading and writing to files or providing a series of functions when an event such as a button click occurs. For example, when a button is pressed, a text box is filled with data stored in a text file. This could be accomplished as follows:

```
On button_click
    open "textfile.txt" for input
    do while not end-of-file
            get line_of_text
            textstuff = textstuff + line_of_text
    loop
    close file
    put textstuff into textobject
end
```

The programming language usually contains the following capabilities:

- Declaration of variables based on a variety of data types such as integers, real numbers, strings, and arrays.
- Math and data functions to set and modify variables.
- Control structures for decision support such as if/then, select; and loop structures such as for/next, do/loop, and while.

Additionally, some systems will allow you to create functions and subroutines for repetitive activities.

Page-Based Authoring

Page-based authoring tools are very similar to the previously mentioned simple interactive page-based tools. The major difference lies in the ability to add **scripting** to various objects in the environment. Scripting, as shown in Figure 9-6, usually handles specialized functions such as graphic transitions, jumping to pages according to programmed conditions (using an IF-THEN or SELECT statement), timing, and other complex presentation metaphors.

Page-based authoring systems with programming capability are a natural transition from those tools without the

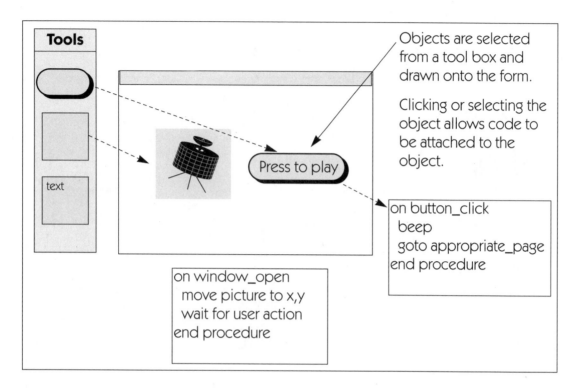

Tools

text

Press to play

Objects are selected from a tool box and drawn onto the form.

Clicking or selecting the object allows code to be attached to the object.

on button_click
  beep
  goto appropriate_page
end procedure

on window_open
  move picture to x,y
  wait for user action
end procedure

programming features. In fact, if you have conventional programming experience in C, Pascal, or BASIC, these tools are very easy to learn and apply.

Figure 9-6 Attaching scripts to page layout software

Temporal-Based Authoring

Temporal or time-based authoring systems provide the developer with the ability to develop an application that runs like a movie. Frames are created with objects that are sequentially played or halted to allow user input to change the flow of the program. Temporal-based systems include the following features:

- A page or display frame on which objects such as buttons, text, or audio/video data are placed. Objects may have code attached for special processes such as jumping to a different page or loading a data file.

- An array for keeping track of pages/frames including their sequence, timing, and content.

- A controller for playing, stopping, stepping, or rewinding a presentation.

Code embedded in button to start the sequence.

Complex Tools

Start

Frame 1

Tools
Tools allow for the
creation and editing
of a presentation.

Frame 2

Content
Provide tools for creating
and editing presentations.
Content is placed on a
series of pages.

Return

Frame 3

Array for managing system			
	Frame 1	**Frame 2**	**Frame 3**
Action	wait for button press	wait to proceed	wait for button
Time		10 seconds	
Content	caption = "..."	caption = ""	caption = ""
Content	button	text	text
Content	picture		button

Figure 9-7 Components of a temporal-based authoring tool

Figure 9-7 provides an overview of the system components for a temporal-based system.

The primary advantage of temporal-based tools is the ability to create complex animation and transitions. A sequence of pages or frames played in rapid succession, for example, one per $\frac{1}{30}$ of a second, will create a movie-like effect. Unfortunately, if a single page within a sequence is flawed, for example, a picture is out of place, it can be difficult to isolate the flawed page from the larger set of good pages.

Icon-Based Authoring

Icon-based authoring enables complex interaction and layering of multimedia products. This is accomplished by let-

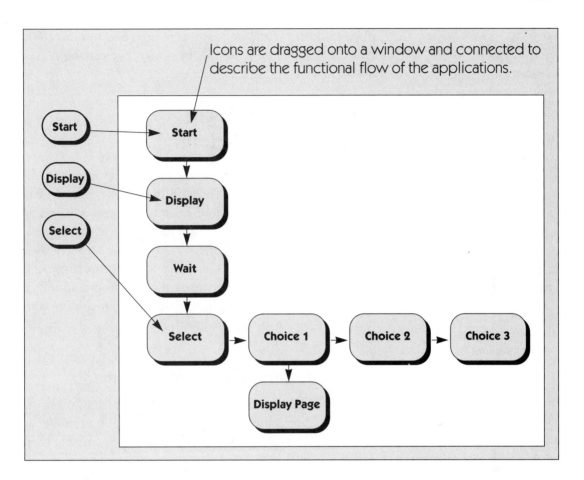

Figure 9-8 Icon-based authoring

ting the author select objects, timing, and sequencing "de-vices" in the form of icons and placing them on a layout screen where they are interconnected as shown in Figure 9-8. As icons are selected and linked, screens can be defined with text, graphic, buttons, and other objects. As with the other advanced authoring tools, code or script can be attached to objects such as buttons to facilitate user interaction or pro-gram execution. One of the major advantages of this ap-proach is the ability to graphically design complex interactions for repetitive applications. Templates can be constructed that are "filled in" by the developer and reused within the application or across similar applications. Tem-plates often contain data and controls that are common to a number of pages within the application. For example, a tem-

Check the CD-ROM for multimedia authoring product demonstrations.

The Web site contains links to commercial multimedia authoring tool vendors.

plate could contain a standard page title, background color, and positioning of recurring buttons, that can be reused over and over during development.

Selecting the Right Authoring Paradigm

Given the types of authoring paradigms that exist and the corresponding number of tools on the market, how do you select the best tool for the job? Selection should be based on a number of issues including the requirements for the project, which tools are available, available skills to use a tool, and cross-platform needs. Generally, more complex projects require tools with more features; that is, programming or complex interactive tools. Simpler projects, including prototypes are often best served with lower cost, easier to use presentation packages.

Internal Expertise versus Requirements

In many instances, corporate staffs develop significant expertise in using a limited number of tools over a number of projects. When new projects are proposed, the existing tools are often applied as opposed to selecting a tool based on the specific needs of the project. Each approach, as shown in Table 9-1 has a number of trade-offs.

In many cases, given the advanced capabilities of some multimedia authoring tools, selection based on corporate expertise will not significantly impact a new project. However, it is critical that if this approach is taken, a thorough requirements study is performed to completely understand the unique features for the application. This ensures that the internal product will handle those needs or, if it cannot, it can be acknowledged that certain requirements will not be met for this particular project.

Prototyping with Different Tools

A novel approach for taking advantage of the large number of tools that are available is to apply different tools to the devel-

Advantage	Disadvantage
Tool Selection is Based on Product Requirements	
If requirements are thorough, tool selection can be mapped to functionality of tools.	If requirements not complete, tool selection could be erroneous.
Opportunity to look at a number of tools providing broader expertise for development team.	Development team may have to learn the selected tool requiring additional development time.
Allows emerging technologies to be applied to applications.	
Tool Selection is Based on Internal Corporate Expertise	
Development team is already trained on the tool.	Tendency to force fit old habits and techniques into a new project.
May have reusable templates or prototype code, which could reduce cost.	Limits exploration of new ideas or approaches.
	Available tools may be outmoded or commercial availability is waning.

Table 9-1. Trade-off Criteria for Selection of Multimedia Authoring Tools.

opment process. Simple tools may be used to describe initial concepts and storyboards with advanced tools used for the final product. This approach is useful because non-technical personnel can present ideas on the computer without requiring them to have advanced multimedia authoring skills.

Cross-Platform Tools and Products

A number of tools support more than one platform or operating system. This is accomplished by either:
- Authoring on one platform and creating a program that runs on the other, or
- Authoring on either platform with the source code that is interchangeable.

	Programming	Word processor, presentation	Page-based	Time-based	Icon-based
Easy and quick to develop; effective for prototyping; easy to update and modify		●			
Greater flexibility for development (= better interface for end user)	●		●	●	●
Extensive training and experience required for developers	●		●	●	●
Programming features included			●	●	●
Cost (1=lowest, 5=highest)	1	2	3	4	5

Figure 9-9 Tool selection and use issues

There are however some issues to be considered when authoring for cross-platforms:

- Data formats are not always directly transportable between different platforms. Two versions of a graphic or video may be necessary to be displayed or presented in both environments. For example, bitmap graphic file formats may be different between various platforms.
- System level functions that are used on one platform may not exist on the other platform. This usually requires some degree of specialized programming to build compatible features.
- Performance may vary from platform to platform impacting things such as program loading or video playback.

The important thing to remember whenever cross-platform development is undertaken is that testing the

Application/Product	Choice for Tool
Informal briefing or presentation	Simple authoring tool—presentation package
Formal briefing—needs to look classy	Simple interactive authoring tool
Standalone kiosk	Complex interactive authoring tool—page based
Database application, or needs to communicate with a database	Programming language
Complex training application	Complex interactive authoring tool—icon based
Entertainment product	Complex interactive authoring tool—temporal based
Interactive game	Complex interactive authoring tool—temporal based

Table 9-2 Correlation of Applications to Selection of Authoring Tools

product must be accomplished on all platforms to ensure compatibility and stability.

One Strategy for Selecting a Tool

When selecting a tool, there are a number of factors to consider including functionality, cost, availability, training, and maintenance. Figure 9-9 provides an overview of comparing some of these factors across the different types of tools. There is some degree of correlation between tool cost, complexity, and training required to use the tool as shown in Table 9-2.

This table is not meant to imply that these are the best choices, but rather likely choices based on what is needed for the product versus what features are available in various tools. The best choice should always be based on a careful assessment of the product requirements, which tools are available, and how well they satisfy the requirements.

SUMMARY

Multimedia authoring tools are the high technology easel and paint for the creation of multimedia products. In this chapter we discussed the features and types of multimedia

Current tools and technologies from commercial multimedia authoring tool vendors

authoring tools that are available. Selection of authoring tools depends on criteria including function, content, hardware, software, and performance. In order to select a tool, you must understand its features—the page, controls, data, and execution. Finally, you must select a type of authoring environment ranging from programming tools to complex interactive development.

These tools apply primarily to the CD-ROM and workstation environment. The advent of high-speed telecommunications and the Internet is promising to change the way we look at authoring tools for multimedia products. Chapter 10 will look at some of the things that will drive these tools and the future of multimedia authoring.

REVIEW QUESTIONS

1. Describe the basic characteristics or requirements for selecting a multimedia authoring tool.

2. What requirements for selecting a multimedia authoring tool are most critical? Which are least critical?

3. What are the basic features of multimedia authoring tools?

4. Compare and contrast the various types of multimedia authoring tools? For what multimedia products would you select one type of tool over another?

5. What experiences have you had with multimedia authoring tools? Which types? What features did you find to be the most or least useful?

6. If you were assigned to develop a multimedia training product for a large corporate sales management system, how would you select a tool for implementing the product? What would functionality, availability, cost, and prior expertise play in your tool selection?

CHAPTER TEN

Multimedia and the Internet

The delivery of multimedia content in a timely fashion is the heart of this chapter. Conventional multimedia delivery via CD-ROM has a rather lengthy delay to market which can make or break the success of a product. For example, assume you finish the content for a multimedia product today, how long will it take to deliver it via commercial channels to a typical end user at home? If the content is prepared and placed on a master CD-ROM, it could take a couple of weeks to generate 10,000 copies. Packaging and distributing the CD-ROM copies could easily take a month. Delivering the product to stores, setting up displays, purchasing the product, and bringing it home could easily add another couple of weeks. Bear in mind that this scenario reflects the minimum amount of time and the maximum effort required to get the product to the end user. The reality is that the delivery time is three to six months.

What is needed is a faster means by which multimedia content can be delivered. The key is to find a method of delivery that is universally accepted, easy to use, and reliable. Fortunately, arising from a United States Department of Defense initiative started in 1969 to link United States government agencies and universities, the answer is already upon us—the Internet. The Internet offers a developer the ability to publish up-to-the-moment information. This chapter discusses both the issues and the surrounding technologies utilized for publishing multimedia on the Internet. It is not intended to be a tutorial on the inner workings and operations of the Internet and related technologies, but

OBJECTIVES

After completing this chapter, you should know:

- What the Internet is.
- What technology issues are involved in developing and delivering multimedia on the Internet.
- How World Wide Web pages are put together.
- How the Internet can be used to deliver content for multimedia products.

rather a discussion on how multimedia and the Internet can come together to deliver timely products—products that will change the way we look at information delivery for both multimedia and the Internet.

The Internet

The Internet is a combination of telecommunications and computer technologies and services that enables information to be shared around the world. Understanding the technology is critical for realizing the potential and the limitations of computers and how they share information. The services, such as file transfer, Telnet, and hypertext transport protocol, provide the tools to move information for multimedia products. Together, Internet-based telecommunications and computers provide the basis to communicate, manage, and distribute information to users throughout the world.

Client/Server Technology

The Internet, as shown in Figure 10-1, is a vast network of computers around the world that share data and information. The key to Internet operation is the Client/Server Model in which multiple computers, called clients, can simultaneously access a single server. The server runs applications for functions such as mail services and file transfer that are accessed by the remote clients. The basic hardware that comprises the Internet includes:

- Workstation (Client): A single computer for a local end user that is uniquely identified on the Internet; that is, it has an address that can be used to link that workstation with other computers. Besides an operating system and application software, each workstation has specialized network software that enables communication with the entire network.

- **Local area network (LAN):** Two or more workstations that are physically connected by a server. Although LANs are typically located within a single

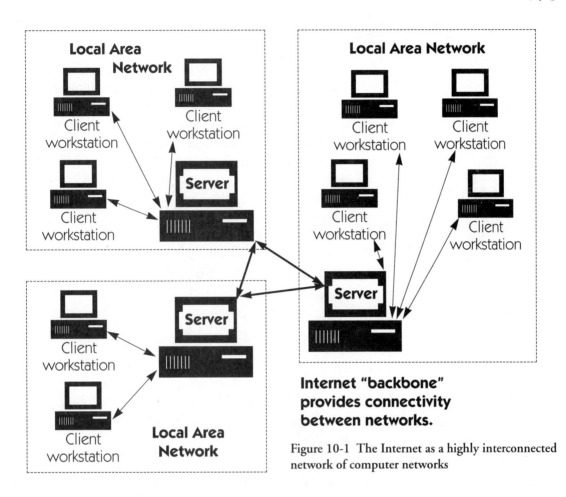

Figure 10-1 The Internet as a highly interconnected network of computer networks

facility or location, they can also be spread across a localized region. Each LAN has a unique identifier or name that sets it apart from other LANs.

- Server: Central point of a LAN, the server provides connectivity and services between the workstations. Services include centralized storage and mail and printing capabilities. The server is also responsible for communication with other LANs.

- Internet "Backbone": Provides connectivity and services between servers. Depends on high-speed communication lines to rapidly move information and commands between servers and, ultimately, individual workstations.

Communications Protocol

The Internet is based on a communications protocol called the "transmission control protocol/Internet protocol," or TCP/IP for short. TCP/IP is a computer communications protocol based on a standard established by the **International Standards Organization (ISO)** called the Open System Interconnection (OSI) Reference Model. The OSI architecture, shown in Figure 10-2, defines a seven-layer set of processes for computers to share information across a network. The seven layers consist of:

1. Physical—physical connection between electrical components.

2. Data Link—data is "packaged" for shipment across the physical network.

3. Network—manages the logical connection between computers including addressing and routing.

4. Transport—guarantees that transfer of information occurs correctly.

5. Session—provides rules to manage the establishment and termination of data streams between workstations in a network.

6. Presentation—transforms data, including format and syntax, into a format appropriate for the receiving and sending devices.

7. Application—provides a window for workstation applications to gain access to the services provided by the network.

Workstations communicate with other workstations across a network by "moving" data from the application layer to the physical layer to send information and from the physical layer to the application layer to receive information. As you can see, the layers are a combination of hardware and software that implement the functions described in the OSI protocol.

TCP/IP is the backbone of the Internet. It implements the OSI protocol in a way that enables different kinds of computers in different kinds of networks to communicate in

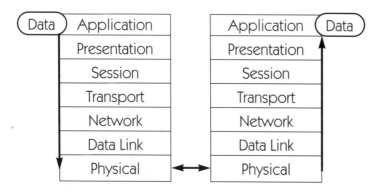

Figure 10-2 The OSI architecture in which data is moved through layers on each workstation and then physically routed to its destination

a standardized fashion. Each computer that uses TCP/IP has a unique identifier or address based on 12 digits. This address makes every machine on the Internet unique so that it can be easily and quickly located to transmit or receive data.

Internet Addressing

The Internet carries addressing one step further by assigning unique "English-like" names to networks of computers making it easier to link computers and share information between them. This naming system, called the Domain Name System (DNS), was developed in 1983 to uniformly assign names and addresses to computers that access the Internet. The DNS actually operates on three layers:

1. Top-Level Domains—describe categories of use: commercial (com), educational (edu), United States federal government (gov), international (int), United States military (mil), network providers (net), miscellaneous and non-government organizations (org), and ISO 3166 List of Countries (2 letter codes such as "jp" for Japan).

2. Second-Level Domains—describe specific users and/organizations within the first-level domains such as "whitehouse" for the White House and commercial company names like "microsoft" and "ibm".

3. Third and subsequent domain layers—provide greater specificity for a particular organization down to a specific name or user. Two or more layers may be needed to identify a particular computer or user.

Domain names are separated by periods (called "dots") with individual users or computers separated by the "@" sign. The following are examples of user and third-layer domain names on the Internet:

- johnsmith@companyname.com—"johnsmith" is a particular person at "companyname" which is a commercial organization ("com").
- tomjones@compnet.bignet.collegename.edu— "tomjones" is a particular user on a network called "compnet" which is part of a larger network called "bignet" at a university ("collegename"), an educational institution ("edu").

Internet Functions

Although there is a great deal of technology involved in making the Internet work, the bottom line is that it provides a variety of useful functions such as:

- File transfer between computers
- Mail services, including simple mail transfer and post office functions
- The ability to access and work on a computer from a remote computer
- Real time text messaging or chat
- Document sharing

File transfer and mail services provide useful functions for distributing information between computers and networks. File transfer enables a user to locate and access a remote computer in order to upload and download files. Mail services are used to disseminate messages and information to a large number of users through a easy-to-use, predominantly text-based service. Telnet enables remote logging and interaction with computers allowing access to their programs and information. Real time messaging or chat is popular because it encourages interaction between people in remote locations.

Origin of the World Wide Web

Although mail service, file transfer, and telnet provide powerful services, it is its ability to share documents that made the Internet one of the the fastest growing technologies of the 1990s. Document sharing, through the Internet "hypertext transfer protocol" (HTTP), is responsible for the World Wide Web, WWW or, simply, the Web. HTTP enables a computer to store multimedia documents that can be accessed by remote users. The documents are based on the HyperText Markup Language (HTML), which enables presentation of multimedia content including text, graphics, audio, and video, and allows the document to be linked to other documents in both local and remote servers.

The Web is becoming a popular place to find content for multimedia projects and to publish multimedia information products. Some typical Web products include:

- Personal information including resumes and autobiographies
- Educational research and publishing projects for K-12 and university-level students
- Reference materials, including manuscripts, reports, and technical data from commercial, public, and government institutions
- Corporate marketing and promotional materials

The Web has actually changed the landscape of personal, corporate, and commercial publishing by providing a medium that is accessible to everyone, anywhere in the world, 24 hours a day.

HTML and Web Authoring

The World Wide Web started out in 1990 as a hypertext-based information system. Although Web documents were primarily text with links to other documents, they have undergone considerable evolution in capability since the early 1990s to include graphics, audio, and video. This evolution was driven by a number of factors:

- Dramatic increase in access and use of the World Wide Web for presenting and communicating information.
- Significant increases in communications bandwidth: that is, the amount of information that can be trans-

Descriptions of advanced Internet and Web technologies

Resources and vendors for Internet-based multimedia technologies

mitted in a fixed period of time. For example, modem speeds have increased from 300 bits per second to 28,800 bits per second enabling much more data to be transmitted.

- Improvements and enhancements in HTML viewer software.
- End users' increased expectations in terms of Web content.
- Developers' increased experience in creating Web content.

Increases in communications speed have resulted in Web pages adding graphic, audio, and video content with an expectation that end users will be able to download larger data files within a reasonable period of time. HTML viewer software advancements have offered more efficient presentation of HTML encoded content as well as adding new data formats and software tools for presenting information. Finally, increased expectations of the users coupled with the increased experience of developers means that more elaborate content is developed, thereby pushing the communications bandwidth and viewer software capabilities.

A Brief Overview of HTML

Web pages are based on the Internet Hypertext Transfer Protocol or HTTP, which allows information to be shared between two computers. HTTP enables an exchange of information between a server and client based on the following sequence of events as shown in Figure 10-3:

1. A client workstation establishes a connection with a server computer.
2. The client computer requests a document from the server.
3. The server sends the document to the client.
4. The connection is closed between the client and the server.

Once HTTP has transmitted the document to the client computer, the client computer presents the document

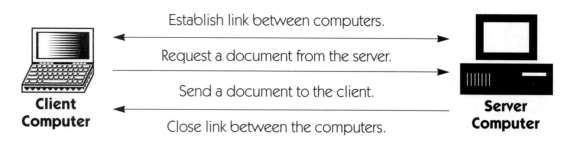

Figure 10-3 Using HTTP to communicate Web pages

to the user. The document is composed using the hypertext markup language or HTML, which is a document encoding scheme that combines text, images, and links to other documents. In Chapter 4, we discussed tagging documents, HTML does the same thing. HTML is based on tags that ascribe how data is formatted for presentation by the Web viewer software. Tags are contained by angle brackets, "<" and ">". Formatted content is preceded by a tag and followed by a tag that starts with a "/" to indicate the end of the tagged information. Typical tags for HTML include:

- <HTML>document </HTML> —these tags surround all of the content contained within a Web document.

- <HEAD>header information </HEAD> —first part of a Web document, contains document setup and document identification.

- <BODY>document content </BODY> —second part of a document, contains the content that will be viewed by the end user.

- <H1>Document Title </H1>, <Hn></Hn> —these tags surround titles and captions; "n" ranges from 1 to 6 for largest to smallest bolded, font sizes. For example, <H1>Main Title</H1> would be presented in the largest, bolded, font size.

- <IMG SRC="IMAGE.GIF"> —places an image (in a separate file with a name of: IMAGE.GIF) in-line with previous content.

- <A HREF="FILENAME.HTM">Anchor description</A>—places a hyperlink to a local or remote document.

Examples of HTML
pages

Resources for late-
breaking information on
Web technology

Tags can tag other tagged content creating complex presentations such as a "text centering" tag surrounding a "header tag" surrounding the actual header content:

<H1>This is the title</H1r>

These additional tags would move the left justified header to the center of the display page. HTML standards describing tags and their functions have been established by international agreements with variations and additions being added by commercial developers of HTML viewers. Figure 10-4 shows what a typical HTTP encoded document using the previously described tags would look like and how the content would be presented in a Web page viewer or browser.

Web Page Browsers

Web page viewers, also known as browsers, are software tools that are capable of presenting HTML encoded content. Web browsers act as HTTP clients by connecting to a server, requesting a specific document, and displaying that document. If the document is HTML-encoded, the browser formats the content accordingly. Web browsers have a number of user and document display features that make them very popular, such as the ability to:

- Track and locally store recently viewed documents for faster subsequent access
- Keep track of addresses to favorite documents (bookmarks)
- Limit display of document to text-only which will speed their display

Any user using a Web browser can enter the address of the document in order to retrieve and view it. The address, called a Uniform Resource Locator or URL, identifies a specific Web server and document and allows the end user to retrieve and load the document into the browser. A URL takes the form of

www.domain_name.domain_category/server_path/filename

resulting in, for example,

www.companyname.com/busplan.html

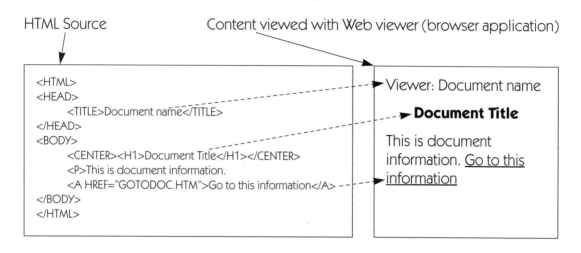

Figure 10-4 Web document source and presentation

Browsers can also be used to view documents on a local computer by identifying and accessing the path and filename of the document.

Hyperlinks, identified by HTML tags in Web documents, can be selected and the browser will display the appropriate document. Hyperlinks usually appear as text that is meaningful to the user rather than as a URL. For example, the user would read:

Click here for more information

while the embedded hyperlink is encoded as:

http://www.companyname.com/moreinfo.html

When the user clicks on the hyperlink text, the browser will access, load, and display the document specified by the URL.

Most browsers can implement bookmarks that keep track of previously viewed document addresses or URLs for the end user. This makes it easier for end users to quickly recall favorite documents in future sessions. In addition to keeping track of URL addresses, many Web browsers will cache or store documents by loading them onto the local hard disk. This allows pages to be retrieved from the local disk if they are reaccessed within a short period of time.

In addition to the ability to view HTML-encoded documents, many browsers enable users to access, download, and view ASCII text, graphics, audio, and video as separate files. These capabilities make the Web browser a useful tool for viewing multimedia content.

Web Page Development

Web page development is similar to other multimedia product development except that on the Web, a developer is able to rapidly update content. Figure 10-5 provides an overview of the Web publishing process:

- Preparation of source data including text, graphics, audio, and video. Supporting files for graphics, audio, and video are maintained separately from the Web document and are linked by URL addresses usually on the local server, although links can be made to remote servers to access multimedia content.

- An HTML editor that assists the user in generating tagged content. They range from simple text editors to WYSIWYG editors. Text editors require the developer to manually insert HTML tags into the document. WYSIWYG, or what-you-see-is-what-you-get, editors are similar to word processors—their key advantage is that they automatically embed HTML tags in the document.

- Transfer of Web documents and supporting files to the HTTP server. This is usually accomplished via File Transfer services between the client and the server.

One important thing to remember when creating Web pages and basic HTML-encoded documents is that although the author determines what a header or text is and where a picture falls in line with other content, the Web browser determines font selection and the specifics of layout based on the size of the browser window. This applies to basic HTML-encoded documents; however, there are techniques that will enable presentation formatting that is completely managed by the author and HTML document. Some of these techniques involve advanced HTML tags that specify font styles and document formatting.

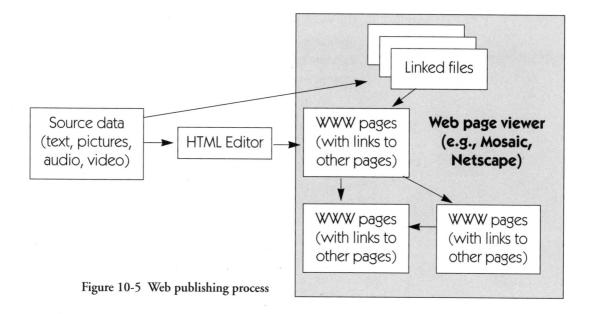

Figure 10-5 Web publishing process

Multimedia Considerations for the Internet

The key advantage of the Internet is that it provides a widely used and uniform communications medium to link users together to access or deliver multimedia information. However, when using the Internet as a vehicle for multimedia delivery, one must be aware of the following considerations:

- Bandwidth: Determines how much information can be transmitted efficiently. The bandwidth depends primarily on the type of data being transmitted. Text has the lowest bandwidth requirement at one byte per character with graphics, audio, and video requiring significant increases in bandwidth to move information.

- Application: The type of software used for delivery of the information. The Internet has spawned the development of a number of facilities such as mail services, file transfer, and the Web to store and deliver information. Traditional multimedia products can benefit from the real time nature of data delivery across the

Internet. For example, a multimedia product could update its content by embedding Web documents into the application and/or downloading files such as graphics from the server.

Bandwidth Considerations

Bandwidth is based on how much information can be transmitted in a given period of time. Bandwidth is dependent on the function of communication devices and the transmission medium. Data, within the computer, moves at rates of 10 to 50 megabits per second—often using parallel connections within the computer. Unfortunately, outside of the computer, transmission speeds are much slower because they rely on much slower, serial-based local area networks and commercial telephone lines for linking vast numbers of users from home-based computers to Internet service providers. Therefore, typical Internet connectivity speed ranges from:

- Low-end (modem): 14,400 and 28,800 bits per second (1800 to 3600 bytes per second under ideal conditions). Modem speeds for analog commercial phone systems are limited to the speeds well below 50,000 bits per second.

- Mid-range (ISDN or Integrated Services Digital Network): 56,000 bits per second (digital transmission). May include a second channel for 112,000 bits per second.

- High-end (Ethernet network): 10,000,000 bits per second (1,250,000 bytes per second under ideal conditions). Most commonly found in office-based network systems. The speed of the Internet connection is also dependent on the number of users and how the networks are configured.

Before we proceed any further, let us review different multimedia data and their average file size. The typical file sizes for various forms of multimedia data are shown in Table 10-1. Table 10-1 shows how big files are depending on

Data Type	Size	Typical Sample
Text	1 character (ASCII) = 1 byte	Page of text (100 characters/line, 30 lines) = 3000 bytes
Pictures	1 pixel, 256 colors = 1 byte	Full screen (640 x 480 pixels), 256 color bitmap = 330,000 bytes
	1 pixel, 16,000,000 colors = 3 bytes	Compressed graphic format = 75,000 to 200,000 bytes (depends on type, detail, colors)
Audio	Voice quality, 1 second, 8 bit capture rate, 11KHz = 11,000 bytes	Voice, one minute = 600,000 bytes
	CD-Audio (music) quality, 1 second, 16 bit capture, 44KHz, stereo = 176,000 bytes	Music, one minute = 10.5 megabytes
Video	1 second, 24 bit color, 30 frames per second, 320 x 240 pixels = 6.9 megabytes	One minute, uncompressed = 414 megabytes
	Compressed video, 1 second = 200,000 bytes	One minute, compressed = 10–15 megabytes (depends on compression scheme)

Table 10-1 Multimedia Data Types and File Sizes

the data. Now consider the size of files in relation to transmission speeds given in Table 10-2.

It should be noted that the transmission speeds listed in Table 10-2 for a modem or Ethernet network are ideal and do not account for actual conditions such as telephone transmission limitations, number of users sharing a network, and physical hardware limitations. Actual network performance would probably be 5 to 20 times less than the values shown in the chart. For example, downloading a full-screen bitmap picture would take up to five minutes via a modem operating at 28,800 bits per second. Table 10-3 gives more realistic expectations of data transmission for network systems.

Data Type/Sample		Time to Transmit…(assumes ideal conditions)	
Data Type	Typical Sample (from Table 10-1)	At 28,800 bits/second (3600 bytes/second)	At 10 megabits/second (1.25 megabytes/second)
Text	Page of text (100 characters/line, 30 lines) = 3000 bytes	1 second	.0002 seconds
Pictures	Full screen (640 x 480 pixels), 256 color bitmap = 330,000 bytes	91 seconds	0.26 seconds
	Compressed graphic format = 75,000 to 200,000 bytes (depends on type, detail, colors)	Compressed file, 20 to 55 seconds	Compressed file, .06 to .13 seconds
Audio	Voice, one minute = 600,000 bytes	Voice, 166 seconds	Voice, .5 seconds
	Music, one minute = 10.5 megabytes	Music, 3000 seconds (50 minutes)	Music, 8.4 seconds
Video	One minute, uncompressed = 414 megabytes	Uncompressed, 115,000 seconds (1.9 hours)	Uncompressed, 330 seconds (5.5 minutes)
	One minute, compressed = 10–15 megabytes (depends on compression scheme)	Compressed, 2777 seconds (46 minutes)	Compressed, 8 seconds

Table 10-2 Transmission Time for Multimedia Data

Given these more realistic transmission speeds for networks and the obviously slower rates for low-end modem based transmission, it is easy to see how multimedia data transmission is useful for text and graphics, but poses limitations for real time transmission of audio and video.

Application Considerations

Standalone multimedia products depend on local content that is only as current as when it was placed on the delivery medium. Internet applications have the advantage of having content available for delivery as soon as the file is posted on a server. This advantage is significant for developers who rely on real time delivery of information. For example, imagine

Data Type/Sample		Network Time to Transmit (adjusted for realistic performance, factor=10X)
Data Type	Typical Sample (from previous chart)	At 10 megabits/second (125,000 bytes/second)
Text	Page of text (100 characters/line, 30 lines) = 3000 bytes	.002 seconds
Pictures	Full screen (640 x 480 pixels), 256 color bitmap = 330,000 bytes	2.6 seconds
	Compressed graphic format = 75,000 to 200,000 bytes (depends on type, detail, colors)	Compressed file—.6 to 1.3 seconds
Audio	Voice, one minute = 600,000 bytes	Voice, 5 seconds
	Music, one minute = 10.5 megabytes	Music, 84 seconds
Video	One minute, uncompressed = 414 megabytes	Uncompressed, 3300 seconds (50.5 minutes)
	One minute, compressed = 10–15 megabytes (depends on compression scheme)	Compressed, 80 seconds

Table 10-3 Realistic Data Transmission Speeds for Network Systems

a multimedia current-events magazine delivered on a CD-ROM. This example is relatively unique by CD-ROM multimedia standards because it assumes a very deliberate effort to speed up production and delivery. However, even with a maximum effort, by the time a CD-ROM is mastered and distributed the information could be days and even weeks old. However, an Internet-based current-events magazine could forever be just minutes old. The downside to publishing multimedia on the Internet is that content bandwidth must be considered, an issue that is not as critical for a CD-ROM delivery vehicle. For example, if high-quality digital video is desired that requires megabytes of storage, delivery time via the Internet could be prohibitive—at least until very fast connections are available for most users.

There are two basic models for authoring and delivering multimedia using Internet technology:

1. Applications-based—programming or multimedia authoring tools with built-in Internet access (file transfer, web, mail, etc.). For example, a traditional CD-ROM-

based application that is able to present very current content by downloading from an Internet-based resource.

2. Browser-based—software for presenting Web files including associated functions such as hyperlinking and in-line data presentation (for graphics, audio, and video files). This is the classic model for delivering Web-based documents using World Wide Web browser applications.

A variation of these two is a combined approach in which applications call Internet browsers to present Internet-based content. For example, a CD-ROM application might start a Web browser application and have it access and load a document that is remotely maintained.

Application-based Internet Access

The "applications-based" Internet access approach includes standard features we discussed in Chapter 9 on multimedia authoring tools and augments it with Internet-specific features to:

- Access to "real time" multimedia data (text, pictures, audio, and video). This content complements or replaces existing application content that is originally delivered on a CD-ROM.
- Dynamic reorganization of content; that is, downloading new instructions to change the layout, presentation, and even the look-and-feel of a multimedia product.

Internet-specific capabilities expand on these functions with:

- Access to download new files for a multimedia presentation. Multimedia content can be transparently replaced in multimedia products without the user ever knowing.
- Mail access to access or distribute new information. End users of multimedia products can be notified of updates to their applications or new applications that might be of interest.

- Web page presentation to take advantage of hypertext markup language (HTML) document encoding.

Browser-based Multimedia Delivery

Browser-based or Web-based information multimedia delivery technology offers a number of advantages over local data delivery via CD-ROM or other high density storage media:

- Access to server-based resources such as applications and databases. Information on servers can be continuously updated and distributed to large numbers of end users.

- Add-on software modules that enhance the behavior or performance of the browser. Browser software applications can be given new functionality such as the ability to present multimedia animation files, with add-on software modules.

- Programming and scripting languages that add functionality to the browser. Web documents, with embedded scripts, enable programmed functions to be added to browser applications.

In the next section, we will discuss issues for designing Web pages based on the unique features of HTML document encoding.

Design Considerations for Web Pages

Beyond the bandwidth and application considerations one must weigh the pros and cons of designing Web documents for Internet browser software. Web documents, also called pages, are primarily a text delivery medium. HTML includes tags to provide a variety of formatting options for text including header formatting, text bolding, and placing text in lists and tables. Graphics, audio, and video can also be added to Web pages providing a range of multimedia options. Finally, hyperlinking enables documents to be linked to other documents to organize information. Organizing content for

Web pages involves a number of issues that go beyond HTML tags and into the operation of the Web browser itself. This section will address a number of these issues.

Due to the nature of browser software, Web page layout is driven by the browser as much as it is by the actual HTML document encoding. Browser settings such as window size, font size, and background and foreground colors can be set by the user, which will in turn impact the layout of a presentation. This lack of "fine control" is often frustrating to Web page developers but, "fine control" may be a feature of emerging standards for HTML and newer browsers. Specific font selection, graphic positioning, and background and text colors are some of the features added in newer versions of the HTML specification that in the past, developers had no control over. One can bet that other even more advanced features will be added in future generations of HTML standards.

Unlike traditional multimedia products which come complete with software that is responsible for displaying content, Web documents are shipped as text files rather than executable software. Web documents depend on the browser to recognize and present their HTML content. Users with "older" browsers are unable to see the new features, or worse, the new features create havoc with layout in older browsers. The bottom line for Web page developers is to be careful when implementing advanced features in their Web documents that might end up being presented by older browser applications.

Due to a certain level of freedom with layout and relative ease of distribution, the risk of creating "bad" Web pages increases. Bad is, of course, a relative term. At a minimum it means that content is incomplete or poorly organized. It can also mean that aesthetics are overlooked, resulting in too much color, too little color, or too much clutter.

Because of the real time nature of Web page publishing, many Web pages are "currently under construction" which causes annoyance to end users. Too often, developers are in such a hurry to reach a market that they develop a large number of pages (called Web sites) with limited resources and time or with little content, resulting in holes in the product. These "holes" are currently accepted due to the newness of Web technology, but as it becomes more pervasive, end users will be less tolerant of incomplete Web content.

Accessing Content on the Internet

The Internet has opened up new access to content that offers great potential for new developers. Public domain and many commercial Web sites offer text, graphics, audio, and video for the taking to develop content and applications. However, pirating of data is also possible by downloading data files or content that is owned by other parties.

There are basically two approaches for accessing on-line content to be used in local presentations:

1. Web page viewers and browsers that allow copying or downloading of files. Many Web browsers will allow you to download content such as graphics or video and store on the browser computer.

2. Internet file transfer software to access remote sites to upload and download files. File transfer software can be used to access remote sites and download data files.

Browser-based access is useful because much of the content is already organized making it easier to find content. You only need to access a Web page and copy text directly or download an image or in-line data file. File transfer allows direct access to remote data servers that can potentially access more resources depending on the user knowing where the file server is.

SUMMARY

This chapter describes the evolution of multimedia technology from locally installed applications to multimedia presentations that access content on remote servers that many end users can access. The Internet is based on client/server technology in which local computers can access applications and data on remote computers called servers. These remote applications include mail services, file transfer, and the World Wide Web. The World Wide Web enables multimedia documents that include text, graphics, audio, and video that can be accessed by Web browsers designed to understand and present HTML-encoded content. Although Web technology has achieved widespread use, many of the lessons for multimedia design also apply to this rapidly evolving technology.

REVIEW QUESTIONS

1. How does the Internet change the way in which multimedia is produced and delivered?

2. What are the advantages and disadvantages of the client/server model for managing and delivering information?

3. What are the advantages and disadvantages of HTML as a means to present multimedia?

4. How critical are standards for HTML?

5. How does communications bandwidth affect the selection and format of multimedia content?

6. What are the differences in how multimedia is authored for Web pages versus other conventional multimedia authoring tools?

7. What factors have influenced Web page development?

CHAPTER ELEVEN

The Multimedia Development Team

Successful multimedia development, more than most other types of software development efforts, requires a unique combination of skills and talents. As with software development, you need people who can think logically and apply structure to things that often appear unstructured. You also need people who are wildly creative and who can turn the dullest subjects into things that will rivet the attention of both children and adults. Finally, you need someone to pull it all together, someone to take responsibility for planning, follow-up, and disaster management. If you are lucky enough to get all of these people, you may be smart enough to build the best multimedia product of all time. More realistically, though, you will find good people to help you build a project that you will all be proud of.

Team Approach

The complexity of multimedia projects can range from simple one-to-two page quick efforts to hundreds of megabytes worth of information requiring months to complete. Regardless of the size or effort, there are basically two approaches to consider when building multimedia projects: one-person approach and team approach.

The one-person approach is self-explanatory. You are chief cook and bottle washer for the entire effort. Writing, editing, graphics, audio and video production, authoring, testing, packaging, and delivery are the sole responsibility of

OBJECTIVES

After completing this chapter, you should know:

- How to staff a multimedia project.
- What the roles and functions are of the different members of a multimedia team.
- What the critical issues are to consider for the successful development of a multimedia project.

215

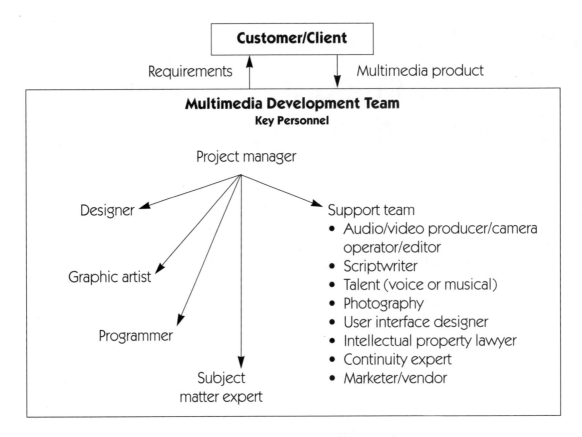

**Figure 11-1 Multimedia
development team**

one person. The team approach, as shown in Figure 11-1,
consists of two groups of people:

1. Key personnel: Primary personnel involved in the lifes-
   pan of the project. Personnel include the project manager, the customer or client, designer, subject matter
   expert, programmer, and graphic artist.

2. Support personnel: Provide limited or specialized functions contributing to the completion of the project and
   includes the editor, audio/video editor, talent, photographer, and user interface designer.

The multimedia team consists of a number of individuals who bring specialized skills and talents to a project. In
some cases, there may be a single person who takes on multiple roles or many people who share one role. Titles will
vary from organization to organization and project to project. Some people will call themselves graphic artists, while

others will call themselves digital artists or computer graphics specialists. A project manager may be a project leader in some organizations, while the customer may be a specific person or agency or even a segment of the population, such as teenagers looking to buy a new and exciting multimedia game system.

Sponsor/Client/Customer

Multimedia products do not simply happen; someone has to want them or be willing to fund the production for future buyers. That is the role of the sponsor or client. Their involvement ranges from simple investor with a hands-off attitude and an expectation of financial gain on product sales to a party with extensive hands-on involvement and who is part of the development team. Sponsors or clients provide the motivation to do a project. They provide the political, financial, and logistical support required to make a product happen. For example, a corporate marketing department allocates part of its budget to develop a multimedia-based product sales presentation to advertise new products.

The sponsors of a multimedia product must be able to:

- Understand the business needs of the product—why is it being developed and who will benefit from it if not the sponsor directly?

- Have and use authority to approve contracts and agreements to set up a development project.

- Provide approval and acceptance of the product. This means the sponsor must be able to understand content and technical issues that will make the product a success.

- Have knowledge of the end users. Specifically, will the completed product meet the expectations of end users?

Multimedia sponsors are as varied as types of businesses and/organizations. They may be:

- Corporate organizations that have their internal "multimedia team" build marketing and technical presentations

- Venture capitalists who invest in a product for the market with payback from commercial product sales
- Training departments who develop classroom lecture or student-based interactive training systems

The key issues that concern the clients are their ability to fund a project and then to ensure that the project is delivered on time, within budget, and of acceptable quality. To do so means that a development team must be assembled with the appropriate management and technical skills to complete the project. The following sections describe the key personnel and the abilities they require to develop a multimedia product.

Project Manager

The project manager is responsible for overseeing and/orchestrating a multimedia development project. At a minimum, the project manager should have knowledge of all aspects of the technology needed for successful multimedia development. Ideally, the project manager should also have very good interpersonal skills enabling him or her to assemble and manage a diverse team of developers.

There are many skills required of a project manager, and not all managers will have a complete skill set. However, the following characteristics will give you some idea of the talents and abilities sought after in multimedia project managers:

- Planner—devises a cost-effective method for developing a project within the constraints of schedule and budget.
- Team builder—assembles a team of developers and then motivates them to work together.
- Organizer—structures the project by applying the best mix of talent to meet the demands of a schedule as well as technical requirements.
- Negotiator—balances the needs of the project, the customer, and the development team.
- Flexible and assertive coach—knows how to get the best out of his or her team. This is accomplished by bending or taking control when necessary to get the job done.

- Work flow manager—schedules activities and tasks in a logical sequence.
- Salesperson—understands the needs of the customer and delivers the solution on time and within budget.
- Problem solver—identifies and rectifies technical and management difficulties.
- Committed to quality—ensures that multimedia products are error free.
- Goal setter—identifies specific tasks and sees to it that they are completed on time.
- Has a creative and analytical mind—has these complimentary abilities that promote novel approaches to solve complex problems.
- Possesses a positive attitude—believes a complex project, despite the things that can go wrong, will get done, no matter what.
- Listener—hears out customers, team members, management, and everyone who has a say in the project, and then makes decision that gets the job done.
- Multi-tasker—juggles a number of things at once, including technical, management, schedule, and budget issues. Possessing this skill is critical and may be the most important skill of all.

Multimedia project managers are not born, they are made. They mature as managers of other types of projects and learn the technology along the way. Or they may grow up as members of a multimedia team and learn to manage through formal schooling or from experience. If there were a formula to follow for creating a good project manager, it would contain:

- Hands-on experience as a multimedia project team member
- Formal training in management with emphasis in planning, scheduling, and budgeting
- An opportunity to understudy a project manager to watch and learn

- A great deal of patience, a desire for hard work, and a little bit of luck

Project Designer

The multimedia project designer is responsible for the technical aspects of a project. He or she usually determines product content, functionality, organization, capability, structure, user interface, navigation, and technical requirements. Next to the project manager, the designer has the second most critical role in the successful completion of a multimedia project. While the manager is responsible for getting the project done, the designer is responsible for doing it right.

Project designers need a variety of skills including:

- Experience with interactive media. The experience should include extensive knowledge about a number of products and tools.
- Creativity in both technical and artistic domains.
- A willingness to accept change.
- Attention for detail.
- Willingness to be a team player.
- Good oral and written communication skills.
- Ability to create structure for themselves and other team members.
- Ability to work well under pressure.
- Skills to use multimedia authoring tools.

Project designers, like project managers, often grow into their jobs and then, later, into project management roles. The designer often matures into the role by combining skills he or she developed as a programmer or graphic artist. They may have become designers through a formal education in computer science or interactive digital design. In other cases, designers may come from fields such as education, communication, or marketing. In these situations, designers need to acquire technical and managerial skills to support a multimedia development project.

The project designer is responsible for developing storyboards. The designer, as shown in Figure 11-2, works di-

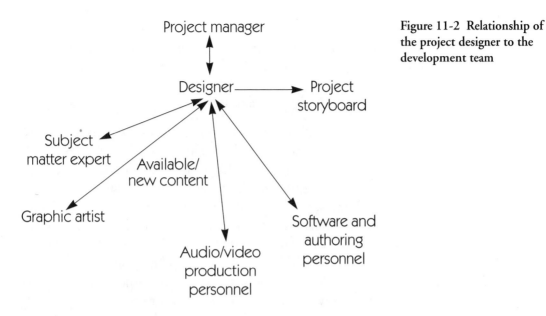

Figure 11-2 Relationship of the project designer to the development team

rectly with a number of key people to develop storyboards that are based on the subject matter available and/or newly developed content. Key to the designer's role is capturing the organization of the product from the subject matter experts. By working closely with the graphics and audio/video production specialists a designer will define what content is available and what content is needed to complete the project. For example, a designer might review hours of videotape from historical archives to select a few minutes of content for a multimedia project. The designer will also work with the software and authoring staff to understand how tools can be applied to present the content. They will report to the program manager for project definition, scheduling, and resource management. As you can see, the project designer possibly plays the most critical and pivotal role not only in designing the operation but also determining the content of a multimedia product.

Other Key Personnel

The key personnel will have extensive involvement with product development. Their efforts often will span a significant portion of the effort and will have a direct impact on defining the requirements of the project, storyboarding, content development, software development, product testing, and product delivery.

Subject Matter Expert

The subject matter expert is someone who is extremely knowledgeable about the subject domain. The expert will meet with and advise the project designer on the nature and/organization of the product content. For example, a well-known expert on the stock market and investing would be essential to develop a multimedia product called "How to Get Rich Playing the Stock Market." In some cases, multiple experts may be called upon to fill in details or to describe a larger domain of subject matter. The expert is also responsible for validating and evaluating the content of the product, which may be accomplished in stages at both the storyboard and authored product levels. The single most important skill of the subject matter expert is knowledge of the subject that is unimpeachable.

Programmer

The programmer prepares software code and/or works with development tools to integrate content and procedures into a multimedia product. The programmer will combine a project storyboard and content to build a product by using a multimedia software authoring package. Critical skills for the programmer to possess include analysis, ability to work with software and authoring tools, and the ability to be a team player. Programmers often have skills in a number of authoring environments and/or programming languages and may be involved in early phases of a project including advising the designer and project manager on the pros and cons of various authoring environments.

Editor

The editor reviews, evaluates, and edits content at both the completed product and detailed levels of text, sound, graphics, and video. The editor is responsible for checking content for continuity, accuracy, and technical correctness including spelling, grammar, and coloring. The editor may provide some level of error checking and correction or resubmit content or software to the appropriate staff for correction. Editors often have backgrounds in graphic arts, copywriting, and other production areas prior to becoming editors.

Copywriter

The copywriter prepares and reviews text content for a multimedia project. The copywriter will often work closely with a subject matter expert and designer to capture critical information and a style of delivery for the application. A copywriter needs to understand the vocabulary constraints of the audience. For example, a children's application requires a level of writing specific to the skills and age of the target audience. Furthermore, when working with the subject matter expert, the copywriter must be able to translate complex ideas into words or stories that are appropriate to the audience. Copywriters prepare text using word processors and usually work closely with graphic artists and programmers to incorporate content into the graphics or the application.

Graphic Artist

Graphic artists are responsible for creating the visual appearance of an application through the creation and editing of graphics. While the designer may determine how an application will function, the graphic artist is responsible for content and visual impact of screens and displays. One or more graphic artists may be involved in a project and expected to complete a range of tasks including creating original art, scanning and editing hard copy materials, creating icons and simple graphic elements, and sifting through clip art and graphic archives in the hope of finding suitable graphics. Although small or simple projects can often survive without the talents of a graphic artist, larger and important projects will most certainly depend on the skills of a talented artist.

Graphic artists come with varied backgrounds but usually have extensive experience with one or more commercial graphic software packages, intimate familiarity with graphic capturing systems (scanners and video digitizers), and of course, artistic skills and abilities. In some projects, graphic artists may have very specialized skills in creating artistic still images, preparation of photographed images, or in developing complex animation. It may be necessary to hire a number of different graphic artists to complete the various types of tasks required in a project.

Support Team

The support team, which is just as important as the primary team, usually has less involvement on a per-person-per-hour basis over the life of the project. A support team is needed to develop one or more pieces of a project or to ensure the overall project is completed. Their efforts typically focus on content production, legal, and marketing issues.

- Audio/Video Producer or Camera Operator/Editor— Professional staff with skills in audio and film production are found in many multimedia projects. Depending on the needs of the project, a project might require a staff to work from beginning to end in producing high-quality audio and video products. For example, a product based on interviews with experts in a particular field could require months to prepare scripts of questions, set up and film interviews, and convert film to digital format.

- Scriptwriter—Works with the Audio/Video staff and the project designer to develop dialogue for voice and screen productions.

- Talent—Professional actors and voice talent who work with the Audio/Video staff to produce analog and digital video content.

- Photographer—Traditional film-based media skills. The photographer works closely with the graphic artist to identify subjects, types of shots, and even the type of film and shutter speed to use.

- Internet Support Specialist—Responsible for technical and operational management of Web sites and Internet-related services. The Internet support specialist will have experience in configuring and maintaining a server and/or knowledge of producing and supporting Web-based content.

- User Interface Designer—Responsible for designing how the various application screens will work. The user interface designer has extensive computer application design experience and works closely with the project designer and graphic artist to achieve the desired working perspective of an application.

- Intellectual Property Lawyer—Provides legal guidance for acquiring content (text, graphics, audio, and video) in the product.

- Continuity Expert—Works with the designer to ensure that a large project appears as a seamless product. A continuity expert is used if a product is related to other or similar products or to ensure consistency across a product line.

- Marketer/vendor/support—Responsible for selling the product. An effective multimedia product salesperson may need a combination of talents and skills involved in the packaging, distribution, sales, and support of an application or product.

- Post-sales support—Responsible for supporting end users of commercial products. They have relatively in-depth knowledge of the product and very good customer support skills.

The makeup of the support team will vary from project to project. Depending on the audio and video production needs, integration of a product line, or the amount and type of public domain and purchased content, the support staff will be assembled and called upon to support the product development accordingly.

Descriptions of skills
found in multimedia
production
organizations

Resources for locating
multimedia developers

Marketing and Sales Support

If the product is a commercial product, then this aspect of the support staff can be the most critical element of the entire process. They may be consulted in the beginning of a project to help define the product and they must certainly be included in the end because they are expected to sell it to the public. Selection of the marketing and sales support staff is usually based on two considerations: first, their familiarity with the product, and second, their sales, marketing, and support skills.

The marketing and sales staff must be able to understand the technical aspects of the product in terms of why and how it was developed. They must be able to answer questions about hardware and operating system requirements as well as how the product will be used. For example, if it is an educational product, a prospective buyer might ask how the student will use it to learn, how it fits into the curriculum, and what learning outcomes should be expected. These are all questions that an informed salesperson will be able to answer.

Assembling a Multimedia Production Team

Assembling a multimedia production team can be a tricky proposition for even the most experienced project manager. The key things to remember are:

- There is no such thing as a "standard" project team. Each project will have unique requirements based on the content and how it works. This will determine the mix of team members.

- Assemble the project designer and key personnel early in the project. Key personnel will make or break a project. Getting them on board early will clarify the vision of the project and build a cohesive team that will work together.

- Schedule the support team to be used as needed so that time and money are not wasted. Having expensive resources sitting around and waiting for direction is a waste of resources and will ultimately reduce the number of things that can be accomplished within a limited budget.

- Get the best talent you can afford. Hiring people who have multiple overlapping skills can save time and money. Be careful however, because too many skills can mean a person is only "average" in some or all of the skills and yield less than acceptable results. A talented graphic artist is often worth the extra money since he or she will mostly create a unique look and feel for the product.

Sizing a Multimedia Team

There is no such thing as the perfect size of a team for a multimedia development project. In fact, multimedia teams are often measured by how many people are involved in the project. Larger project teams are required for applications that feature animation, digital video, games, and special effects. On the other hand, smaller products such as ten or twelve page marketing presentations may require one or two people. Generally speaking, if you look at most multimedia projects, they can be categorized as:

- Small or one person efforts
- Average sized teams of five to fifteen developers
- Large teams of developers, typically twenty or more

Obviously, the scale of the projects is directly related to the size of the team required. Furthermore, project size may also be dictated by how fast a project needs to be completed. A shorter schedule may require more resources concurrently, while a longer schedule can accommodate resources that are spread out and a smaller staff. The following sections describe the three types of efforts in terms of who makes up these teams for developing multimedia projects.

Small or One Person Project

A small or one person project is like assembling a camping tent—it is assembled in a couple of hours by one person in which the product is prefabricated and has a limited life span. One-person projects tend to very small efforts and typically include:

- Briefings or marketing presentations
- Small prototype and demonstration projects
- Small training modules

Projects created by one person are usually short duration efforts with a very limited set of goals. As you can imagine, these projects are very limited in scope and may, in the case of corporate briefings, be used once and discarded. In many cases the one-person project will depend on other sources for text copy, graphics, audio, and video components usually in the form of clip art or reusable material from other projects.

The advantage of a one-person effort is that a single vision for a product is realized, which coincidentally, is also the primary disadvantage. The one-person project is limited to the individual's skills—he or she may be very good at developing graphics and much weaker at authoring software, or have great technical skills but poor storyboarding and writing skills. The one-person project is best suited for those with a broad range of skills, with particular emphasis in design and multimedia programming, as they can always find clip art and similar resources to fill the content of a project.

Average Team Project

The average team project is like building a house. It is assembled in a couple of months by a dedicated team of generalists (carpenters) and specialists (plumbers and electricians) in which the product is long lived. The average team project consists of anywhere from five to fifteen developers. In most cases, the entire staff is not all on board at the same time but rather called in as needed to complete specific phases of a project. The members of an "average" project are:

- Project manager
- Designer
- Programmer
- Graphic artist
- Content staff (writer, editor, continuity)
- Support staff (audio/video production, photographer, talent)

At any given time there will be at least four or five people directly involved in the project with other members used to provide product design guidance, development and editorial content expertise, and review of the project.

A project of even average size requires significant planning to ensure product deadlines can be met while still maintaining a reasonable budget. It is common that a number of projects may share resources or that resources are contracted outside of the local organization. For example, a firm that develops educational products may develop a series of them in parallel with all of the projects, sharing graphic arts and authoring personnel. Finally, although external resources may be short lived, and not even part of the organization, they should be viewed as significant contributors to the project team.

Big Project

The big project is like constructing an office building. It is assembled over many months, sometimes even years, by a very large team of workers with various levels of management and large numbers of generalists and specialists. The final product is a very large, long-lived structure. The big project may include a staff of dozens or even hundreds of developers. From a functional viewpoint, the project members fill the same roles as the average project but there are often large numbers of individuals with similar skills that contribute to the overall project. For example, a single graphic artist may have a number of collaborators who develop content. This is particularly true of projects with extensive amounts of animation and digital video.

Project management for the big project is critical. It is essential that detailed planning and scheduling be performed to manage personnel and budgets. It is common for big projects to have additional support staff for planning and tracking resources including:

- Detailed management support including budgeting and scheduling specialists.
- Contract specialists who set up and manage subcontracts with vendors for services, equipment, and *ad hoc* project support.
- Equipment support specialists for coordinating computers, copiers, scanners, and plant resources.
- Quality assurance and configuration management personnel.
- Administrative support for documentation.
- Marketing and support staff for pre-sales, distribution planning, and initial product support.

Big projects often last many months and sometimes even years. Large commercial products take extensive animation efforts or very large data sets. Animation projects require dozens of artists who generate original and edited material that must be cross-checked for consistency and quality on a daily basis. Depending on the raw volume of data, data configuration specialists may be required to keep track of what data is available, what version it is currently in, and where it is stored.

Examples of big projects are not that common. The shear cost of a big project in technology-based multimedia markets that are rapidly changing makes corporate investment in such a project very difficult to obtain. However, there are examples of multiple products that are developed simultaneously by a single firm that are similar to big projects. These efforts often involve the same application delivery environment that can be used for cookbooks, health guides, encyclopedias, and a number of other reference-type products. These efforts often involve large sets of data that must be carefully managed by large staffs.

SUMMARY

This chapter provides the foundation for assembling the team that will build a multimedia product. The sponsor or client, project manager, and designer are complemented by a key staff of subject matter experts, graphic artists, copywriters, programmers, and editors. A support team that varies from project to project includes audio/video specialists, scriptwriters, talent, and lawyers. A good marketing and sales team for commercial products can make the difference in the success or failure of a product. Finally, we discussed the various scales of multimedia projects from one or two person efforts to very large teams of developers.

REVIEW QUESTIONS

1. What skills and abilities do you possess or have you seen in others that characterize an effective project manager or designer in a multimedia project?

2. Given the various functional roles discussed in this chapter, what skills are common? What skills tend to be unique?

3. What criteria would you use to locate and hire a subcontractor to provide support services, such as a photographer, for a multimedia product effort?

4. What kind of experience would you expect to find in a senior member of an "average" or "big" project?

CHAPTER TWELVE

The Multimedia Development Process

Multimedia application development is part science and part art. In Chapter 11 we discussed the multimedia development team and the roles the various individuals play in developing a multimedia product. This chapter focuses on the actual tasks involved and the relationships of those tasks in creating a product. The key to this is understanding how creative and technical processes can be combined effectively and efficiently. Five sample multimedia projects are used to describe how the development process is applied. Finally, we will discuss costing issues and how they can be dealt with to make multimedia development affordable.

Multimedia Development Issues

Multimedia development is unique from most software development efforts. Developers of traditional software applications usually focus on the operational function of the software, while multimedia developers must also consider the content of the application. Therefore, multimedia product development is based on a number of factors that determine the success of the development effort and the product itself.

- Concept Validity: Is this an idea that will sell? This is especially true for commercial products, which are often faced with fickle customers and competing products. For example, game products are constantly

OBJECTIVES

After completing this chapter, you should know:

- What technical issues are involved in developing a multimedia project.

- What the advantages are of a structured approach to developing a multimedia product.

- What the phases or steps are for developing a multimedia product.

- How different types of multimedia products are impacted by the development process.

- What techniques can be used to estimate the cost of a multimedia project.

competing for attention by a youth-oriented market that is always looking for new challenges and is often bored very quickly. For other applications, the questions include: will the product fill a previously empty void, improve efficiency, or maximize profit?

- Technology Dependence: Is this product state-of-the-art? Multimedia products are often based on the current or next generation technology tools that may not be completely tested and ready for commercial use. This leads to questions such as: can the end users run it on their computers and do we have developers who can take advantage of the technology?

- Availability of Content: Even with a great concept and suitable technology, the most important question is: can we fill the disk with relevant and useful content? There are two sides to this issue: a product for the sake of content and not enough content for a product. For example, early multimedia developers, in a rush to get any kind of product on the market, created shovelware applications. Shovelware applications consist of bulk collections of text, pictures, audio, and video that are often of poor quality, or worse, barely related to the product concept. As product concepts evolve, the more common problems are the time and cost to generate new, high-quality content.

- Tool Selection: Closely related to the technology dependence issue is the need to pick the best tool for the job. Many multimedia productions have been based on tools that were not selected because they were best for the application but because the developers knew how to use them. Many multimedia development shops have staff members that are trained on a particular authoring tool and when they are posed with a new project, will work to make the project fit within the capabilities of their tool as opposed to finding a better tool.

- Authoring: If done correctly, authoring is the simplest job in development. The author merely uses the authoring tool to integrate the content and provide functionality. Unfortunately, a number of productions fall into the trap of developing functionality during the authoring process. This can result in schedule overruns and significant deviations from the original concept.

- Testing: There can never be enough product testing. Unfortunately, many projects leave little time for extensive testing depending instead on error-free authoring. Testing should be scheduled as a significant effort within the product development cycle.

- Delivery and Product Support: Unlike film and other static media products, when a multimedia product leaves the developer, it must be packaged, delivered, and installed on end users' computers. Even simple business applications are often prepared and then delivered on someone else's machine. Developers often leave delivery and support as an afterthought, putting too much dependence on the skills of end users to install and use the product. Even a very good application will generate questions such as: Is my machine powerful enough or how do I start the program? It is critical for the developer to stay on top of the product long after it has been shipped.

- Maintenance: Multimedia products are updated for a number of reasons, including performance improvement, error corrections, and new content availability. Developers should consider extensibility in the product design to ensure that updates are easy and cost effective to make.

These are some of the major issues to keep in mind when developing multimedia products. Multimedia development is best done with a structured process that covers all the issues just discussed. Throughout this chapter we will discuss a structured approach to product development based on a set of processes that manage the schedule, resources, and costs to create a useful product.

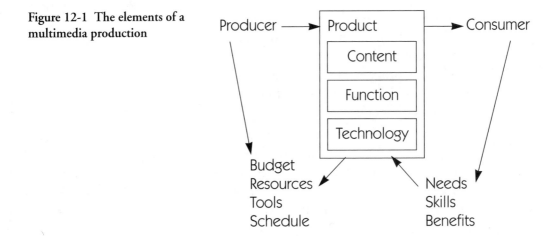

Figure 12-1 The elements of a multimedia production

The Multimedia Project

Every multimedia project, like any other project, depends on three things: a consumer, a producer, and a product. Each has a role in the project, as shown in Figure 12-1, that will directly impact the potential for success. These roles are:

1. Producer: The creator of the product. The producer is responsible for managing the budget, resources, tools, and schedule. The personnel described in Chapter 11 will use the processes described here to build a product.

2. Consumer (also known users or sponsor/client): The agency who will buy the product. They define the need, skills of the end users, and benefit of the product. The consumer may be an agency that the producer deals with directly or a market segment that will purchase the product through intermediate retailers.

3. Product: The multimedia product that will be developed, including:

   • Content: Usually in the form of text, pictures, audio, and video.

   • Function: How the product works

   • Technology: What the product needs to work and which tools will be used to develop it

In Chapter 11 you learned about the various roles of the development team and consumer in producing multimedia products. These roles depend on the type of product under development and a strategy for using the team to develop the product. Given the specific roles described for managers, designers, programmers, and the other members, it is easy to imagine how chaos could ensue if there was no plan to organize the talents of the various personnel. Furthermore, as content and software are developed for the product, a series of steps must be put in place to ensure that all elements come together efficiently within a specified budget and time schedule.

A multimedia product can be developed in one of two ways:

1. A haphazard, free-form approach often taken by single person projects that are not defined very well.

2. A structured approach required for complex and thorough product development.

The haphazard approach is not recommended for obvious reasons, including fiscal responsibility and a desire to complete a project on time in order to reach a competitive commercial market. It is mentioned here to point out that it is a method that is used, and that it is not a particularly effective or economic model to follow.

It is essential that the producer understand the consumers—what they need, what their skills are, and how they will benefit from the product. Then, given the budget, resources, tools, and schedule, they must develop a product. A haphazard approach usually means that no one is paying attention to how long it is taking or how much is spent in developing the product. Worse, they may not be paying attention to making sure the product is what the consumer needs, will be able to use, or will benefit from.

This leaves the structured approach. The structured approach to multimedia product development means that specifically defined steps or processes are used to produce an application. Each step is assigned a specific amount of time and resources to be accomplished. Each step is preceded and/or followed by steps that ensure that the consumer's requirements for the product are met. In this fashion, the producer can determine, or at least realistically estimate, how much will be spent in advance. A structured development effort means that creative processes can be managed to produce the best possible product.

Structured Multimedia Development

Multimedia application development requires structured and methodical processes to seamlessly blend the technology with the creative process. A successful multimedia product can follow many of the same production processes as:

- Book publishing
- Music production
- Film and video production
- Software development

Each of these processes requires the development of content and functionality that is similar to that found in a multimedia product. In fact, multimedia development shares many common characteristics such as:

- Thorough understanding of the market and consumers, especially for commercial products that will be sold to the public
- Planning and managing resources, activity timing, scheduling, and budgeting
- Understanding the product requirements
- A story or message that the application can present
- Content in the form of text, pictures, audio, and video
- Development of the product using appropriate multimedia tools
- Testing to determine if the product works
- Delivery, marketing, and support of the product

Although there are a number of models that have been developed, Figure 12-2 provides a model based on the points we just discussed.

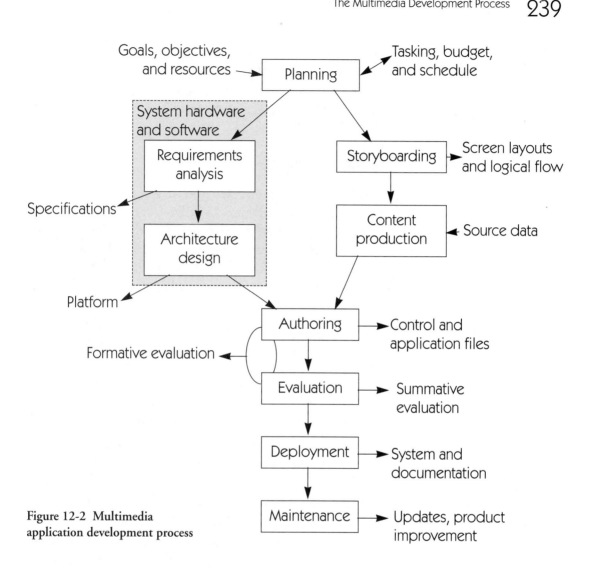

Figure 12-2 Multimedia application development process

Multimedia Project Timing

Although Figure 12-2 presents a linear series of events for product development, some of the steps occur in tandem, which raises the issue of project timing. Generally speaking, there are activities that occur in parallel because they are practical and cost effective. However, there are always inter-related activities that will influence each other even though they appear in separate paths. For example, the selection of a multimedia authoring tool may influence the type of content that can be presented. Although the selection of the tool and content occur in separate paths, they have a significant influence on each other. It is necessary for the developers to be aware of how these activities impact each other and to make allowances in both scheduling and the completion of the activities themselves.

Sample Projects

The following sections describe in greater detail the elements presented in Figure 12-2. Each section also provides examples of projects that will help you to understand how structured process leads to both functional and creative multimedia productions. Five sample projects have been chosen to help you understand how to apply a structured process to multimedia development:

1. Commercial—a for-profit game product which will be developed, produced, and sold through commercial retail outlets to the general public.

2. Kiosk—a standalone information delivery system located in a shopping mall. The kiosk will be periodically updated to include new information.

3. Briefing—a corporate technical sales presentation that will be used a limited number of times and discarded.

4. Trainer—a computer-based training system for individuals to learn new processes and products. The trainer is a **just-in-time (JIT)** training system, which means it is designed to provide employee training at the time when they need it to get a particular job done.

5. Web site—a multimedia-based World Wide Web application for providing information to corporate customers.

As we discuss each of the stages of multimedia development, specific comments will be provided that are not necessarily comprehensive for any one project but provide useful commentary on things for developers to consider.

Planning

Planning is the beginning phase of multimedia development and can make the difference in project success and failure.

Planning attempts to answer questions about what a product is before it is created. Planning will:

- Define the project and product goal. What is the vision of the product? Who will use it? How will they benefit from it?

- Specify project objectives. What resources are available and how will they contribute to product creation? How long do we have to complete the project?

- Scope the technical issues and content. What content, hardware, and software are to be used to develop the product?

- Allocate personnel and equipment resources. Who and what will be involved in design, programming, testing, and deployment of the product?

- Determine schedule. How long will each major activity require? How long will subtasks take to complete? What are the critical dependencies between activities and tasks?

- Establish and monitor a project budget. Most projects have a limited budget and must be managed within that budget.

- Manage risks that would hinder the project. What can go wrong and how can those problems be prevented or managed to have minimal impact on the development of the product?

The answers to these questions are detailed in a planning document that is both fixed and dynamic. The fixed component describes the project, product, objectives, and initial allocation of resources, schedule, and budget. The dynamic component is that of tracking resources and project costs as the project unfolds. The planning document can be very useful not only in providing a view of what is to come, but what has happened so that future projects are managed more efficiently.

In each of the following projects, the goal and background are provided as a basis for developing a plan:

- Commercial—A fixed budget is established to develop a multimedia game product that must be on shelves within six months to compete with currently emerging products. The game will reflect common features found in comparable products.

- Kiosk—The goal is to develop a prototype system that provides information about local and state government resources. It will be deployed in key public locations such as shopping malls, and government offices such as licensing offices.

- Briefing—A relatively low-budget effort to develop a marketing presentation for new manufacturing products that have been released in the last six months. It will be used by nontechnical personnel at a variety of trade shows and marketing demonstrations.

- Trainer—A just-in-time training system that will provide multimedia training of employees for a sales and product support system. The system must be able to train and assess the skills of employees.

- Web site—Build a World Wide Web site that provides user support for new products. The site must be able to present product information as well as collect and process customer orders.

Requirements and Architecture

The requirements analysis and architectural design process as shown in Figure 12-3, defines and specifies the hardware and software required for a multimedia product. This process is directly related to classic software development in that it describes the operational aspects of the software, hardware, and operating system, and complements the content development effort. The requirements process specifies:

- Program and hardware function. Describe the functional characteristics of the application in terms of what is expected, the date it is expected, and where it is to be delivered.

- Performance. Describe the expectations for speed, size, and efficiency of the hardware and software.

- User interface. Describe who will use the software and how they can expect to use it.

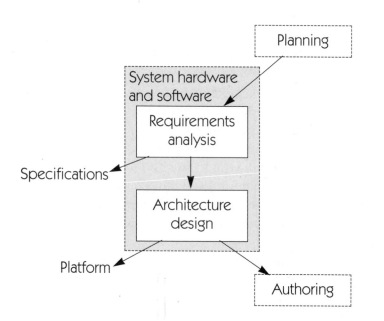

Figure 12-3 The requirement analysis and architectural design processes

- Hardware. Describe specific features of hardware such as what the end user is expected to have or the type of hardware platform the application is to be deployed.

- Hardware and software interfaces. Describe how the software is to behave on the hardware platform. This may also take the form of how the software operates on the hardware. For example, how a touch screen display monitor would interface to the application.

Requirements describe the expected behavior of the hardware and software and form the basis from which the architecture is designed. For example, some of the requirements of a multimedia product include:

- Functional requirements: the software will be started by clicking an icon in the operating system; if left unattended the first page of the application will be automatically displayed after 5 minutes; each page will provide access to Help and Quit functions.

- User requirements: all controls will be displayed as large gray buttons; an audio indication will be used when a new page is displayed; Help information will explain all user accessible functions.

- Performance requirements: the application will load in less than 10 seconds; audio and video clips will operate smoothly.

The product of the requirements process is a specification that describes the software and hardware to be designed and developed. The specification is useful to identify all aspects of the system early in the development effort so that nothing is overlooked and left out. It is also useful for testing in later activities to make sure everything works the way it was intended. The requirements specification is reviewed and signed off by all interested parties to agree on the product expectations.

The architecture transforms the requirements into a design by identifying or selecting:

- Specific software including the application development environment and operating system

- Specific hardware that supports the software

- How the software is installed onto the hardware

- How new software will be implemented to satisfy specific requirements

The product of the architecture activity is the design approach for the software and hardware to be used in product development.

Multimedia products are developed using a number of software authoring tools as discussed in Chapter 9, Multimedia Authoring Tools. In some cases, the authoring tool is complete and provides all of the functionality required for the application. In other cases, software modules are written to satisfy unique or specialized requirements that the authoring environment does not directly support. For example, server-based software would be written to support Internet-based multimedia products to access database information or provide client-based user information.

Requirements and architecture specifications vary a great deal from project to project. The following examples of requirements and architecture will give you an idea of the kinds of information and concepts derived from this activity:

- Commercial—The application is targeted for children ages twelve to eighteen and will run on a commercially available game platform that connects to a television. The user hardware is a hand-held game control with four directional buttons and three control buttons.

- Kiosk—A 19-inch diagonal touch screen monitor will be mounted in a durable cabinet. The system will be self-starting on initial power application and capable of operating for extended periods of time.

- Briefing—The software will be used by nontechnical personnel and will start by clicking on an icon from the operating system. It will operate on laptop hardware that may be connected to computer projection equipment.

- Trainer—Employees will be able to install and run the training software on all corporate hardware that is already on employee desktops. The training software will track each employee by employee identification number to determine how often and long they used the software. Testing information on all employees will be collected and stored.

- Web site—The specifics of the server will be defined in addition to the expectations for the client-side browser software and hardware platform. Internet and remote applications are often limited by the capabilities of the client-side platform.

Storyboarding

Storyboarding is the process of defining the message and describing the user interaction with content and the application. Storyboarding involves a complex effort to develop panels for screen layouts that describe content, flow, and format. Storyboards are described in Chapter 9 from a technical perspective. The focus here is on how storyboarding fits into the overall development process.

Storyboarding is similar to the requirements activity in that it describes what the application is going to do and how it is going to do it in terms of the content. For example, an educational product starts out with a menu of choices that leads to content that is followed by testing to determine what has been learned. Depending on the testing, the user is led through review material and then directed to the next topic. The product designer, subject matter expert, and educational experts will develop and review storyboards to ensure that the subject matter is comprehensively covered in a fashion that the anticipated end user can learn.

Continuing with our sample projects, storyboarding will provide the following:

- Commercial—Detailed character animation is described on a frame-by-frame basis dictated by game options that the user selects or are program determined.

- Kiosk—Standard information storyboards are defined for each government agency that identify the agency, what they do, points of contact, operating hours, and other important information. The standard storyboards are applied to each agency involved in the kiosk project.

- Briefing—Storyboards that are both entertaining and informative are prepared and submitted for review and comment by the product teams, management, and marketing organizations. The storyboards in this model tend to be linear although the presenter can go back or jump to a specific page via a drop-down menu selection.

- Trainer—Specific learning objectives are identified and transformed into storyboard modules. Existing training courseware is reviewed to identify available content that can be adapted into the application.

- Web site—The complete set of pages are structured to ensure that the user can view marketing and sales information without having to go more than three pages from the initial page.

Content Production

Content production follows storyboarding so that story ideas and concepts can be turned into reality. Content production, depending on the availability of existing resources or the need to create new materials, includes:

- Identification of new resources to be created or selected from existing resources of text, pictures, audio, and video.

- Obtaining rights to existing materials whenever necessary.

- Digitizing of source pictures, audio, and video into formats compatible with the multimedia authoring software and delivery environment.

- Production of original materials including text, graphics, audio effects, and animation by the graphics production staff.

- Format source data for presentation in the product. Content may be modified by clipping unused portions; coloring (converting color to black and white, or increasing and decreasing the color depth); converting digital audio bit rate sample, frequency, and channels; or modifying digital video frame rate, size, or color depth.

Many multimedia projects are based on having content resources available prior to the start of the project. In reality, the project may happen to take advantage of some set of content. For example, a "History of Eighteenth Century Art" title is based on the painting, sculpture, and artwork of famous artists. The content is available from two resources: prior digitized content from other projects, and actual artwork and photographic images from museums. Storyboarding proceeds from the premise that an educational title is being developed that explains eighteenth century artists and their efforts. However, because a set of content is already available, these resources and the history they represent may be featured in the product. This can result in a more cost-effective production because it takes advantage of existing resources.

Content production can also proceed when there is no existing content prior to the start of the project. This is especially true for entertainment projects such as multimedia games where new characters and situations are created to provide fresh concepts for consumers. In cases where new content is required, a complete set of storyboards is essential to ensure that only the content that is required is actually created. In this fashion there is little waste and it will also help the content producers such as writers and graphic artists to have a strong sense of what they are creating and how it will fit into the final product.

Continuing our discussion of sample projects, content production will vary as we have just described depending on what is new versus what can be reused or adapted from other efforts:

- Commercial—Extensive animation segments are created matching storyboard sequences. The animation sets are matched to background color palettes to prevent distracting color shifts. All animation clips will be matched with audio tracks.

- Kiosk—Text and graphics are obtained from the participating offices describing organizational functions. Local maps are digitized and edited to show office locations relevant to the kiosk locations. Video and audio tapes of government officials are digitized for introductory segments to explain the use and benefits of the kiosk and to introduce participating agencies.

- Briefing—Existing marketing and technical materials, already in digital format, are converted and used in the effort. Due to limits on the budget, new content production is kept to a minimum. Clip art and music are used for backgrounds and continuity.

- Trainer—Following the storyboard model of using existing courseware materials, content is adapted from training documents and materials. Instructors provide audio tracks describing training objectives and to clarify key points. Most of the content is text and graphic material with audio and video is used for supplementing delivery for users with audio/video-capable hardware.

- Web site—Original artwork is prepared by graphic artists. All graphics are converted to World Wide Web compatible compressed formats to minimize file sizes for Internet delivery. No audio and video content was developed due to concerns about delivery bandwidth. Extensive text segments were written and edited to ensure readability.

Authoring

Authoring is the process of assembling the content into the multimedia software development environment following the map provided by the storyboards. It is the focal point of the software design and storyboarding/content efforts. There are two kinds of authoring that occur:

1. Content assembly—the content is put together and linked to other content.

2. Functional programming—software is created to provide specific behavior.

In Chapter 9 we described the operation of various authoring tools and environments. Some authoring tools merely allow content to be placed on pages that are presented in a simple linear sequence. Other, more complex, tools enable a range of interactive behaviors, including jumping to pages out of sequence, accessing databases, or downloading information across networks.

It is critical that the selection of the authoring tool and the storyboarding be mutual. There are many considerations in selecting the appropriate authoring environment such as:

- Level of interactivity required. Is the application a simple page turner or does it have complex interactive behavior?

- Platform requirements including type and features of hardware and operating system.

- Interaction with other software and systems such as databases and networks.

The authoring process will implement the desired feature set using the prescribed tool. If the tool is inadequate, the project can just as easily fail as if the storyboards or content are incomplete.

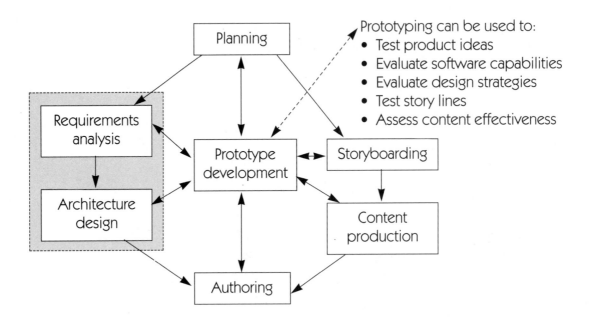

Prototyping can be used to:
- Test product ideas
- Evaluate software capabilities
- Evaluate design strategies
- Test story lines
- Assess content effectiveness

Figure 12-4 Prototyping as part of the development process

Although authoring follows the software design and storyboarding/content efforts, it may also be called into play as early as the planning phase. Figure 12-4 presents the use of a limited authoring segment to prototype a multimedia product. Prototyping is a process in which a limited set of the application is created to demonstrate features or functions. Prototyping a product may be used to sell the concept or to test ideas for capabilities to be included into the design. Whatever reason is used for prototyping, it is important to note that prototypes are usually discarded after they have been used. Prototypes are often limited versions of a final product with incomplete features. Discarding the prototype helps to ensure that the final product is complete and fully functional.

Authoring, if other activities are completed well, can be a smooth and trouble-free process for multimedia product development. On the other hand, if storyboards are not complete, content is not ready, or requirements and architecture are not well considered, authoring can be a time consuming and costly process. The following project examples illustrate some of the benefits and problems encountered when authoring:

- Commercial—A programming language is used to author the game product. Animation segments are assembled with audio tracks in predetermined sequences described in storyboards. User game scoring was implemented and designed to allow games to be played from one session to the next by saving the game situation and scoring in a limited amount of memory provided by the game system hardware.

- Kiosk—A multimedia authoring tool is used to assemble the content. Significant time was lost when various agencies failed to provide content elements according to schedule. Extensive authoring rework was required when content finally arrived and had to be adapted to the product.

- Briefing—A commercial, linear presentation authoring tool was used to author the content. Various product lines were presented in interchangeable segments that could be inserted and removed for various customer presentations.

- Trainer—A commercial multimedia authoring tool designed specifically for training applications was used to develop the product. Built-in features of the tool provided for monitoring user time spent on the program, testing of users, and tracking which training modules they had completed.

- Web site—A commercial HTML (HyperText Markup Language) authoring tool was used to create the World Wide Web pages. Server-based programming provided access to corporate sales databases so that end users could order via the application.

Evaluation

Evaluation is the process that tests and assesses a multimedia product to make sure it is what was ordered and it does what it is supposed to do. It starts the moment storyboards and requirements analysis activities begin. In-process evaluation that occurs during development, such as review of storyboards and content, is called formative evaluation. Evalua-

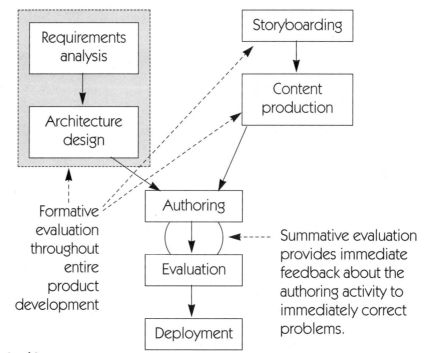

Figure 12-5 The relationship between authoring and evaluation

tion conducted following the authoring process is called summative evaluation.

Evaluation starts with the requirements and storyboards. All requirements are checked to make sure they are satisfied in the product. The storyboards are compared to the operation of the product to make sure that all buttons, menus, and program links operate as intended. Figure 12-5 shows the relationship between evaluation and authoring in which immediate feedback to the authoring phase is used to correct deficiencies. As deficiencies are corrected they are rechecked to ensure the original problem has been fixed and no new problems have been created.

Usability testing focuses on the operation and performance of the product from the end user's perspective. It is carried out by end users or testers with similar backgrounds, skills, and attitudes to end users. Usability testing may be applied to:

• Prototype versions of the product

- Data elements such as graphics, audio and video segments, and animation clips
- The completed product

Usability testing can be used to correct deficiencies and to improve the product by correcting problems with the operation, performance, or user interface design.

Alpha and Beta Testing

A strategy for evaluating multimedia products is to allow users to evaluate the product prior to final release. End user testing often exposes problems or issues that in-house testers would overlook because they have a vested interest in the application. Outside testers are less likely to make assumptions about the application performance or behavior. For example, in-house testing may be done on hardware that is more powerful than that used by end users.

Alpha and beta testing occur at different stages of development:

1. Alpha Testing—The product is evaluated relatively early in the development phase; in fact, the application may be missing part of the content or functionality. The main interest in alpha testing is to review the application concept, format, user interface, and page layouts.

2. Beta Testing—The product is evaluated just prior to final release; the product should be relatively bug free and complete. The main interest in beta testing is to find bugs and content mistakes.

Alpha testing is usually done in-house or with end users who agree to keep their comments and experiences confidential. This protects the developer from competitors and keeps problems from becoming common knowledge, which might hurt future deployment of the application.

Evaluation of multimedia products during development is the only way to ensure that the product will meet requirements and operational expectations:

- Commercial—Animation segments are thoroughly reviewed and prototype versions of the game are tested for usability by sample groups of end users.

Deficiencies are corrected and tested prior to final acceptance of the product.

- Kiosk—Extensive usability testing is accomplished by placing the kiosk in a local shopping mall. Test participants are given surveys to complete prior to and following their hands—on use of the kiosk. Results were used to improve the user interface and system performance.

- Briefing—Limited testing was required because of the linear nature of the product. All content was reviewed by the various corporate contributors. Marketing staff end users were also shown the product to get last minute input on the product.

- Trainer—The initial training module was given to two groups: those experienced in the subject matter, and those with little or no prior knowledge. Input on the completeness of the product was solicited from the experienced group. Pre- and post-interviews were used to evaluate the effectiveness of the training material with the second group.

- Web site—On-line testing was performed to assess the performance of the World Wide Web pages. Access via modem and network connections were both evaluated. All functional requirements including server functions such as user input and sales support are thoroughly tested.

Deployment

Product deployment is the release of the product to the end user or market. Depending on the type of product there are a number of tasks that may occur during this stage:

- Documentation for the product is written including user and installation guides and troubleshooting instructions.

- Mass production of CD-ROMs or other delivery media.

- Packaging of product for mass distribution.

- Marketing of the product.

- Mass production of hardware for kiosks or other delivery platforms.
- Installation of the software.
- Training of personnel to use the software.

The sample projects all have different deployment schemes:

- Commercial—The product is delivered via hardware specific game cartridges and CD-ROMs. A user and installation guide is created for users with limited computer skills. Appropriate packaging is created and the product is sold via commercial software and computer game vendors.
- Kiosk—Kiosk hardware and software are installed in predetermined locations over a phased delivery schedule that included extensive initial monitoring to verify that the systems operate with minimal support.
- Briefing—Marketing staff are trained to use the product. The software is installed on portable laptop computers.
- Trainer—The software is deployed on the corporate network and subsequently installed on end user computers for training purposes.
- Web site—The World Wide Web site is advertised via conventional commercial marketing channels including radio, television, and periodicals. The product is registered with commercial Internet search engines and mutual marketing agreements are established with existing Web sites to advertise the new Web site.

Maintenance

Books, film, and audio media are completed when they are shipped, whereas multimedia products often take a life of their own following deployment. Maintenance is the process in which a product can evolve and grow with emerging technologies or to meet new user demands. It may also be used to correct software or hardware errors called bugs that are missed during development. Depending on the product, maintenance releases may take on various strategies:

Check the CD-ROM for alternative strategies and views of multimedia product development.

Tools for managing multimedia product development

- Complete redistribution of the product.
- Distribution of portions of the product to replace faulty or deficient segments of software or data.

Depending on the extent of the rework, maintenance activities may be accomplished by completing a new development cycle from planning through authoring and evaluation. This situation is where documentation of the old project is critical to the new project effort. By reviewing the previous effort you may be able to find ways to improve the efficiency and cost effectiveness of the new maintenance effort.

Although some products have no second generations or add-on product development efforts, product and customer support may be a necessity. This typically requires that product support personnel be trained and made available for a reasonable amount of time.

Maintenance efforts for the sample projects range from no further product enhancement to limited enhancement and onto extensive enhancement and development cycles to add content and functionality to the original project:

- Commercial—The product was only moderately successful with limited sales. There were no follow-on efforts except for limited customer support.
- Kiosk—Updates to the content are provided on a quarterly basis. A content support office was established to track and implement updates. Backup hardware units were developed to rapidly replace failed systems for subsequent repair.
- Briefing—Marketing personnel were very happy with the product and requested extensive additions to improve the use of the tool.
- Trainer—Training modules were created for additional areas identified for corporate training. Templates were developed to speed up the development of new modules.
- Web site—Updates were made to the sales database as required for new products. The user interface for the World Wide Web site was reworked in stages to reflect customer inputs to Web site performance and desired functionality.

Costing a Multimedia Project

Multimedia projects cost money, whether the project is a short-term effort to build a simple linear marketing presentation or a long-term, complex effort to build the next commercially successful multimedia game. In either case, being able to cost the project is critical. Multimedia project costs are based on:

- Content costs—the price of text, pictures, audio, and video content regardless of how it is created, purchased, or if permissions need to be secured.

- Labor costs—salaries, benefits, bonuses, and other costs associated with hiring or contracting personnel to do the work. This includes costs for design, authoring, content production staff, testers, and production.

- Equipment costs—purchase, rent, lease, and maintain computers, software programs, and other equipment.

- Talent and production costs—fees for actors, voice talent, and similar resources as well as taping, editing, and processing costs.

- Facility and location costs—fees for owning or renting a place to work; may also include monies to rent stages, film locations, and production studios.

- Marketing and production costs—documentation, CD-ROM duplication, packaging, distribution, and advertising costs.

- Maintenance and support costs—salaries, equipment, and other costs to provide Help desk, Internet server support and connectivity, and similar costs incurred to provide long-term product support.

- Miscellaneous costs—other money spent on specific project needs that do not fit into the other categories; for example, purchasing rights to prior product versions in order to develop add-on products.

Labor and content costs tend to be the highest single cost items for multimedia development, while the other costs will vary significantly depending on the type of product.

Cost Modeling

The problem with multimedia project costing is that no one model exists that is appropriate for all projects. The best approach for developing an effective cost model is to make sure that you have a thorough understanding of:

- Product requirements
- Operational expectations of the product (derived from storyboards)
- What resources are available to develop the project

The first two components are based solely on the product. The third component is based on prior project experience and knowing what is available to get the work done.

The development model described earlier in this chapter and shown in Figure 12-2 is effective for managing the relationship of activities and establishing schedules. It is not nearly as effective a tool for costing the overall project. The basic problem lies in estimating costs for a product that has not been completely defined. It is critical that the following questions be answered in order to realistically determine overall costs. How many pages? How complex is the subject matter? How many pictures? How many minutes of audio and video?

There are two basic models to follow when estimating costs:

1. Labor-driven model—an estimate, determined by the number of hours of labor that will be used to develop the product
2. Content-driven model—an estimate, determined by the number of pages and amount of content

Both of these models must also consider:

- Costs to obtain content
- Equipment, facilities, and other costs

Labor Model

The labor-driven model for cost estimation is based on the amount of labor and time estimated for the project. For example, for each activity below, estimate the number of hours for each labor category:

- Project Planning—Project manager and designer
- Requirements Analysis and Architecture Design—Project designer and programmer
- Storyboarding—Project manager, designer, subject matter expert
- Content Production—Graphic artist, audio/video production, talent
- Authoring—Programmer, project designer
- Evaluation—Project designer, programmer, editor, testing personnel
- Deployment—Marketing staff, production staff, support staff
- Maintenance—Project manager and designer

Project management costs may be included as a percentage of the overall effort. For example, if 3,000 hours of effort is expected across all tasks, project management would be added at a rate of 300 hours or 10 percent of the total project. Remember to include content, facility, and other costs. Please note that this is an example, and that labor categories can and will vary from project to project.

The key to this approach is knowing how much labor costs run and having a reasonable estimate of the overall product effort. If the product's needs dramatically increase due to new requirements or operational functionality, then the total project cost is at significant risk or the improvements will be limited by the budgeted resources.

Content Model

The content model is based on what it costs to create a single page and the cost per element of content. For example, the average cost of a multimedia page might be $90 for authoring and $200 for one minute of audio. These costs can be applied and extended to the total number of pages estimated for a complete project. This model assumes that you can estimate the number of pages and amount of content. For example:

- Number of pages for the entire product includes pages for titles, menus, content, help, credits, and support. A per page price can be assigned that accounts for design, programming, testing, and management.

- Number of elements of content. This may be measured as 100 words of text, a single graphic, or one minute of audio or video content. A per unit cost can be developed that accounts for graphics and audio/video production, editing and processing.

As in the labor-driven model, you must also account for content costs that are unique for this effort; for example, cost to use a specific graphic or video footage.

The key to using this model is having a history of prior projects from which to derive costs for authoring and content production. If this data is not available, then reasonable estimates may be applied to determine costing. Like the labor-driven model, this model depends on a reasonable estimation of the product. This may be more practical if the new project is similar to completed products in terms of functionality and content size.

Other Costing Issues

Selection of a cost model is best left to the specific project and its organization. However, there a number of cost items and issues that must also be considered when developing a product:

- Management Cost—Overhead costs for nondirect management that are incurred by the project; for example, the prorated costs of corporate management such as the president of the company.

- Quality Assurance—External quality assurance may be desirable to validate the quality and acceptability of the product. What percentage of the effort is required or mandated by the developing organization for quality assurance?

- Realism—Is the development team experienced for this type of effort? Is the technology available?
- Source (in-house versus contract)—The best place to develop a project may be an external organization with already available and appropriate personnel, resources, and equipment.
- Scheduling—Does the effort fit into the availability of existing resources and programs?
- Talent—Is the desired acting or voice talent available to complete the project? What is acceptable for substitutes?

These items may or may not impact a typical project; however, they should be considered in the estimation of a project cost.

SUMMARY

Once you know about the different types of multimedia data, the tools, and how to design a multimedia product, the final ingredient is having a process to follow. The process provides a structure that will help you to cost-effectively manage product development. We discussed planning, requirements analysis, architectural design, storyboarding, content production, authoring, evaluation, deployment, and maintenance as activities for development. Finally, we correlated the structured process to costing so that reasonable estimates could be developed. Multimedia products do not simply happen, but are built one piece at a time by developers who understand the technology and how to apply it.

REVIEW QUESTIONS

1. Why is management of multimedia product development so critical?
2. What is the relationship between a multimedia product, the consumer, and the producer?

3. How would you relate experiences in management of other activities to management of multimedia activities?

4. Given the process described in this chapter for developing multimedia products, develop a plan for a one-person effort to build a simple multimedia presentation. Justify any exceptions that you would apply to the process.

5. Given the process described in this chapter for developing multimedia products, develop a plan for a five-person effort to build a relatively complex multimedia product. Explain any exceptions you would apply to the process.

6. In which situations are requirements analysis and architectural analysis less critical as elements of multimedia production?

7. What issues are important for multimedia products that depend on the new creation of significant amounts of content?

8. Describe the cost estimation of a sample multimedia project using both the content and labor models. How is costing similar? How is it different?

Glossary

A

amplitude: The power or intensity of sound.

ANSI (American National Standards Institute): A non-profit organization that serves as the national clearinghouse and coordinator for establishing standards in the United States.

analog video: Video information that is stored using television video signals, film, videotape, or other non-computer media.

anti-aliasing: Blending a font into the background by transitioning the color from darker to lighter over a series of pixels.

application: A computer program that serves a specific purpose or use such as a word processing or spreadsheet program. Multimedia products include games, educational programs, and corporate briefings to name a few. Multimedia products may also be referred to as applications.

ASCII (American Standard Code for Information Interchange): A standard table of 7-bit codes for the digital representation of letters, numbers, and special control characters.

aspect ratio: The ratio of an image's width to its height.

asynchronous: Applications or activities using a store and forward method in which data is transmitted and stored for future presentation.

authoring tools: Software programs for developing and delivering multimedia products. Tools include programs for text and graphic editing, audio and video capture and editing, and multimedia authoring.

AVI (Audio Video Interleaved): A file format for digital video under Microsoft Windows. AVI files include both raw and compressed video.

B

bandwidth: The amount of information that can be transmitted across a network within a fixed period of time. It is often measured in kilobits per second (Kbit/s) or megabits per second (Mbit/s) that can be carried by a network.

bitmap: Pixel-based image with a color depth typically ranging from 1 to 24 bits.

bookmarks: Pre-defined locations in a document that can be referenced by hyperlinks.

bus: A network in which devices are logically connected in a line to a signal cable. At any one moment, one device has control of the network and is allowed to transmit. A computer bus is used for moving both data and instructions.

byte: A unit of information in a computer consisting of 8 bits. A byte can represent 256 (28) values.

C

CBT (Computer-Based Training): The use of computers for training and education in which direct computerized instruction forms the main component of the teaching process.

CD-DA (Compact Disk-Digital Audio): The digital audio version of the computer disk. The Red Book standard specifies a 12 cm disk capable of storing up to 72 minutes of high-quality sound encoded using 16-bit digital audio at 44.1 kHz.

CD-I (Compact Disk-Interactive): A specification (the Green Book) proposed by Philips and Sony for a self-contained multimedia system that supports the simultaneous interactive presentation of video, audio, text, and data.

263

CD-R (Compact Disk-Recordable): Orange book CD-ROM specification for media that can be read-only and read-write.

CD-ROM (Compact Disk-Read Only Memory): A version of the compact disk for the storage of digital data. The Yellow Book specifies a 12 cm disk which can store up to 550 MB of text, still images, graphics, and audio.

CD-ROM XA (Compact Disk-Read Only Memory Extended Architecture): An extension of the CD-ROM specification (the Yellow Book), which is compatible in some respects with CD-I. It supports the interleaving of sound and picture data for animation and sound synchronization.

cels: The individual frames of movie film.

chrominance: The color information part of a video signal.

clip art: Ready-to-use graphics that can be placed in multimedia products. Clip art collections are often grouped by subject or types of images (i.e., file format).

codec (compressor/decompressor): A processor that can code analog audio or video information in digital form and decode digital data back into analog form.

color depth: The number of colors that a computer's display system is capable of. Also refers to the number of colors in a graphic image.

color flashing: This occurs when images change the basic color palette. It occurs with animation or consecutively displayed images with different palettes in each successive image.

component signal: A color signal in which luminance and chrominance information are transmitted separately.

composite analog video: All the video components, including brightness, color, and synchronization combined into one signal.

composite signal: A color signal in which luminance and chrominance information are combined in a single signal and transmitted across a single wire.

composite video: Used in an analog video signal, each frame of the video is represented by a fluctuating voltage signal known as an analog wave form.

compositing: The combining of video components: brightness, color, and synchronization. The quality of composite video is considered marginal.

compression: The process of reducing the number of bits required to store or transmit information in digital form. Compression is most often used in graphics and digital video.

compression ratio: Comparison of file sizes between uncompressed and compressed video.

computer: A machine that is capable of gathering, processing, storing, and disseminating data.

computer animation: The process of displaying a series of discrete images in rapid succession creating the illusion of natural movement.

content: Specific information for a multimedia product in the form of text, pictures, audio, and video. Multimedia products typically contain a set of multimedia content that is specific and unique to that application.

control: Within a computer, it is instructions in the form of software that control the operation of the computer.

controllers: Electronic devices that enable computers to control the operation of video equipment.

D

data bus: A group of conductors, operating in parallel, that transfer data and instructions from one part of a computer to another.

decompression: The process of decoding a compressed image or digital video and expanding that data to its original length.

developers: Managers, designers, programmers, graphic artists, and other skilled individuals who participate in the development of multimedia products sometimes referred to as producers.

digital: A signal that varies discretely (typically measured as 0 or 1).

dithering: Process through which colors are changed to meet the closest available color based on the current palette.

domain: A domain, in the multimedia world, is a relatively narrow or focused area of information or knowledge such as astronomy or famous authors, but it can also be a broader area of organized information such as an encyclopedia.

DPI: The number of dots per inch, used as a measurement of image resolution in documents. A dot is equivalent to a pixel.

F

fair use: The limited use of copyrighted material for purposes of criticism, comment, news reporting, teaching, scholarship, and research.

fields: In video technology, electromagnetic scan lines projected onto a phosphor tube for display to create a television image. In databases, elements of a data table that represent discrete groupings of information.

font: A particular size of typeface (see also typeface).

frame: A single complete image in a film or moving video recording.

frequency: The rate at which sound is measured in cycles per second or Hertz (Hz).

G

gray scale: An image whose pixel values represent shades of gray.

GUI: Graphical user interface.

H

halftone: An image that creates the illusion of continuous tone on a bitonal display.

HTML (HyperText Markup Language): An embedding scheme used for World Wide Web documents.

hypermedia: A term used to describe hypertext, which contains a large proportion of non-text information (e.g., graphics, image, video, sound).

hypertext: Nonsequential information consisting of linked pieces of text or other media (nodes) joined together by a network (of links). The hypertext reader navigates through the network of information, choosing when to follow a link.

I

information: Facts, ideas, beliefs, and stories that when communicated, provide value to the receiver. In the context of multimedia, information comes in many forms including text, pictures, audio, and video.

input: The collection and conversion of analog data into a computer via the keyboard, data files, or other device.

interactivity: A stimulus-response behavior in which a computer program presents options that the user can select from that lead to further options. Multimedia software applications are designed to logically organize information, making it easily accessible to users.

interframe compression: The removal of redundant information that is repeated from one frame to another in a moving video sequence.

interlaced video: Television display of analog video signals. Odd lines are presented first, and even lines second.

intraframe: Occuring within a single frame. Typically applies to video compression.

ISA (Industry Standard Architecture): A 16-bit bus for the IBM PC/AT and compatible PCs.

ISO (International Standards Organization): The worldwide coordinating standards body with a membership composed of national institutions for standards in individual countries such as the British Standards Institution (UK) and ANSI (U.S.).

ISO 9660: A standard for the format of the directory on CD-ROM, for use under different operating systems, originally developed by the High Sierra Group.

J

JIT (Just-in-time): An approach to training in which help and information are given to the user as required.

JPEG (Joint Photographic Experts Group): An ISO sponsored group that has developed a general purpose compression standard for continuous tone still images.

K

kiosk: Multimedia device that is very easy to use that provides quick access to information. Often includes a touch screen interface in lieu of a keyboard or mouse.

L

LAN (Local Area Network): A communications system for workstations and computer systems (nodes) within a local site to enable passing of data between nodes on the network and the sharing of peripheral devices such as printers.

line art: A bitonal (two color) image or mode of scanning that generates a bitonal image.

linear: A series of actions or events happening in sequence with no branching. They are typically found in briefing type multimedia presentations.

lossless: Any form of compression in which the original data can be recovered without loss.

lossy: Any form of compression in which the data is not exactly recoverable.

luminance: The brightness of an image.

M

MCI (Media control interface): Allows Windows-compatible applications to control multimedia devices such as CD-ROM drives.

memory: The ability to store data for both short and long term use.

MIDI (Musical Instrument Digital Interface): A standard published by the International MIDI Association that defines communication between musical devices.

motherboard: A device that integrates the processor, memory, and other devices of a computer.

MPC (Multimedia PC): The (trademarked) name for a minimum specification for a personal computer to run multimedia products.

MPEG (Moving Picture Experts Group): An ISO activity to develop a standard for the storage of video and associated audio on digital media.

multimedia: The use of text, pictures, audio, and/or video to deliver information.

N

non-interlaced video: A computer display process in which the entire frame is displayed thirty times every second.

NTSC (National Television Systems Committee): The standard for color video in the United States, Canada, and Japan established by the National Television Systems Committee. It specifies a 525-line screen updated at 30 frames per second.

O

OCR (Optical Character Recognition): An electronic process in which characters printed in a standard typeface can be automatically read and encoded.

OLE (Object Linking and Embedding): A Microsoft software technology that allows users to insert multimedia elements into software programs.

optical disk: A disk on which information is read and written using a light, usually a laser.

output: The production and transmission of analog data from a computer via the monitor, data files, audio speaker, or other device.

overlay: The technique of placing computer-generated graphics (e.g., titles) over standard video.

overscan: A method of display in which an image is extended to fill the whole screen, as on a television set.

P

page: A single instance of a multimedia presentation.

PAL (Phase Alternate Line): The standard for color video used in most of Europe, Africa, Australia, and South America. It specifies a 625-line screen updated at 25 frames per second.

PCM (Pulse Code Modulation): The standard method of encoding digital audio signals. The input wave form is sampled at regular intervals and the amplitude converted to a binary code.

Photo CD: A type of CD disk used for large collections of images.

pixel: A picture element forming the basic element in a digital image.

processor: A very fast device for performing arithmetic and logic calculations.

product: A completed multimedia product that is distributed for use by end users. Products are often sold to consumers via commercial outlets.

progressive scan: The refreshing of a computer display one line at a time from top to bottom.

R

random access: The ability of a computer storage device, such as a hard disk, to jump to any point in the storage medium and access data.

raster: Images that are created as two-dimensional sets of points on a computer display (see also bitmap).

rasterization: The creation of a font on a computer display using one pixel at a time.

resolution: The number of dots per unit length measured in one of two directions. The number of pixels measured across and down the screen is also frequently referred to as its resolution.

RGB (Red-Green-Blue): An output signal and image-encoding scheme for color displays on computers that consists of separately controllable red, green, and blue elements.

S

sampling frequency: The cycles per second at which digital audio files are recorded.

script: Programming found in multimedia authoring tools.

SECAM (Système Electronique Couleur Avec Memoire): The television standard developed in France. It specifies a 625-line screen updated at 25 frames per second.

SGML (Standard Generalized Markup Language): An ISO standard for the content and logical structure of an electronic document.

storyboard: Building a story on paper that describes and details the message or story of the product, Storyboarding is used to link content to the message so that it can be translated into product software.Symmetric compression: An approach to the encoding and decoding of digital information in which the decompression process is a step-by-step reversal of the compression process. The two processes thus take the same length of time.

synchronous: Applications that are able to transmit and receive data in real time allowing the end user to view or hear data as it is being captured or created.

T

text: Symbols usually in the form of letters, numbers, and special characters such as periods and commas used for written communication.

typeface: Graphic representations of the alphabet, numbers, and special characters. Typefaces are usually organized by type sizes and styles.

U

users (also known as end users): Those individuals or groups who use and/or apply multimedia products and products for work or play.

V

VCR (Video Cassette Recorder): A device that can record and play back video signals using removable tape cassettes.

VHS (Video Home System): A trademark for the half-inch videotape format developed by JVC and Matsushita.

video capture: The process of transforming a video input signal from a VCR or camera into a series of graphic images that can be stored on a computer.

videodisk: An optical disk that can be used to store analog video and audio information. Some forms may also be able to store digital audio.

Index